MAH CET

B.Ed. (ELCT)

Latest Edition Practice Kit

15 Tests

15 Practice Test

Based On Real Exam Pattern

✓ Thoroughly Revised and Updated

✓ Detailed Analysis of all MCQs

Title	: MAH CET B.Ed. (ELCT)
Author Name	: Mr. Rohit Manglik
Published By	: EduGorilla Community Pvt. Ltd.
Publishers Address	: 12/651, First Floor Opp. Arvindo Park, Near Jama Masjid, Indira Nagar, Lucknow, Uttar Pradesh-226016, India

Copyright EduGorilla

ISBN : 978-93-55568-75-5

First Edition

Disclaimer EduGorilla

Compiled and created by EduGorilla Community Pvt. Ltd

Printed By EduGorilla Community Pvt. Ltd.

ROHIT MANGLIK
CEO, EduGorilla

Dear Applicants,

People say *"Success comes to those who work hard."* But I've seen people working hard for their exams day in and day out for marginal success. While others succeed in their examinations by putting in just half the work. So are they God Gifted? No! I believe that it's because they work *smart* and not just *hard*. Similarly, for your exams, you should strategize your preparation so as to increase the likelihood of success. Well with EduGorilla get ready to increase your *chances of selection* in your exam by *16x*.

EduGorilla helps you in not only working *hard* but also working in a *smart and strategic* manner. With EduGorilla's preparation package, you get a chance to make your exam preparation easy, and a fun learning path towards selection. Finding the right path to your preparations can be difficult if you don't know in which direction to head. Don't worry, we have you covered! EduGorilla will be your guide to success in your journey. With our Preparation Package, you can prepare strategically and beat the exam in just one attempt.

EduGorilla's Preparation Package includes-

- **Test Series**
- **Books**

Our preparation package is handcrafted as per the latest changes, expert opinions, and students' discretion. Thus, enabling you to get through each stage of the selection process for your exam.

Our Books are designed by the teachers and experts of the respective exam with a combined 150+ years of experience; to provide you with easy, efficient, and effective learning. Our books are smart, in the sense that not only do they give you the answers to the questions but also provide similar questions for practice.

EduGorilla's competent Test Series gives you real-time experience and confidence through which you can clear your offline or online exam in just one attempt. We currently host 109,000+ mock tests for 1,520+ competitive and academic exams.

Thus, EduGorilla misses no chance to assist you in your preparation and covers all stages of the exam, so that you don't have to look anywhere else.

We provide complete preparation packages for defense, banking, teaching, and other National & State-Level exams. Hence, it doesn't matter which exam you aspire to because you will reach your success.

ALL THE BEST !

Let EduGorilla be your Guide to Success.

Rohit Manglik,
Founder and CEO, EduGorilla

INTRODUCTION

EduGorilla focuses on guiding students to succeed in their examinations. With that in mind, our book, titled "MAH CET : B.Ed. (ELCT)", has been drafted through the collective efforts of our distinguished experts with 150+ years of combined experience. This book consists of questions that are created following the latest changes in the syllabus and exam pattern. We compiled the book on the basis of questions that are most likely to appear in the MAH B.Ed. (ELCT) CET. Through EduGorilla's "MAH CET : B.Ed. (ELCT)" your chances of success will increase 16x.

EduGorilla does this through our Complete Preparation Package. This package consists of well-conceptualized and structured content in the form of questions that are tailor-made according to your needs and will help you practice for exams in a smart way by pinpointing all the necessary information. It also provides hints and solutions, along with a smart answer sheet for your self-evaluation. You can assess your shortcomings and work accordingly on areas that may require more of your attention.

EduGorilla promises to help you succeed in your examination and accomplish your dream goals. We believe in our aspirants and see them at the top of the merit list. And the first step towards the top is to start preparing with us. EduGorilla's "MAH CET : B.Ed. (ELCT)" includes the following attributes.

➤ Well-Researched Content

➤ Top-Notch Quality

➤ Detailed Answers and Analysis

➤ Smart Answer Sheet

➤ Exam Relevant Questions

Therefore, EduGorilla fortifies your preparation and makes it durable enough to help you stand tall and beat the examination.

MAH B.Ed. (ELCT) CET

Scan QR code for Eligibility, Exam Pattern, Syllabus and more.

Book ID: 1434

TABLE OF CONTENTS

Ques (1-4): Directions : Read the passage given below and answer the questions that follow, by selecting the correct / most appropriate options :

1. Kangri Karchok, the Kailash Purana of the Tibetans describes the sacred elephant-mouthed river or Langchen Khambab as a long and extensive river that rises from the 'lake unconquerable', the Tso Maphan or Manasarovar that flows from the mountainous regions of Tibet. According to this holy book, this cold river with its sands of gold, circles the holy Manasarovar seven times before taking its course to the west.

2. The Langchen Khambab flows down from the red coloured mountains of the Kanglung Kangri Glacier in the Trans-Himalayan region of Tibet, channelling its way through the earth forests of Tholing and Tsparang of the Gugi Kingdom. These earth forests are full of pillars formed by rocks that collectively appear like a forest from afar – an 'out of the world' landscape that was formed by geological movements of the earth and erosion by wind and water. The Khyunglung ruins also lies on the northern bank of the Sutlej river in this valley which was once known as the 'Garuda Valley".

3. This mighty river then flows north-west for about 260 km before entering Himachal Pradesh through Shipki La cutting across the formidable Himalayan ranges of Zanskar, the Greater Himalaya and the Dhauladhar. Subsequently, the waters meander through the gigantic Kinnaur Kailash-Jorkanden Range at Reckong Peo creating the terrifying Sutlej gorge. Then it streams into Shimla, Kullu, Mandi and Bilaspur and is responsible for the rich cultivation of grapes, apples and apricots all along its banks. After its confluence with the River Spiti at Khab it is known as Sutlej.

4. It is 1,448 km in length, making it the longest among the five rivers of Punjab. Extensively used for irrigation, it is topographically divided into the Upper Sutlej Basin and Lower Sutlej Basin. It leaves the Himachal boundary to enter the plains of the Punjab at the Bhakra Dam, the second highest gravity dam and a major point of water supply and electricity generation for the North of India.

1. **Langchen Khambab is a boon for the North of India because:**
   (a) it is a major source of water supply and power generation
   (b) it brings along with it mountain soil and minerals.
   (c) the prosperity of the whole of India depends on it.
   (d) it abounds in aquatic animals.

2. **Read the following sentences :**
   A. Kangri Karchok is a holy book of the Tibetans.
   B. Langchen Khambab is responsible for rich cultivation of various types of fruits in the Himachal Pradesh.
   (a) A is true, B is false.   (b) B is true, A is false
   (c) Both A and B are true   (d) Both A and B are false

3. **Which one of the following words is most similar in meaning to the word 'gigantic' as used in the passage (Para 4)?**
   (a) terrifying   (b) high
   (c) formidable   (d) huge

4. **Which one of the following words is the most opposite in meaning to the word 'sacred' as used in the passage (Para 1)?**
   (a) pure   (b) noble
   (c) unholy   (d) moral

Ques (5-12): Direction : In the following passage, some of the words have been left out. Read the passage carefully and select the correct answer for the given numbers out of the four alternatives

India has put out some ____(1) personalities - brave, creative, and brilliant. It'd be great to see biopics made on these people as____ (2). The torchbearer of Indian football didn't____(3) have an easy start. Bhaichug Bhutia's parents were farmers, and ____(4) he was in athletics ____(5) at a young age, they weren't too keen on him for____(6) sports. His father passed away when he was very young____ (7), after which he received a football scholarship at the age of 9, and that's how it all began. The iconic comedian and all____ (8) entertainer Mehmood, actually worked as a driver before he found his way into films. He held several____ (9) jobs, and only started acting properly____ (10) he got married and ne eded to make more money.

5. **Find out the appropriate word for blank no. 2.**
   (a) About   (b) Like
   (c) Well   (d) Too

6. **Find out the appropriate word for blank no. 3.**
   (a) Actually   (b) Precisely
   (c) Indeed   (d) Accurately

7. **Find out the appropriate word for blank no. 4.**
   (a) Erstwhile   (b) During
   (c) When   (d) While

8. **Find out the appropriate word for blank no. 5.**
   (a) To   (b) From
   (c) During   (d) At

9. **Find out the appropriate word for blank no. 6.**
   (a) Presenting   (b) Persevering
   (c) Pursuing   (d) Purveying

10. **Find out the appropriate word for blank no. 8.**
    (a) Keeper   (b) Circle
    (c) Way   (d) Round

11. **Find out the appropriate word for blank no. 9.**
    (a) Common   (b) Odd
    (c) Glorifying   (d) Various

12. **Find out the appropriate word for blank no. 10.**
    (a) Only   (b) Even though
    (c) After   (d) Because

Ques (13-20): Direction : Read the given passage and answer the question that follow by selecting the most appropriate option.

Have you ever wondered what the qualities of a really professional teacher are? I know that all teachers want their students to like them, but being liked isn't the be-all and end-all really, is it? I mean teachers have to make some unpopular decisions sometimes. Teachers can be popular just because they are friendly and helpful, but to be truly professional and effective, we need to be able to identify the skills and behaviour we require in a true professional. A professional teacher needs to be confident without being arrogant. Nobody can expect to have all the answers, so, if a student asks a real stinker, the professional teacher should be able to admit defeat but offer to find out more for the student. And they must carry that promise out. When the teacher enters the classroom, she / he should have all the required materials and the lesson-plan ready. And, in orchestrating the class, the teacher must give everyone their chance to contribute and should be flexible enough to modify lessons if they are obviously not going to plan. Indeed, a fallback position is part of good planning. It stands to reason also that a teacher must observe punctuality and appropriate tidiness and dress : it is not possible to demand such behaviour from students if the teacher doesn't set the standards. The last thing I would mention is that teachers should be able to feel that their professionalism entitles them to back up from the school directors. If a teacher has a problem with class or student, then the school should have procedures for handling the difficulties. The teacher should not have to feel alone and vulnerable if a difficult situation rises. So, yes, professionalism cuts both ways: in the standards we demand of teachers and the framework we have for giving them support.

13. **The expression isn't the be-all and end-all... is an assumption that pertains to the _____ point of view.**
    (a) writer's
    (b) teacher's
    (c) student's
    (d) general

14. **Here, the fallback position is the system where _____ well-prepared.**
    (a) good students are
    (b) good teachers are
    (c) teachers, even if caught out unexpectedly, are still
    (d) students and teachers who support each other are

15. **Here, able to admit defeat implies that:**
    (a) Students can 'catch' a teacher unaware
    (b) teachers easily lose self-confidence as they lack professionalism
    (c) it doesn't matter if students often contradict what their teacher says
    (d) teachers should be confident enough to own up to their unpreparedness

16. **Here, orchestrating the class suggests:**
    (a) the teacher controlling the class to ensure high grades
    (b) the whole class performing uniformly well
    (c) acknowledging the individual differences in the process of achievement
    (d) that music helps academic achievement

17. **Here, ... asks a real stinker... suggests that:**
    (a) teachers are always unprepared
    (b) students can be better informed than their teachers
    (c) students dislike teachers in general
    (d) teachers are unprofessional in students' eyes

18. **A word that can best replace the word entitles in the passage is:**
    (a) warrants
    (b) names
    (c) calls
    (d) gives

19. **The writer's view that professionalism cuts both ways means:**
    (a) teachers are faced with students and trustees hold them accountable
    (b) teachers teach well then trustees pay them well
    (c) trustees and their employees owe each other support
    (d) students and teachers owe respect to the management of their school

20. **Here, framework refers to the overall:**
    (a) school curriculum
    (b) clearly spelt out duties for teachers
    (c) system for assessment of teachers' performance
    (d) transparency in fixing teachers' salary

21. **Direction: Select the correctly spelt word.**
    (a) Manageble
    (b) Manageable
    (c) Managable
    (d) Manegeable

22. **Direction: In the following question, out of the four alternatives, choose the one which can be substituted for the given words/sentence. Place where wine is made**
    (a) Bakery
    (b) Cloakroom
    (c) Tannery
    (d) Winery

23. **Direction: In the following question, four words are given, out of which only one word is incorrectly spelled. Find the incorrectly spelled word.**
    (a) Tomorrow
    (b) Occurence
    (c) Temperature
    (d) Preferable

24. **Direction: In the following question, four words are given, out of which only one word is incorrectly spelt. Find the incorrectly spelt word.**
    (a) Tranquility
    (b) Perseverence
    (c) Resplendence
    (d) Accommodation

25. **Direction: In the given question, a word has been written in four different ways out of which only one is incorrectly spelled. Select the correctly spelled word.**
    (a) Wastness
    (b) Vastness
    (c) Wasteness
    (d) Vasteness

26. **Direction: Select the answer choice that identifies the noun in the sentence.**
    It will take all of your energy and will to be able to walk again.
    (a) Take
    (b) All
    (c) Your
    (d) Energy

27. **Direction: Select the correct active form of the given sentence.**
    The beggar was laughed at by the boy.
    (a) The boy is laughing at the beggar.
    (b) The boy laughs at the beggar.
    (c) The boy laughed at the beggar.
    (d) None of above

28. **Direction : Fill in the blank with the correct word in order to make the sentence grammatically correct.**
    Each of the girls _____ received an award.
    (a) does
    (b) is
    (c) has
    (d) were

29. **Direction : A sentence is given with a blank to be filled in with an appropriate and suitable word. Four alternatives are suggested for each question. Choose the correct alternative out of the four.**
    Are your really desirous .... visiting Japan?
    (a) of
    (b) in
    (c) to
    (d) about

30. **Direction : The question contains a sentence followed by four choices. Select from these choices the one which most logically completes the idea contained in the given sentence or part.**
    It makes me wince when managers grumble that the Internet simply deluges them with customer email,
    (a) making it difficult for them to pick the grain out of the chaff

(b)   making unreasonable demands on their precious time

(c)   driving up their customer service costs

(d)   with a surfeit of specious complaints

31. **Direction: Choose the correct prefix to get a meaningful word.**
     ___pone.
     (a) uni-   (b) in-
     (c) post-   (d) ante-

32. **Direction: Change the following sentence into imperative sentence:**
     You cannot talk to me like this.
     (a) Do not talk me like this
     (b) Can you not talk to me like this
     (c) Do not to talk to me like this
     (d) Do not talk to me like this

33. **Which of the following is not a simple sentence?**
     (a) I have a very costly book in my house.
     (b) She reads what she likes.
     (c) She does not know good manners.
     (d) He is a man of great knowledge.

34. **Direction: Arrange the words to make a meaningful sentence**
     must / eat / leafy / vegetables / green /children /taught /be /to.
     (a) Children must be taught to eat green, leafy vegetables.
     (b) Children must be taught to eat leafy green, vegetables.
     (c) Must be taught to eat children green, leafy vegetables.
     (d) Green, leafy vegetables must be taught to children eat.

35. **In each question below a sentence broken into four or five parts. Join these parts to make a meaningful sentence. The correct order of parts is the answer.**
     1. **Do**
     2. **Today**
     3. **You**
     4. **Must**
     5. **It**
     (a) 34152   (b) 25413
     (c) 12543   (d) 51324

36. **Direction: In the following question a part of sentence is bold. Below are given alternatives to the part of sentence given in bold, which may improve the sentence. Choose the alternative which makes the sentence grammatically and contextually correct. In case the sentence is correct as it is, choose 'No Improvement' as your option.**
     He lives far from the station.
     (a) Away from the station
     (b) A long way from the station
     (c) Off the station
     (d) No improvement

37. **Direction: Fill in the blanks given below to form correct sentence by using the appropriate option:**
     The sun rose bright and fair, and the morning was _______ a cloud.
     (a) In   (b) Without
     (c) From   (d) None of these

38. **Direction: Pick out the most effective word from the given word to fill in the blank to make the sentence** meaningfully complete.
     He has been seriously injured. There is _________ hope for his survival.
     (a) A little   (b) A few
     (c) Little   (d) Few

39. **Direction: The given sentence is of which type.**
     Come to the ball dance with me!
     (a) Declarative sentence   (b) Interrogative sentence
     (c) Imperative sentence   (d) Exclamatory sentence

40. **Direction: Separate the following sentence into Subject and Predicate.**
     He has a good memory.
     (a) Subject: has a good memory; Predicate:He
     (b) Subject: He; Predicate: has a good memory
     (c) Subject: He has a; Predicate: good memory
     (d) Subject: He has; Predicate: a good memory

41. **/beri/ is the correct transcription of:**
     (a) beri   (b) berry
     (c) bury   (d) beary

42. **'Exist' is transcribed as:**
     (a) /cgjhist   (b) /egziest/
     (c) /cg'zist/   (d) /lg'zist/

43. **The correct transcription of 'virtue' is:**
     (a) /wʌchuː/   (b) /v3ːtʃuː/
     (c) /'vɜrtʃuː/   (d) /w3ːtʃuː/

44. **Direction: Select the most appropriate meaning of the underlined idiom in the given sentence.**
     He runs for two hours <u>at a stretch</u> to build his stamina.
     (a) easily   (b) painfully
     (c) comfortably   (d) continuously

45. **Direction: Select the most appropriate meaning of the underlined idiom in the given sentence.**
     He knows the <u>ins and outs</u> of the case and has been chosen to defend the accused.
     (a) expense involved   (b) time needed to complete
     (c) high stakes   (d) complete details

46. **Direction: Select the most appropriate meaning of the underlined idiom in the given sentence.**
     If the audit report shows anomalies, the finance manager will be <u>brought to book.</u>
     (a) Held accountable   (b) Rewarded suitably
     (c) Supported fully   (d) Given a promotion

47. **Directions: Select the most appropriate meaning of the underlined idiom in the given sentence.**
     Information technology has developed <u>by leaps and bounds.</u>
     (a) very gradually   (b) at a rapid pace
     (c) in far off places   (d) through unfair means

48. **Direction: Complete the proverb.**
     A ______ in the hand is worth two in the bush.
     (a) Bird   (b) Sheep
     (c) Fish   (d) Fruit

Ques (49-50): Direction: Point out the figure of speech used in the sentence given below.

49. **He was a learned man among lords, and a lord among**

learned men.

(a) Epigram

(b) Metonymy

(c) Oxymoron

(d) Antithesis

50. And thou, Dalhousie, the great god of war Lieutenant-Colonel to the Earl of Mar.

(a) Apostrophe

(b) Epigram

(c) Anticlimax

(d) Paradox

// Smart Answer Sheet //

Correct Percentage of students who answered correctly.

Skipped Percentage of students who skipped.

Q.	Ans.	Correct / Skipped	Q.	Ans.	Correct / Skipped	Q.	Ans.	Correct / Skipped
1	A	57.39% / 1.2%	2	C	67.9% / 1.57%	3	D	25.96% / 4.13%
4	C	56.11% / 1.67%	5	C	41.96% / 1.06%	6	A	59.33% / 1.6%
7	D	46.33% / 1.85%	8	B	54.62% / 1.33%	9	C	65.45% / 1.24%
10	D	51.77% / 1.63%	11	B	68.47% / 1.06%	12	C	61.84% / 1.48%
13	A	64.8% / 1.17%	14	B	55.26% / 1.82%	15	D	46.64% / 1.85%
16	C	40.51% / 1.43%	17	B	84.5% / 0.0%	18	A	46.43% / 1.47%
19	C	57.63% / 1.52%	20	A	63.1% / 1.87%	21	B	85.22% / 0.0%
22	D	84.84% / 0.0%	23	B	86.22% / 0.0%	24	B	66.13% / 1.79%
25	D	45.61% / 1.76%	26	D	78.86% / 0.0%	27	C	42.38% / 1.45%
28	C	64.93% / 1.29%	29	A	51.23% / 1.25%	30	C	49.61% / 1.54%
31	C	50.1% / 1.24%	32	D	88.7% / 0.0%	33	B	80.76% / 0.0%
34	A	46.09% / 1.05%	35	A	40.32% / 1.14%	36	D	49.83% / 1.72%
37	B	58.04% / 1.08%	38	C	47.99% / 1.86%	39	C	81.7% / 0.0%
40	B	44.7% / 1.66%	41	B	66.53% / 1.13%	42	D	48.75% / 1.82%
43	C	89.64% / 0.0%	44	D	79.68% / 0.0%	45	D	60.97% / 1.66%
46	A	79.28% / 0.0%	47	B	47.72% / 1.65%	48	A	68.9% / 1.48%
49	A	42.86% / 1.73%	50	C	43.03% / 1.8%			

// Hints and Solutions //

1(A). It is mentioned that "It leaves the Himachal boundary to enter the plains of the Punjab at the Bhakra Dam, the second highest gravity dam and a major point of water supply and electricity generation for the North of India." Clearly, no other option mentions the appropriate reason.

2(C). It is mentioned that "Kangri Karchok, the Kailash Purana of the Tibetans describes the sacred elephant-mouthed river or Langchen Khambab as a long and extensive river that rises from the 'lake unconquerable', the Tso Maphan or Manasarovar that flows from the mountainous regions of Tibet" and "Then it streams into Shimla, Kullu, Mandi and Bilaspur and is responsible for the rich cultivation of grapes, apples and apricots all along its banks." It can clearly be deduced that Kangri karchok is a holy book.

Also, it can be inferred that Langchen Khambab is responsible for rich cultivation of grapes, apples and apricots in Shimla, Kullu, Mandi and Bilaspur.

3(D). Gigantic: of very great size or extent; huge or enormous. Let us look at the meanings of the options-

- Terrifying means causing extreme fear.
- High means of great vertical extent.
- Formidable means inspiring fear or respect through being impressively large, powerful, intense, or capable.
- Huge means extremely large; enormous.

Clearly, 'huge' is correct.

4(C). Sacred means connected with God or a god or dedicated to a religious purpose and so deserving veneration. Let us look at the meanings of the options-

- Pure means not mixed or adulterated with any other substance or material.
- Noble means belonging by rank, title, or birth to the aristocracy.
- Unholy means sinful; wicked.
- Moral means concerned with the principles of right and wrong behaviour.

Clearly, 'unholy' is the correct word.

5(C). The sentence tells the 'these people' should have their biopics too. For such adding up of subjects, we use 'as well'.

6(A). Actually means really; in fact or although it may seem strange. In this context, the torchbearer of Indian football didn't actually have an easy start. This means that although his success seemed easy in reality, his start was not as it seemed.

7(D). While is used when two actions occur simultaneously. In the given sentence, two actions (Bhutia being athletic and his parents not being keen) occur simultaneously. Erstwhile means former, or previously. During is used to show the whole duration of action. When is used to indicate a point of time.

8(B). 'From' tells about the start of something (being athletic). Here it indicates that from a young age he was in athletics. 'To' is used for directions or indications. 'During' is used to show the whole duration of action. 'At' describes a location.

9(C). Pursuing means to try to achieve something or to continue to do something over a period of time. Present means give an exhibition of to an interested audience. Persevere means be persistent, refuse to stop. Purveying means supply with provisions.

10(D). All-round is a verb phrase meaning able to do many different things well; good in many different ways. Here, it is used because Mehmood was a comedian, entertainer, and good at many other things at the same time.

11(B). Odd means beyond or deviating from the usual or expected. Here, it means that earlier Mehmood had to do many irrelevant jobs before he started acting. Common means having no special distinction or quality; widely known or commonly encountered; average or ordinary or usual. Glorifying means bestow glory upon. Various means of many different kinds purposefully arranged but lacking any uniformity.

12(C). The sentence is talking about a sequence of events. In such cases, we use 'after'. 'After' is a preposition, conjunction, and an adverb as well that means later than something or repeated many times or continuing for a long time.

13(A). **According to the passage:** "Have you ever wondered what the qualities of a really professional teacher are? I know that all teachers want their students to like them, but being liked isn't the be-all and end-all really, is it? I mean teachers have to make some unpopular decisions sometimes. Thus, it can be conclude that from the writer's point of view, being liked isn't the be-all and end-all really." The expression isn't the be-all and end-all... is an assumption that pertains to the **writer's** point of view.

14(B). **According to the passage:** "Indeed, a fallback position is part of good planning. It stands to reason also that a teacher must observe punctuality and appropriate tidiness and dress : it is not possible to demand such behaviour from students if the teacher doesn't set the standards."
Here, the fallback position is the system where good teachers are well-prepared.

15(D). **According to the passage: "** A professional teacher needs to be confident without being arrogant. Nobody can expect to have all the answers, so, if a student asks a real stinker, the professional teacher should be able to admit defeat but offer to find out more for the student. And they must carry that promise out."
Here, able to admit defeat implies that teachers should be confident enough to own up to their unpreparedness.

16(C). **According to the passage: "** When the teacher enters the classroom, she/he should have all the required materials and the lesson-plan ready. And, in orchestrating the class, the teacher must give everyone their chance to contribute and should be flexible enough to modify lessons if they are obviously not going to plan."
Here, orchestrating the class suggests acknowledging the individual differences in the process of achievement.

17(B). **According to the passage:** "A professional teacher needs to be confident without being arrogant. Nobody can expect to have all the answers, so, if a student asks a real stinker, the professional teacher should be able to admit defeat but offer to find out more for the student. And they must carry that promise out."
Here, ... asks a real stinker... suggests that students can be better informed than their teachers.

18(A). **According to the passage:** "The last thing I would mention is that teachers should be able to feel that their professionalism entitles them to back up from the school directors. Entitles means to furnish with a right or claim to something. Warrants means officially affirm or guarantee something."
A word that can best replace the word entitles in the passage is warrants.

19(C). **According to the passage:** "If a teacher has a problem with class or student, then the school should have procedures for handling the difficulties. The teacher should not have to feel alone and vulnerable if a difficult situation rises. So, yes, professionalism cuts both ways: in the standards we demand of teachers and the framework we have for giving them support."
The writer's view that professionalism cuts both ways means trustees and their employees owe each other support.

20(A). **According to the passage:** "The teacher should not have to feel alone and vulnerable if a difficult situation rises. So, yes, professionalism cuts both ways : in the standards we demand of teachers and the framework we have for giving them support."
Here, framework refers to the overall school curriculum.

21(B). The correct spelling is manageable.
Meaning of Manageable: Something that can be managed.

22(D). Winery: A place where wine is made
Bakery: A place where bread and cakes are made and/or sold
Cloakroom: A room in a public building where people can leave coats, bags, etc. for a time
Tannery: A place where animal skins are tanned and made into leather

23(B). Occurrence is the right spelling of occurence, which means an incident or event.
Tomorrow means the day after today.
Temperature means how hot or cold something is.
Preferable means better or more suitable.

24(B). 'Perseverence' is incorrectly spelt its correct spelling is 'Perseverance'. It means persistence in doing something despite difficulty or delay in achieving success.
'Tranquility' means calmness, peacefulness.
'Resplendence' means a very bright or beautiful appearance.
'Accommodation' means a place for somebody to live or stay.

25(D). Wastness means the state of lying barren or being waste.
Vastness means very great extent or size; immensity." the vastness of the Atlantic Ocean"
Wasteness means the quality or state of being waste.
Vasteness is an incorrectly spelled word

26(D). Energy is a noun.
Energy means the ability to put effort and enthusiasm into an activity, work, etc.
A noun is a word that refers to a thing (book), a person (Betty Crocker), an animal (cat), a place (Omaha), a quality (softness), an idea (justice), or an action (yodeling). It's usually a single word, but not always: cake, shoes, school bus, and time and a half are all nouns.

27(C). Given sentence is in Past indefinite (Past simple) tense and it is in the passive voice.
Rule for the Passive voice of Past indefinite (Past simple) tense is:
Object + (was /were) + V3 + by + subject + other agents.
Passive voice: The beggar was laughed at by the boy.
Active voice: The boy laughed at the beggar.

28(C). **Has** is used when we talk about receiving by one particular individual or for having something by one particular individual.
Does is used when an action is stated in general in present tense.
We use **is** when we state about one particular thing.
Were is plural form of past tense was which tells us about the existence of a number of things in the past.
Has fits appropriately in this context.
Each of the girls **has** received an award.

29(A). Looking at the meaning of the word given here:
desirous (Adj.): having a wish for something; wanting something; desirous agrees with the preposition 'of'.
Here, 'of' is the right usage.
Complete sentence: Are your really desirous of visiting Japan.

30(C). The author is pained. This means that he believes the managers are not realising the potential of customer email.

Thus, complete sentence is It makes me wince when managers grumble that the Internet simply deluges them with customer email, driving up their customer service costs.

31(C). The prefix is a letter or a group of letters that appears at the beginning of a word and changes the word's original meaning.

The word legal consists of the prefix 'Post'- which means 'after' combined with the root (or stem) word 'pone' the word becomes Postpone.

There are some words related to the prefix 'Post' that are - post-natal, post-mortem.

32(D). The given sentence is an assertive sentence.

To change an assertive sentence into an imperative sentence, we follow the steps mentioned below:

- If the given assertive sentence starts with 'you' and contains an auxiliary verb and negative adverb 'not', while changing it into imperative sentence, subject 'you' should be removed. And the sentence will start with 'do not'.
- 'Do not' will then be followed by main verb and extra information.

Following the rules mentioned above, we get the required imperative sentence as following:

- Do not talk to me like this

33(B). A simple sentence contains one independent clause.

A compound sentence contains more than one independent clause.

For example:

- He plays football. (Simple)
- He dances and sings as well. (Compound)

The option (B) is a combination of two sentences i.e. She reads and She likes.

So, it isn't an example of a simple sentence.

34(A). Follow the subject – verb – other words order. Also take care of the comma – since it is placed after 'green' this word has to be written before 'leafy.' It is also the order of adjectives.

35(A). "You must do it today"= 34152 is correct.

"Today it must do you"= 25413 is incorrect.

"Do today it must you"= 12543 is incorrect.

"It do you today must"= 51324 is incorrect.

36(D). The adverb far showing distance indicates at, to, or from a great distance in space or time:

Ex: (1) How far is it from Australia to New Zealand?

(2) He doesn't live far from here.

37(B). Without should be there as the sentence describes the weather of the day. ' without the clouds' means a bright sunny day. Without is defined as outside of, free from or not with. So, the correct sentence is "The sun rose bright and fair, and the morning was without a cloud. "

38(C). Few is a quantifier used with plural countable nouns. Little is used with singular uncountable nouns. Hope is singular uncountable nouns.

He has been seriously injured. There is little hope for his survival.

39(C). The given sentence is an Imperative sentence.

Whenever a demand is expressed, it's an imperative sentence. It could also be instructions, requests, a wish or demands. Basically, anything you want to make happen can be expressed in what we call, imperative sentence.

40(B). Subject: He; Predicate: has a good memory

The pronoun he is being talked about here. He is the topic of discussion and is, therefore, the subject. The rest of the sentence consists of what is being said about the subject, i.e., the predicate, starting with the verb has.

41(B). /beri/ is the correct transcription of berry.

Phonetic alphabets include symbols, which can be used to describe the sounds or words, sentences, and phrases of all the languages of the world. It is known as phonetic or phonic transcription.

It is based on the principle of "one symbol one sound" which is a symbol that represents one and only one sound.

Some English words with their phonic transcription are given below:

cell - /sel/

- Berry - /beri/
- does - /d^z/
- admit - /əd'mɪt/

This allows language teachers to teach pronunciation to remedy it and helps students to compare the different varieties of the same language.

The pronouncing dictionaries of the English language include the phonetic transcription of the words in addition to their meaning.

42(D). 'Exist' is transcribed as /ɪg'zist/.

- Phonetic transcription, also known as phonetic script or phonetic notation, is the visual representation of speech sounds or phones by means of symbols.
- The most common type of phonetic transcription uses a phonetic alphabet, such as the International Phonetic Alphabet.
- The word 'exist', according to IPA is transcribed as '/ɪg'zist/'.

43(C). The correct transcription of 'virtue' is /'vɜrtʃuː/ .

- Phonetic transcription, also known as phonetic script or phonetic notation, is the visual representation of speech sounds or phones by means of symbols.
- The most common type of phonetic transcription uses a phonetic alphabet, such as the International Phonetic Alphabet.
- The word 'virtue', according to IPA is transcribed as '/'vɜrtʃuː/'.

44(D). He runs for two hours continuously to build his stamina.

At a stretch means continuously; without stopping.

Example: She worked for six hours at a stretch.

45(D). He knows the complete details of the case and has been chosen to defend the accused.

The meaning of the given idiom 'ins and outs' is 'complete details'.

Ins and outs: the detailed or complicated facts of something.

Example: I know how to use computers, but I don't really understand the ins and outs of how they work.

46(A). The correct answer is 'held accountable.'

Brought to book- to reprimand or require (someone) to give an explanation of his conduct.

Example:

If policemen have lied, then they must be brought to book.

47(B). The correct answer is- at a rapid pace.

Given Idiom: By leaps and bounds means rapidly or in fast progress.

Example - Her French is improving by leaps and bounds

48(A). A Bird in the hand is worth two in the bush.
A Bird in the hand is worth two in the bush means i t's better to be content with what you have than to risk losing everything by seeking to get more.
A proverb is a short sentence that people often quote, which gives advice or tells you something about life.
Example: The enemy of my enemy is my friend.

49(A). He was a learned man among lords and a lord among learned men. The figure of speech in this sentence is Epigram.
- Epigram is a rhetorical device that is a memorable, brief, interesting, and surprising satirical statement. Another example is: "Mankind must put an end to war, or war will put an end to mankind."
- Metonymy: the substitution of the name of an attribute or adjunct for that of the thing meant, For Example - Suit for the business executive or the turf for horse racing.
- Oxymoron: a figure of speech in which apparently contradictory terms appear in conjunction, For Example- Faith unfaithful kept him falsely true.
- Antithesis: a person or thing that is the direct opposite or negation of someone or something else, For Example- Love is the antithesis of selfishness.

50(C). The figure of speech in above sentence is Anticlimax.
Anticlimax is a figure of speech in which statements gradually descend in order of importance. Here Dalhousie is considered to be 'the great god of war' and later as a Lieutenant Colonel to the Earl of Mar. Thus, the titles given descend in order of importance. Another example is: She is a great writer, a mother and a good humorist.

Practice Test 02

Ques (1-6): Direction : Read the given passage and answer the question that follow by selecting the most appropriate option.

Anthropology is the holistic study of humankind. It studies all aspects of human life in all geographic regions of all time periods, from its evolution as Homo sapiens to its diverse manifestations within cultures and societies, both past and present. Since recorded history, people have sought answers to such probing questions as, Who are we? How have we come to be we are? How can diverse people peaceably coexist? and What might the past and present tell us about our future? Anthropology seeks to answer these and many other fundamentally humanistic questions. Anthropology employs both qualitative and quantitative research methods within its numerous sub-disciplines. Common to all anthropologists is the method of fieldwork. A physical anthropologist may observe wild or captive primates, or dig prehistoric sites to discover clues about humankind's origins and early migration patterns while an applied anthropologist plays games with disadvantaged schoolchildren to advise school administrators on how to create conflict reducing after-school programmes. A socio-cultural anthropologist may live in a hut among tribal communities to learn the meanings of their unique rituals and political economy, while a linguistic anthropologist interacts with native language speakers at a family function to discover clues to their cultural retention amidst a globalizing society. Within each of these and the myriad other ways and places in which anthropologists conduct day-to-day research, they seek answers to benefit humankind. Anthropology has been described as "the reformer's science", and "the most humanistic of the sciences and the most scientific of the humanities".

1. **The prime function of an anthropologist is to ____ human history and behaviour.**
   (a) watch
   (b) record
   (c) predict
   (d) analyze

2. **The writer suggests that Anthropology is a discipline that leads to:**
   (a) removal of diversity of human cultures
   (b) greater globalization
   (c) promotion of diversity and individuality in human society
   (d) deeper understanding of human diversity which leads to harmony

3. **A word that can best replace the word holistic in line 01 of the passage is:**
   (a) spiritual
   (b) comprehensive
   (c) mystical
   (d) healthy

4. **A / An ______ anthropologist studies human and non-human primate evolution, human variation and its significance, and the biological bases of human behaviour.**
   (a) physical
   (b) linguistic
   (c) socio-cultural
   (d) applied

5. **The discipline is referred to as the reformer's science because:**
   (a) necessary changes can easily be introduced
   (b) laws can be applied with little resistance
   (c) of being a favoured field of study for scientists
   (d) of its potential to improve human lives in general

6. **An antonym for the word 'countable' from the passage is:**
   (a) captive
   (b) diverse
   (c) disadvantaged
   (d) myriad

Ques (7-13): Direction : Read the passage and answer the question that follows.

1. June came and the hay was almost ready for cutting. On Midsummer's Eve, which was a Saturday, Mr. Jones went into Willington and got so drunk at the Red Lion that he did not come back till midday on Sunday. The men had milked the cows early in the morning and then had gone out rabbiting, without bothering to feed the animals. When Mr. Jones got back he immediately went to sleep on the drawing-room sofa with the News of the World over his face, so that when evening came the animals were still unfed. At last they could stand it no longer. One of the cows broke in the door of the store-shed with her horn and all the animals began to help themselves from the bins.

2. It was just then that Mr. Jones woke up. The next moment he and his four men were in the store-shed with whips in their hands, lashing out in all directions. This was more than the hungry animals could bear. With one accord, though nothing of the kind had been planned before, they flung themselves upon their tormentors. Jones and his men suddenly found themselves being butted and kicked from all sides. The situation was quite out of their control. They had never seen animals behave like this before, and this sudden uprising of creatures frightened them out of their wits. They gave up trying to defend themselves and took to their heels. Soon all five of them were in full flight down the cart-track that led to the main road with the animals pursuing them in triumph.

3. Mrs. Jones looked out of the bedroom window, saw what was happening, hurriedly flung a few possessions into a carpet bag, and slipped out of the farm by another way. Meanwhile the animals had chased Jones and his men out into . the road and slammed the five-barred gate behind them. So, almost before they knew what was happening, Jones was expelled and the Manor farm was theirs.

7. **The word 'flung' means the same as:**
   (a) Covered
   (b) Attacked
   (c) Throw
   (d) Hit

8. **Jones' men didn't bother to feed the animals because:**
   (a) Their master had gone to Willington.
   (b) Each thought the other would feed them.
   (c) They were angry with their master.
   (d) They just forgot to do the job assigned to them.

9. **After one of the cows had broken in the door of the store-shed, the hungry animals:**
   (a) Began kicking Jones' men.
   (b) Started damaging things.
   (c) Ran out of the shed
   (d) Started eating the fodder from the bins

10. **When Jones and his men started lashing out at the animals, they (the animals):**
    (a) Started bellowing agonisingly.
    (b) Started kicking and butting their tormentors.
    (c) Felt terrified.
    (d) Ran out of the farm house.

11. **For the readers the scene described in Para-2 is highly:**
    (a) Comic
    (b) Intriguing
    (c) Pathetic
    (d) Outrageous

12. **The fierce attack launched by the animals shows that:**
    (a)   Animals are thinking beings.
    (b)   Injustice leads to rebellion.
    (c)   Anger is a destructive emotion.
    (d)   Animal behaviour is unpredictable.

13. **The word/words which is/are similar in meaning to 'immediately' is/are:**
    (a)   Slowly   (b)   Usually
    (c)   At once   (d)   Tardily

Ques (14-20): Direction : Read the passage given below and answer the questions that follow by choosing correct/most appropriate option:

1. There is consistent, strong evidence to prove that the SARSCoV-2 virus, behind the COVID-19 pandemic, is predominantly transmitted through air, according to a new assessment published on Friday in The Lancet journal. The analysis by six experts from the UK, the US and Canada says public health measures to fail to treat the virus as predominantly the airborne route leaves the people unprotected and allows the virus to spread. Although some studies in the past have suggested that COVID-19 may spread through air, overall scientific literature on the subject has been inconclusive. In July last year, over 200 scientists from 32 nations wrote to WHO, saying there is evidence that the Corona virus is airborne, and even smaller particles can infect people. "The evidence supporting airborne transmission is overwhelming, and evidence supporting large droplet transmission is almost non-existent", said Jose-Luis Jimenez, from the University of Colorado Boulder in the US. "It is urgent that the world Health Organization and other public health agencies adapt their description of transmission to the scientific evidence so that the focus of mitigation is put on reducing airborne transmission," Jimenez said. Studies have confirmed these events cannot be adequately explained by close contact or touching shared surfaces or objects, the researchers said in their assessment.

2. They noted the transmission rates of SARS-CoV-2 are much higher indoors than outdoors, and transmission is greatly reduced by indoor ventilation. The term cited previous studies estimating that silent - asymptomatic or pre-symptomatic transmission of SARS-CoV-2 from people who are not coughing or sneezing accounts for at least 40 percent of all transmission.

14. **Which of the following statements is not true about the transmission of SARS-CoV-2?**
    1. It is transmitted through air.
    2. Transmission rates of the disease are much higher indoors than outdoors.
    3. It is not transmitted via close contact or touching shared surfaces or objects.
    4. It could be transmitted through asymptomatic patients to a healthy person.
    (a)   1   (b)   2
    (c)   3   (d)   4

15. **According to experts from the UK, the US and Canada the SARS-CoV-2 virus:**
    1. spreads through human contact.
    2. affects the elderly the most.
    3. proves fatal to people with weak immune system
    4. the airborne route leaves people unprotected.
    (a)   1   (b)   2
    (c)   3   (d)   4

16. **What, according to Jimenez, should WHO and other public health organisations do to effectively deal with the problem?**
    1. To find a scientific cure for permanent extinction of the virus.
    2. To find scientific ways to reduce the airborne transmission
    3. Issue guidelines regarding Covid-19 protocol and make them mandatory for all.
    4. To adapt their description of transmission to scientific evidence to reduce airborne transmission.
    (a)   1   (b)   2
    (c)   3   (d)   4

17. **Choose the correct option to fill in the blank in the following sentence.**
    ____________ was the first to establish the fact that COvid-19 pandemic prominently spreads through air.
    1. World Health Organisation
    2. Jose-Luis Jimenez
    3. Research studies
    4. Lancet Journal
    (a)   1   (b)   2
    (c)   3   (d)   4

18. **Which of the following words has the same meaning as the word, 'overwhelming' as used in paragraph 1 of the passage?**
    1. strong
    2. transparent
    3. clear
    4. close
    (a)   1   (b)   2
    (c)   3   (d)   4

19. **Which of the following words is opposite in meaning to the word, 'consistent' as used in para 1 of the passage?**
    1. excellent
    2. dependable
    3. marvellous
    4. astonishing
    (a)   1   (b)   2
    (c)   3   (d)   4

20. **Which part of the following sentences contains an error?**
    He asked him/(a), why was he reluctant/(b), to accept/(c), such a good offer./(d)
    1. (a)
    2. (d)
    3. (b)
    4. (c)
    (a)   1   (b)   2
    (c)   3   (d)   4

21. **Direction: Out of the four alternatives, choose the one which express the right meaning of the word.**
    Augment
    (a)   Increase   (b)   Decrease
    (c)   Save   (d)   Mention

22. **Direction : Out of the four alternatives, choose the one which expresses the similar meaning of the given word.**
    Dubious
    (a)   Doubtful   (b)   Disputable
    (c)   Duplicate   (d)   Dangerous

23. **Direction : Out of the four alternatives, choose the one which expresses the similar meaning of the given word.**
    Flabbergasted
    (a)   Scared   (b)   Embarrassed

(c) Dumbfounded   (d) Humiliated

24. **Direction : Out of the four alternatives, choose the one which expresses the similar meaning of the given word.**
Eternal
(a) Innumerable   (b) Unmeasurable
(c) Prolonged   (d) Perpetual

25. **Direction : Choose the word opposite in meaning to the given word.**
Despair
(a) Belief   (b) Trust
(c) Hope   (d) Faith

Ques (26-27): Direction: Fill in the blanks with the appropriate pair of words.

26. **Discipline can be explained as _____ that will develop one's moral character and helps to _____ a particular type of behaviour.**
(a) procedure, train   (b) training, support
(c) training, produce   (d) None of these

27. **Global _________ effort is essential to addressing _________ such as climate change, and delivering on the promise of technology.**
(a) important, views   (b) economic, harmful
(c) wonderful, things   (d) cooperative, challenges

28. **Direction: In the given question, a part of the sentence is underlined. Below are given alternatives to the underlined part as (A), (B), and (C), which may improve the sentence. Choose the correct alternative. In case 'no improvement' is needed, your answer is (D).**
After several days' tour, we became convinced that the climate of this place was like Srinagar in winter .
(a) was like that of Srinagar in winter
(b) was like Srinagar&aposs in winter
(c) in winter was like Srinagar
(d) No improvement

29. **Direction: In the following question, one part of the sentence has an error. Read the sentence to find the error and mark the corresponding option.**
If you live (A)/ in one of the (B)/ country he is visiting, (C)/ how will you welcome him? (D)
(a) (C)   (b) (A)
(c) (B)   (d) (D)

30. **Direction: Pick out the most effective word from the choices below to fill in the blanks to make the sentence meaningfully complete.**
The strike in the paper mill has resulted in a _____ loss.
(a) commendable   (b) voluminous
(c) colossal   (d) comprehensive

31. **Direction: Pick out the most effective word from the choices below to fill in the blanks to make the sentence meaningfully complete.**
A cup of water was enough to _____ his thirst.
(a) satisfy   (b) appease
(c) quench   (d) extinguish

32. **Direction: Identify the degree in the sentence:**
There are many large cricket stadiums in India.
(a) Positive Degree   (b) Comparative Degree

(c) Superlative Degree   (d) None of these

33. **Direction: Choose the correct part of speech for the underlined word.**
Tarry walked toward the back door <u>inside</u> the office.
(a) Adverb   (b) Preposition
(c) Verb   (d) Conjunction

34. **Direction : Choose the option that best transforms the given sentences into one.**
The speaker had just finished his speech. The people started shouting slogans.
(a) Hardly had the speaker finished his speech before the people started shouting slogans.
(b) Hardly had the speaker finished his speech then the people started shouting slogans.
(c) Hardly had the speaker finished his speech when the people started shouting slogans.
(d) Hardly had the speaker finish his speech and the people started shouting slogans.

35. **Direction : Rearrange the following words/phrases to make meaningful sentence by choosing the correct sequence.**
Snowfall (A)/ heavy (B)/ the (C)/ everything (D)/ covered (E)
(a) CBAED   (b) BAECD
(c) DECBA   (d) CABED

36. **Direction : Rearrange the following words/phrases to make meaningful sentence by choosing the correct sequence.**
Waved (A)/ she (B)/ greeted (C)/ and (D)/ cheerfully (E)/ us (F)
(a) BCDFEA   (b) CADBEF
(c) ADBFEC   (d) BADCFE

37. **Direction: Separate the Subject and the Predicate in the following sentence:**
All matter is indestructible.
(a) Subject: indestructible; Predicate: All matter is
(b) Subject: All; Predicate: matter is indestructible
(c) Subject: All matter; Predicate: is indestructible
(d) Subject: matter; Predicate: All is indestructible

38. **Direction : Choose the option that best transforms the given sentences into one.**
This is my cousin. His name is Anil.
(a) Anil is his cousin brother.
(b) This was my cousin brother Anil.
(c) This is my cousin, Anil.
(d) He is not my cousin brother Anil

39. **Direction: Separate the following sentence into Subject and Predicate:**
Nature is the best physician.
(a) Subject: Nature is the; Predicate: best physician
(b) Subject: physician; Predicate: Nature is the best
(c) Subject: the best physician; Predicate: Nature is
(d) Subject: Nature; Predicate: is the best physician

40. **Direction : Given below are six sentences with the first and the last in their correct order; however, the remaining four are jumbled. Pick the option that gives the correct order.**
Sentence 1. Emilia and her family lived on the island of Sebesi-one of the largest islands in the Sunda Strait-

located near the Anak Krakatau volcano.

P. Sebesi island is one of several areas that was badly hit by the tsunami, which was triggered after volcanic activity at Anak Krakatau caused undersea landslides.

Q. Vast waves engulfed coastal towns on the islands of Sumatra and Java leaving at least 430 dead and more than 150 missing.

R . It destroyed hundreds of buildings, sweeping away cars and uprooting trees in several popular tourist destinations on Saturday.

S. At least 16,000 people still remain displaced and rescue workers are struggling to reach remote areas of the country that have been hit by the tsunami.

Sentence 6. Emelia is one of 90 people who have been hospitalised at the Bob Bazar hospital in the nearby town of Kalianda.

(a) SPQR   (b) PRQS
(c) RSQP   (d) RQPS

41. Identify the word in which the end sound is different from the other words.
(a) Concept   (b) Percept
(c) Sect   (d) Conceit

42. Which of the following words has a diphthong sound?
(a) Speed   (b) Liquid
(c) Paternal   (d) Out

43. Which of the following words begins with the consonant sound /j/?
(a) Jealous   (b) Zeal
(c) Yeast   (d) Gist

44. Direction: In the given sentence, one phrase has been printed in bold. Select the correct meaning of the phrase from the options given below.
The National Human Rights Commission is all bark and no bite as it lacks the authority to penalize those guilty of human rights violations.
(a) Impressive action   (b) Intimidating action
(c) Low on action   (d) Threatening action

45. Direction: In the given sentence, one phrase has been printed in bold. Select the correct meaning of the phrase from the options given below.
Agriculture stocks gained ground after the finance minister proposed to raise institutional credit for agriculture to Rs.11 lakh crore for 2018-19.
(a) Increase in quantity   (b) Become Popular
(c) Lose momentum   (d) Market capitalization

46. Direction : In the following questions, four alternatives are given for the meaning of the given Idiom/Phrase. Choose the alternative which best express the meaning of the Idiom/Phrase.
To pick holes
(a) To find some reason to quarrel
(b) To destroy something
(c) To cut some part of an item
(d) To criticise someone

47. Direction: Select the most appropriate idiom (in the context) to fill in the sentence.
That student of yours has such sound values. She's indeed a _____.
(a) pot calling the kettle black

(b) barrel of laughs
(c) pain in the neck
(d) rare bird

48. **Direction:** Complete the proverb.
Man proposes, _______ disposes.
(a) Friend   (b) Man
(c) Mother   (d) God

Ques (49-50): Direction: Point out the figure of speech used in the sentence given below.

49. **Her voice is music to ears.**
(a) Hyperbole   (b) Metaphor
(c) Idiom   (d) Alliteration

50. **Silence is sometimes more eloquent than speech.**
(a) Personification   (b) Bathos
(c) Oxymoron   (d) Antithesis

// Smart Answer Sheet //

Correct Percentage of students who answered correctly.

Skipped Percentage of students who skipped.

Q.	Ans.	Correct / Skipped	Q.	Ans.	Correct / Skipped	Q.	Ans.	Correct / Skipped
1	D	48.83% / 1.51%	2	D	52.21% / 1.46%	3	B	69.28% / 1.79%
4	A	40.89% / 1.27%	5	D	50.29% / 1.44%	6	D	25.08% / 3.69%
7	C	88.19% / 0.0%	8	D	44.53% / 1.82%	9	D	76.73% / 0.0%
10	B	47.34% / 1.65%	11	D	61.73% / 1.31%	12	D	62.55% / 2.0%
13	C	84.17% / 0.0%	14	C	57.99% / 1.24%	15	D	40.89% / 1.45%
16	D	63.43% / 1.7%	17	D	66.79% / 1.84%	18	A	69.28% / 1.53%
19	B	83.86% / 0.0%	20	C	57.89% / 1.94%	21	A	51.25% / 1.94%
22	A	65.77% / 1.43%	23	C	53.78% / 1.5%	24	D	55.2% / 1.88%
25	C	63.22% / 1.35%	26	C	47.84% / 1.77%	27	D	55.26% / 1.72%
28	A	67.52% / 1.66%	29	A	63.37% / 1.98%	30	C	58.55% / 1.66%
31	C	68.82% / 1.96%	32	A	60.3% / 1.85%	33	B	65.21% / 1.44%
34	C	48.17% / 1.59%	35	A	57.21% / 1.97%	36	D	61.75% / 1.4%
37	C	55.57% / 1.26%	38	C	85.34% / 0.0%	39	D	21.79% / 4.39%
40	B	29.91% / 3.72%	41	D	76.88% / 0.0%	42	D	80.8% / 0.0%
43	C	69.32% / 1.13%	44	C	56.77% / 1.96%	45	B	77.69% / 0.0%
46	D	68.32% / 1.35%	47	D	86.75% / 0.0%	48	B	80.2% / 0.0%
49	B	66.17% / 1.6%	50	D	51.74% / 1.05%			

// Hints and Solutions //

1(D). The prime function of an anthropologist is to analyze human history and behaviour.

The above passage talks about Anthropology and its various sub- disciplines. According to the author, An anthropologist researches human life by various methods in order to satiate the curiosity of People's curiosity about their very existence. Let's refer to last lines of para 2 which states 'anthropologists conduct day-to-day research, they seek answers to benefit humankind'.

2(D). **According to the passage:** "Since recorded history, people have sought answers to such probing questions as, Who are we? How have we come to be we are? How can diverse people peaceably coexist? and What might the past and present tell us about our future? Anthropology seeks to answer these and many other fundamentally humanistic questions".

The writer suggests that Anthropology is a discipline that leads to deeper understanding of human diversity which leads to harmony.

3(B). 'Holistic' means 'dealing with or treating the whole of something or someone and not just a part'. Ex: My doctor takes a holistic approach to disease. The marked option 'comprehensive' means 'complete and including everything that is necessary'. Ex: We offer you a comprehensive training in all aspects of the business.

A word that can best replace the word 'Holistic' in line 01 of the passage is comprehensive.

4(A). A/An physical anthropologist studies human and non-human primate evolution, human variation and its significance, and the biological bases of human behaviour. Physical anthropologists study the biology of human beings. They are concerned with origin and evolution of people. For this purpose, they may observe wild or captive primates, or dig prehistoric sites to discover clues about humankind's origins and early migration patterns.

5(D). The discipline is referred to as the reformer's science because of its potential to improve human lives in general. Reformer refers to someone who tries to improve a system or law by changing it.

6(D). The question word 'countable' means 'capable of being counted'. Ex: The apples are countable. The marked option 'myriad' means 'a very large number of something'. Ex: And now myriads of bars and hotels are opening up along the coast.

An antonym for the word 'countable' from the passage is 'myriad'.

7(C). According to the passage, Flung means to throw, especially with force or abandon.

8(D). Jones' men didn't bother to feed the animals because t hey just forgot to do the job assigned to them.

9(D). According to passage, when evening came the animals were still unfed. At last they could stand it no longer. One of the cows broke in the door of the store-shed with her horn and all the animals began to help themselves from the bins.

10(B). According to the passage, If we look at these lines of the second para, ' With one accord, though nothing of the kind had been planned before, they flung themselves upon their tormentors. Jones and his men suddenly found themselves being butted and kicked from all sides.'

11(D). Outrageous means shocking and morally unacceptable. If we look at these lines of the second para, we can conclude that the behaviour of the animals was frightening and bad, thus, outrageous is the apt answer.

12(D). According to the passage, They had never seen animals behave like this before, and this sudden uprising of creatures frightened them out of their wits.

13(C). Immediately means occurring or done at once; instant.

14(C). According to the passage, 'The term cited previous studies estimating that silent - asymptomatic or pre-symptomatic - transmission of SARS-CoV-2 from people who are not coughing or sneezing accounts for at least 40 percent of all transmission.'

So, it is concluded that 'It is not transmitted via close contact or touching shared surfaces or objects' is not true.

15(D). According to the passage, 'The analysis by six experts from the UK, the US and Canada say public health measures to fail to treat the virus as predominantly the airborne route leaves the people unprotected and allows the virus to spread.'

So, it is concluded that according to experts from the UK, the US and Canada the SARS-CoV-2 virus the airborne route leaves people unprotected.

16(D). According to the passage, "It is urgent that the World Health Organization and other public health agencies adapt their description of transmission to the scientific evidence so that the focus of mitigation is put on reducing airborne transmission," Jimenez said.'

Upon the perusal of the above lines, it can be concluded that 'to adapt their description of transmission to scientific evidence to reduce airborne transmission' is true.

17(D). According to the passage, " There is consistent, strong evidence to prove that the SARS_CoV-2 virus, behind the COVID-19 pandemic, is predominantly transmitted through air, according to a new assessment published on Friday in The Lancet journal."

So, the fact was first established by The Lancet journal.

18(A). The meaning of the given words:
- Overwhelming: very great in amount.
- Strong: having the power to move heavy weights or perform other physically demanding tasks.
- Transparent: (of a material or article) allowing light to pass through so that objects behind can be distinctly seen.
- Clear: easy to perceive, understand, or interpret.
- Close: only a short distance away or apart in space or time.

So, strong is similar in meaning to the word overwhelming.

19(B). The meaning of the given words:
- Consistent: acting or done in the same way over time, especially so as to be fair or accurate.
- Dependable: trustworthy and reliable:
- Excellent: extremely good; outstanding.
- Marvellous: causing great wonder; extraordinary.
- Astonishing: extremely surprising or impressive; amazing.

So, dependable is opposite in meaning to the word consistent.

20(C). Part (b) contains an error.

In indirect speech, the exact meaning is expressed but not necessarily using the speaker's words i.e. we convey the message of the speaker in our own words to another person. In the indirect speech of interrogative sentence, the subject is put before the helping verbs (is, am, are, was, were).

This sentence is in indirect speech but not correctly written in indirect speech as the subject is not used before the verb in this sentence.

So, we change 'why was he reluctant' into 'why he was

reluctant' to make the sentence grammatically correct.
Correct Sentence: He asked him why he was reluctant to accept such a good offer.

21(A). Augment means make (something) greater by adding to it; increase.
So 'increase' is the correct option.
For example, The goal is to augment social interactions during collaborative learning.

22(A). Dubious means hesitating or doubting.
Doubtful means feeling uncertain about something.
For example, Steve tells Catherine he wants to plead manslaughter on grounds of temporary insanity, but she looks dubious about the idea.

23(C). Flabbergasted maens greatly surprised or astonished.
Dumbfounded means so shocked that you cannot speak.
For example, While Dean was flabbergasted, his emotions were conflicted. He said he's " a bit flabbergasted " to win.

24(D). Eternal means lasting or existing forever; without end.
Perpetual means never-ending or changing.
For example, His kindness and support earned him her eternal gratitude.

25(C). Despair means the state of having lost all hope.
Hope means the feeling of wanting something to happen and thinking that it will.
For example, He soon gave up the attempt in despair.

26(C). Complete Sentence: Discipline can be explained as training that will develop one's moral character and helps to produce a particular type of behaviour.
For the first blank, we need a word whose meaning is close to the act of teaching.
For the second blank, we need a word whose meaning is close to generate.
Training: the action of teaching a person or animal a particular skill or type of behaviour.
Produce: to make something or bring something into existence.

27(D). Complete sentence: Global cooperative effort is essential to addressing challenges such as climate change, and delivering on the promise of technology.
In the context of the sentence, the only combination of words that lead to a meaningful sentence is "cooperative" and "challenges". All other options are incorrect either contextually or grammatically. The sentence wants to convey that it is essential for all the countries in the world to unite in order to address issues such as climate change and developing relevant technology.

28(A). The climate should be compared with the climate of Srinagar and not with Srinagar itself. It can be rightly expressed by the phrase 'like that of' as given in option (A). Using preposition 'of' is preferred over apostrophe with Srinagar, maintaining parallelism with 'climate of this place'.

29(A). In the given sentence, the form of the noun 'country' is not correct.
The phrase 'one of the' is used to describe something/ someone from the same group.
The noun following the phrase "one of the" is always a plural noun, whereas the use of verbs as singular or plural will entirely depend upon the subject of the statement, i.e. singular verb for singular subject and plural verb for the plural subject.
Thus, the singular noun 'country' should be replaced by the plural noun 'countries'.

30(C). The correct answer is "colossal".
Let us explore the given options:
Commendable means deserving praise.
Voluminous means very lengthy and detailed.
Colossal means extremely large or great.
Comprehensive means including or dealing with all or nearly all elements or aspects of something.
Complete Sentence: The strike in the paper mill has resulted in a colossal Loss.

31(C). The correct answer is "Quench".
Let us explore the given options:
Satisfy means to meet the expectations, needs, or desires of someone.
Appease means to satisfy a demand or a feeling.
Quench means to satisfy one's thirst by drinking.
Extinguish means put an end to; destroy.
Complete Sentence: A cup of water was enough to quench his thirst.

32(A). Let's discuss the marked option first i.e. Positive degree.
Positive degree is the simplest form of an adjective that merely indicates simple quality, without offering or suggesting any comparison.
• Ex: Sherlock was a great detective.
In the question sentence, adjective 'large' is just denoting the simple quality of being big in size without making any comparison.
'Large' means 'big in size or amount'.

33(B). Here, in the given sentence the underlined part 'inside' is a Preposition.
A preposition is a word or group of words used before a noun, pronoun, or noun phrase to show direction, time, place, location, spatial relationships, or to introduce an object.
Example: The squirrel hid the nuts under a pile of leaves.
• Here, in the given above example, the preposition 'under' is a Preposition.

34(C). 'Hardly....when' is used to combine sentences denoting two past simultaneous actions.
'Hardly' is written at the beginning with the past perfect tense form.
The second part is written after using 'when'.
The most appropriate answer is option (C) which combines the sentences without changing the meaning.
Hardly had the speaker finished his speech when the people started shouting slogans.

35(A). The basic object of words in a sentence is - subject + verb + object.
In the given words subject is the heavy snowfall, covered is verb and everything is object.
So, the sentence will be "The heavy snowfall covered everything."

36(D). The basic object of words in a sentence is - subject + verb + object.
In the given words subject is she, waved is verb and greeted us cheerfully is object.
So, the sentence will be "She waved and greeted us cheerfully."

37(C). All matter is being talked about, followed by the verb is, indicating that the work is being done by the former. Thus, the subject is all matter, and the rest of the sentence, talking about the subject, is the predicate.

38(C). The only sentence which does not change the meaning of the original sentence is option (C).

Options (A) and (D) change the meaning.
Option (B) changes the tense to past tense.
This is my cousin, Anil.

39(D). The word nature is the topic of discussion, doing the work in the sentence, as indicated by the verb is. Thus, nature is the subject and the rest of the sentence, talking about the subject, is the predicate.

40(B). P should be the first sentence as it gives the introduction about the tsunami. Q, R and S describe the effects of the tsunami.
The sixth sentence states about people being hospitalized. So, the fourth and fifth sentences must be about the people (Q and S).
The word 'still' in sentence S hints that S comes after Q. R is therefore, the third sentence. The correct order should be PRQS.

41(D). IPA: It stands for the International Phonetic Association which was first published in 1888. Its objective is to define sounds of speech that applies to all languages. Pronunciations of some of the words are:

Word	Pronunciation
Concept	'kɒnsept
Percept	pə(r)'sept
Sect	Sekt
Conceit	kən'siːt

So, we conclude that 'conceit' has a different pronunciation.

42(D). "Out" has a diphthong sound.
- International Phonetics Association is also known as IPA is the oldest phonetic notation system.
- It was founded for the standardization of speech sounds in written form.
- Diphthongs are vowel sounds. It is also known as glided vowel since two vowels are combined here.
- For example, bound, though loan, all have adjacent vowels.

43(C). "Yeast" begins with the consonant sound /j/.
- International Phonetics Association is also known as IPA is the oldest phonetic notation system.
- It was founded for the standardization of speech sounds in written form.
- The sound /j/ in IPA represents the y sound.
- This sound /j/ can also be found in yes and yellow.
- It should not be confused with the [y] sound as it stands for a non-English vowel.

44(C). All bark and no bite: Full of talk that is more threatening or impressive than that which one can or will actually do, pretentious, often making cutting remarks, but having a gentle personality underneath.
Example: He always threatens to call the police if I don't stay off his lawn, but he's all bark and no bite.
From the meaning given above, option (C) is the best fit here.

45(B). Gain ground: It means to become popular, to make progress, to advance. If something such as an idea or an ideal gains ground, it gradually becomes more widely known or more popular.
Example: The new product gained ground in a very short time.
From the meaning given above, option (B) is the best fit here.

46(D). To pick holes means To make an effort to find flaws or negative aspects in something through excessive analysis or criticism.
Sentence: He then goes on to pick holes in the article before reaching his conclusion.

47(D). The speaker is talking about how the student has sound values i.e., an unusual thing.
Rare bird means an unusual person.
Complete Sentence: That student of yours has such sound values. She's indeed a rare bird.

48(B). Man proposes, Man disposes.
Man proposes, Man disposes means p eople can make plans; God determines how things will turn out.
A proverb is a short sentence that people often quote, which gives advice or tells you something about life.
Example: The enemy of my enemy is my friend.

49(B). The correct answer is Metaphor.
A Metaphor is a figure of speech that makes an implicit, implied, or hidden comparison between two things that are unrelated, but which share some common characteristics.
In the given sentence, her voice is being directly compared to music which means it is very lovely. So, metaphor is the correct answer.

50(D). The correct answer is: Antithesis
Silence is sometimes more eloquent than speech is a famous saying in English which is a classic example of Antithesis
Antithesis: Juxtaposition of two words, phrases, clauses, or sentences contrasted or opposed in meaning in such a way as to give emphasis to contrasting ideas.

Ques (1-5): Direction : Read the passage and answer the question that follows.

My father was a lover of his clan, truthful, brave and generous, but short-tempered. To a certain extent he might have been even given to pleasures. But he was incorruptible, and had earned a name for strict impartiality in his family as well as outside. His loyalty to the state was well known. A Political Agent spoke insultingly of his chief, and he stood up to the insult. The Agent was angry and asked him to apologize. This he refused to do and was therefore kept under detention for a few hours. But when the Agent saw that he was adamant, he ordered him to be released.

My father never had any ambition to accumulate riches, and left us very little property.

He had no education, save that of experience. At best, he might be said to have read up to the fifth standard. Of history and geography he was innocent. But his rich experience of practical affairs stood him in good stead in the solution of the most intricate questions and in managing hundreds of men. Of religious training he had very little but he had that kind of religious culture which frequent visits to temples and listening to religious discourses make available to many Hindus. In his last days he began reading the Gita at the instance of a learned Brahman friend of the family, and he used to repeat aloud some verses everyday at the time of worship.

1. **The word 'adamant' most nearly means:**
   (a) Aggressive   (b) Determined
   (c) Rugged   (d) Angry

2. **'His loyalty to the state was well known.'**
'Tense' in the above sentence has been correctly changed into 'past perfect' in:
   (a) His loyalty to the state is well known.
   (b) His loyalty to the state will have been well known.
   (c) His loyalty to the state had been well known.
   (d) His loyalty to the state has been well known.

3. **The word which is similar in meaning to 'learned' is:**
   (a) Shrewd   (b) Alert
   (c) Clever   (d) Scholarly

4. **The author praises his father for his:**
   (a) Incorruptibility and impartiality.
   (b) Outspokenness and impartiality.
   (c) Learning and impartiality.
   (d) Patience and incorruptibility.

5. **When the author's father refused to apologize to the Political Agent he was?**
   (a) Beaten   (b) Detained
   (c) Humiliated   (d) Heavily fined

Ques (6-13): Direction: Read the passage given below and then answer the questions given below the passage.

Bioengineering combines the design and problem-solving techniques of engineering with biological and medical sciences to improve health-related and medical problems. Bioengineers have made many positive changes in many lives today. It has become a growing field over the past couple of years. The new advances and research that stem from biomedical engineers can solve problems that would have never been able to be solved before. Many great inventions have been made through research in biomedical engineering, for example, genetic engineering, cloning, and insulin. After insulin had been invented, there were still a lot of problems with the purity and the quantity of the insulin produced.

Biomedical engineering devised a way to produce large quantities of insulin with a higher level of purity, which has saved a lot of human lives. Engineers have been working on new technology that will utilise stem cells in order to save lives and treat diseases. By designing life-saving objects such as artificial hearts, dialysis machines, and surgical lasers bioengineers have helped save many lives. Biomedical engineers can be traced back to over 3000 years with the Egyptians. The Egyptians created a wooden prosthesis to replace the big toe. Since then, bioengineering has developed a great deal. A big improvement this century has been the development of artificial lungs. When polio hit the states, many patients were put into a respirator made of two vacuum cleaners and an iron box. This invention, designed by Philip Drinker and Louis Agassiz Shaw, was nicknamed the "iron lung". The iron lung pumped air in and out of the patient, allowing the patient to breathe. Iron lungs are replaced today with artificial lungs, which are more advanced and are put inside the patient, allowing him or her to be mobile and enjoy life to a fuller extent.

6. **Why does bio-engineering combine techniques of engineering with biological and medical sciences?**
   (a) To improve health-related and medical problems
   (b) To improve financial problems
   (c) To make life easier for the poor
   (d) To solve medical problems in developing countries

7. **Since how long has bio-engineering been a growing field?**
   (a) Since 3000 years back
   (b) Since the Egyptians came into being
   (c) Over the past couple of years
   (d) Since Philip Drinker made the iron lung

8. **How was the problem of purity and quantity of insulin handled?**
   (a) Bioengineers got the help of medical sciences
   (b) Bio-engineers came up with a way to make high quantities of pure insulin
   (c) Bio-engineers were stumped at the problem
   (d) Bio-engineers had to seek the help of other professionals

9. **Which of the following is CORRECT in the context of the paragraph?**
   (a) Egyptians created a wooden prosthesis to replace the big toe
   (b) The first biomedical engineers were Africans
   (c) Iron lungs cannot be replaced with anything
   (d) Biomedical engineers were unable to design artificial heart

10. **Which word of the following means the SAME as devised?**
   (a) Adjunct   (b) Perfunctory
   (c) Concocted   (d) Convoyed

11. **Which word of the following means the OPPOSITE of utilise?**
   (a) Unexploited   (b) Requisite
   (c) Stilted   (d) Enforced

12. **What was done when the states were affected by polio?**
   (a) Many patients were left to die
   (b) Many patients were treated but couldn't be saved
   (c) Many patients were put into a respirator

(d) The governments paid no heed to the affected people

13. Why are artificial lungs more effective than iron ones?
(a) They are more advanced
(b) Iron was hard to find and hence only some patients could be helped
(c) Allowed the patient to be mobile and enjoy life to a fuller extent
(d) Both (A) and (C)

Ques (14-20): Direction : Read the autobiographical story given below and answer the question that follows by selecting the correct/most appropriate options.

1. Let me tell you about a young boy who made a model car all on his own. The boy is me. Six years ago when I was just 11 and the car was small and simple but in my imagination it was a high-speed, Formula-1 racing car, speeding along the race track.

2. It was during the summer holidays and workmen were building a new driveway and garage beside our house. While watching the workmen I had an idea. I'd build a car to drive into the garage in celebration of the new addition to our home. I told my mother and drew up complicated plans but I couldn't find the right material. So I gave up and spent a miserable couple of days doing nothing. My mother noticed that I'd stopped working and asked me why. She suggested that maybe I should change my plans to fit the material I had, rather than give up.

3. And that's just what I did. I found pieces of wood in my father's workshop and made my car from anything that was lying around the house. I found a small engine from a toy plane of mine, I added that. The power came from a battery attached with some wire I found in a cupboard.

4. By the time the garage was finished, so was my car. I called my family outside the house, connected the wires, started the engine and placed the car on the driveway. It was fast and I had to run to the garage to rescue it before it crashed into the new door. My family clapped and I smiled proudly. Thanks to my mother, I learnt the value of seeing a project through to its end. Soon I was making plans for my next project: a helicopter!

14. The underlined word in the expression 'six years ago' is a/an:
(a) Conjunction
(b) Preposition
(c) Adverb
(d) Verb

15. In the sentence 'And that's just what I did', the word 'that's' is used as a/an:
(a) Verb
(b) Pronoun
(c) Adjective
(d) Article

16. Read these statements carefully and arrange them in proper sequence as suggested in the text:
(A) Family was called outside the house
(B) Car ran fast and was stopped before it crashed into the door
(C) The garage and car were completed
(D) Engine started after wires were connected
(a) (B) (A) (D) (C)
(b) (C) (A) (D) (B)
(c) (A) (B) (C) (D)
(d) (D) (A) (C) (B)

17. What was the writer's age when he wrote this experience?
(a) 17 is correct, 6 is incorrect
(b) 11 is correct, 17 is incorrect
(c) 11 is correct, 6 is incorrect
(d) 17 is incorrect, 11 is correct

18. Which word in para 2 means the opposite of the word 'easy'?
(a) Addition
(b) Complicated
(c) Celebration
(d) Miserable

19. Why did the writer start building the car ?
(a) To show the workers that he could build something too.
(b) To pass time during school holidays.
(c) To give his mother a special present.
(d) To celebrate the family's new garage.

20. How did the writer feel initially when he started making his car?
(a) Sad that he was unable to find suitable things to make the car
(b) Annoyed that his father wouldn't let him borrow any material
(c) Frustrated by how much time he had wasted on his project
(d) Embarrassed by the poor quality of his model car

21. Find out the words which mean the same as 'eventually'.
(a) Finally
(b) Instantly
(c) Constantly
(d) Abruptly

22. Find out the words which mean the same as 'empowered'.
(a) Excluded
(b) Abolished
(c) Allowed
(d) Activated

23. Find out the words which mean the same as 'revolved'.
(a) Fixed
(b) Automated
(c) Circumduct
(d) Addressed

24. Find out the words which mean the same as 'evidence'.
(a) Assumption
(b) Suggestion
(c) Indication
(d) Deposition

25. Find out the words which mean the same as 'veto'.
(a) Rebuke
(b) Reject
(c) Ratify
(d) Recline

26. Direction: Fill in the blanks with appropriate words from the option given below.
This is a ______ on his character.
(a) blur
(b) blot
(c) spot
(d) slur

27. Direction: Pick out the most effective word from the choices below to fill in the blanks to make the sentence meaningfully complete.
Some of our external problems have completely ______ our national leaders.
(a) beguiled
(b) belaboured
(c) baffled
(d) blustered

28. Direction : In the following question a part of the sentence is bold. Below are given alternatives to the bold part at (A), (B), and (C) which may improve the sentence. Choose the correct alternative. In the case of no improvement, choose (D) as your answer.
Practically every part of the coconut tree is used by man.
(a) Each
(b) All
(c) Most
(d) No improvement

29. Direction : A sentence has given below, with some errors. Find the best option which is error-free.
The councilor has not and will not file his nomination for

re-election.
(a) The councilor has not and will not file his nomination for re-election.
(b) The councilor has not filed, nor will he file his nomination for re-election.
(c) The councilor has not filed, neither will he file his nomination for re-election.
(d) The councilor has not filed and will not file his nomination for re-election.

30. **Direction: What is the status of two the's in the sentence: This is the last time I will remind you to do the things on time.**
(a) Verb
(b) Indefinite article
(c) Definite article
(d) Preposition

31. **Choose the correct alternative which can be substituted for the below given word/sentence.**
A person who talks in sleep is called as
(a) Philatelist
(b) Somnambulist
(c) Somniloquist
(d) Oneirocritic

32. **Choose the option with the correct meaning of the Idioms in the question given below.**
To smell a rat
(a) To see signs of plague epidemic
(b) To get bad small of a bad dead rat
(c) To suspect foul dealings
(d) To be in a bad mood

33. **A sentence has been given in Active Voice. Out of the four alternatives suggested, select the one which best expresses the same sentence in Passive Voice.**
Let me do this.
(a) Let us do this
(b) This is to be done by me
(c) Let this be done by me
(d) Let I do this

34. **Direction: Pick out the most effective word from the choices below to fill in the blanks to make the sentence meaningfully complete.**
He always stammers in public meetings, but his today's speech _________.
(a) Was fairly audible to everyone.
(b) Was not liked by the audience.
(c) As not received by the audience.
(d) Was surprisingly fluent.

35. **Rearrange the parts of the sentence in the correct order.**
1. Even though
P. the movie 'Avatar'
Q. at the Box Office
R. is doing wonders
S. some depict the movie as
6. being racist.
(a) SRPQ
(b) PRQS
(c) QSPR
(d) RSPQ

36. **Rearrange the parts of the sentence in the correct order.**
1. Miffed over the issue
P. of not being given
Q. Chetan Bhagat continues
R. to spew anger
S. due credit for the film '3 Idiots'
6. through his blog.
(a) RSPQ
(b) PSQR
(c) SPQR
(d) SRPQ

37. **Direction: Pick out the most effective word from the choices below to fill in the blanks to make the sentence meaningfully complete.**
The electricity is _____ than coal.
(a) Cheap
(b) To cheap
(c) Cheaper
(d) Cheapest

38. **Direction: Pick out the most effective word from the choices below to fill in the blanks to make the sentence meaningfully complete.**
__________ know about where the soul goes after the death.
(a) Few
(b) A few
(c) Little
(d) A little

39. **Which one of the following options is the right form of the sentence which has been framed using the given parts:**
next/at least/easy for/the doctor/the patient/take things/ suggested that/two months
(a) The patient suggested that the doctor for at least next two months take things easy.
(b) The doctor suggested things that the patient take easy for at least next two months.
(c) The doctor suggested that the patient take things easy for at least next two months.
(d) The doctor suggested the patient that take things easy for next two months at least.

40. **Direction: Pick out the most effective word from the choices below to fill in the blanks to make the sentence meaningfully complete.**
________ work has been done yet. What about remaining work?
(a) A little
(b) A few
(c) Much
(d) Most of

41. **'Adjust' is transcribed as:**
(a) /ə'd3ʌst/
(b) /adʃust/
(c) /ədjust/
(d) /ɔ'd3ʌst/

42. **'Velar' is the sound formed by:**
(a) the front of the tongue and the hard palate
(b) the lower lip and the upper teeth
(c) the blade of the tongue and teeth ridge
(d) the back of the tongue and the soft palate

43. **Sounds 'f', 'v', 'o', 'r' etc. are:**
(a) Semi-vowels
(b) Lateral
(c) Fricatives
(d) Nasals

44. **Direction: Select the most appropriate meaning of the underlined idiom in the given sentence.**
When the miscreants saw the police they beat a retreat.
(a) ran away
(b) protested strongly
(c) attacked fiercely
(d) marched ahead

45. **Direction: Select the most appropriate meaning of the underlined idiom in the given sentence.**
His probation was extended because his performance was not up to the mark.
(a) lacking in maturity
(b) of the desired height
(c) up to the required standard

(d) up to the required standard

46. Direction: Select the most appropriate meaning of the given idiom.
On the double

(a) on the verge of collapse
(b) at a fast pace
(c) out of order
(d) between two undesirable things

47. Direction : Select the most appropriate meaning of the given idiom.
To call the shots

(a) to be the person in charge
(b) to be blissfully happy
(c) to be in debt
(d) to lack control

48. Complete the following proverb.
While there is life, there is _____ .

(a) hope   (b) None of these
(c) happiness   (d) wealth

Ques (49-50): Direction: Point out the figure of speech used in the sentence given below.

49. Sceptre and crown
Must tumble down,
And in dust be equal made
With the poor crooked scythe and spade.

(a) Irony   (b) Apostrophe
(c) Metonymy   (d) Synecdoche

50. Death lays his icy hands on kings.

(a) Metaphor   (b) Personification
(c) Apostrophe   (d) Simile

// Smart Answer Sheet //

Correct — Percentage of students who answered correctly.

Skipped — Percentage of students who skipped.

Q.	Ans.	Correct	Skipped	Q.	Ans.	Correct	Skipped	Q.	Ans.	Correct	Skipped
1	B	80.47%	0.0%	2	C	84.69%	0.0%	3	D	83.64%	0.0%
4	A	77.24%	0.0%	5	B	77.57%	0.0%	6	A	50.0%	1.71%
7	C	46.63%	1.57%	8	B	44.73%	1.2%	9	A	64.42%	1.21%
10	C	51.33%	1.84%	11	A	50.53%	1.76%	12	C	13.16%	3.68%
13	D	59.9%	1.44%	14	C	62.35%	1.82%	15	B	66.5%	1.1%
16	B	44.42%	1.53%	17	A	51.82%	1.59%	18	B	60.62%	1.07%
19	D	64.23%	1.47%	20	A	52.25%	1.51%	21	A	44.6%	1.78%
22	C	64.43%	1.17%	23	C	67.74%	1.32%	24	D	46.87%	1.25%
25	B	87.17%	0.0%	26	D	89.58%	0.0%	27	C	76.42%	0.0%
28	D	47.52%	1.18%	29	D	54.1%	1.53%	30	C	55.63%	1.39%
31	C	57.11%	1.48%	32	C	86.2%	0.0%	33	C	45.89%	1.13%
34	D	59.42%	1.38%	35	B	60.49%	1.53%	36	B	45.27%	1.43%
37	C	59.94%	1.2%	38	A	56.68%	1.62%	39	C	68.76%	1.3%
40	A	49.57%	1.02%	41	A	88.2%	0.0%	42	D	48.45%	1.56%
43	C	82.04%	0.0%	44	A	79.58%	0.0%	45	C	80.41%	0.0%
46	B	66.36%	1.91%	47	A	61.89%	1.96%	48	A	45.73%	1.6%
49	C	65.17%	1.99%	50	B	89.26%	0.0%				

// Hints and Solutions //

1(B). Adamant means refusing to be persuaded or to change one's mind. Determined means having made a firm decision and being resolved not to change it.

2(C). Past perfect tense is used to describe actions finished in the past before a particular time. The correct answer is "His loyalty to the state had been well known".

3(D). The word which is similar in meaning to 'learned' is s cholarly.

4(A). The author praises his father for his i ncorruptibility and impartiality.

5(B). When the author's father refused to apologize to the Political Agent he was d etained.

6(A). Bio-engineering is another term for genetic engineering. It applies engineering principles of design and analysis to biological systems and biomedical technologies.
As stated in the above paragraph, bio-engineering combines the design and problem-solving techniques of engineering with biological and medical sciences to improve health-related and medical problems.

7(C). Bio-engineering is another term for genetic engineering and bio-engineers have made many positive changes in many lives today.
As stated in the above paragraph it has become a growing field over the past couple of years.

8(B). In general, biological engineers attempt to either mimic biological systems to create products or modify and control biological systems so that they can replace, sustain, or predict chemical and mechanical processes. After insulin was invented, there were a lot of problems with the purity and the quantity of the insulin produced.
As stated in the above paragraph, biomedical engineering devised a way to produce large quantities of insulin with a higher level of purity, which has saved a lot of human lives.

9(A). As stated in the above paragraph, bio-engineering can be traced back to over 3000 years with the Egyptians.
As stated in the above paragraph, they created a wooden prosthesis to replace the big toe. Since then, bio-engineering has developed a great deal.

10(C). 'Devised' means 'planned or invented a complex procedure, system, or mechanism by careful thought.'
Only 'concocted' means the same as 'devised' as it means 'create or devise a story or plan'.
The meaning of other words are:
Adjunct: A thing added to something else as a supplementary rather than an essential part.
Perfunctory: Carried out without real interest, feeling, or effort.
Convoyed: Accompanied a group of ships or vehicles for protection

11(A). Utilise means 'make practical and effective use of.'
Only 'unexploited' gives the opposite meaning of utilize as it means 'not used to maximum benefit.'

12(C). As stated in the above paragraph, biomedical engineering helped the lives of many. When the states were hit by the disease polio, many patients were put into a respirator made of two vacuum cleaners and an iron box.
This invention, designed by Philip Drinker and Louis Agassiz Shaw, was nicknamed the "iron lung".

13(D). The iron lung was invented by Philip Drinker and Louis Agassiz Shaw for patients who had been diagnosed with polio. They were put into a respirator made of two vacuum cleaners and an iron box.
As stated in the above paragraph, iron lungs were replaced with artificial lungs, which are more advanced and are put inside the patient, allowing him or her to be mobile and enjoy life to a fuller extent.

14(C). The underlined word in the expression 'six years ago' is an Adverb.

15(B). In the sentence 'And that's just what I did', the word 'that's' is used as a pronoun.

16(B). The correct sequence of events is: (C) (A) (D) (B)

17(A). The first sentence in the story says "Six years ago when I was just 11..." which means the writer is currently 17 years old (or older) at the time of writing this experience.

18(B). The opposite of the word 'easy' is ' Complicated '.

19(D). The writer started building the car to celebrate the family's new garage, as mentioned in the text: "I'd build a car to drive into the garage in celebration of the new addition to our home."

20(A). The writer was sad that he was unable to find suitable things to make the car.

21(A). The given word ' eventually ' means something which is done after a long time.
The meaning of the given words are:
Finally: after a long time or delay
Instantly: without delay; immediately
Constantly: always; again and again
Abruptly: In a sudden, unexpected, and sometimes unpleasant way

22(C). The given word ' empowered' refers to give power or authority to.
The meaning of the given words are:
Excluded: to leave out; not include
Abolished: to end law or system officially
Allowed: to give permission for somebody/something to do something or for something to happen
Activated: to make something start working

23(C). The given word ' revolved' means to turn or circle.
The meaning of the given words are:
Fixed: already decided
Automated: to make something operate by machine, without needing people
Circumduct: To lead about; to lead astray
Addressed: to write the name and address of the person you are sending a letter etc.

24(D). The given word ' evidence ' means depicts the proof or documentation.
The meaning of the given words are:
Assumption: something that you accept is true even though you have no proof
Suggestion: a plan or idea that somebody mentions for somebody else to discuss and consider
Indication: something that shows something
Deposition: the natural process of leaving a layer of a substance on rocks or soil; a substance left in this way

25(B). The given word 'veto' means to reject something by exercising a veto power.
The meaning of the given words are:
Rebuke: to speak angrily to somebody because he/she has done something wrong
Reject: to refuse to accept somebody/something
Ratify: to make an agreement officially acceptable by voting for or signing it
Recline: to sit or lie back in a relaxed and comfortable way

26(D). Slur→ It is a noun that means 'insinuation or allegation'
Blur→ make or become unclear or less distinct.
Blot→ It is a noun that means a dark mark or stain, especially one made by ink.'
Spot→ A small round or roundish mark. It is a noun
According to grammar, we need a noun in the blank hence all the options are nouns but 'Slur' is correct contextually because someone will make allegations on someone hence it is the correct answer.

27(C). The correct answer is "baffled".
Let us explore the given options:
Beguiled means a charm or enchant someone, often in a deceptive way.
Belaboured means to attack someone physically or verbally.
Baffled means faced with difficulty or uncertainty about what to say, think or do.
Blustered means to talk in a loud, aggressive, or indignant way with little effect.
Complete Sentence: Some of our external problems have completely baffled our national leaders.

28(D). With the adverbs like "almost, practically and nearly" always 'every' is used.
So, no improvement is required as the given sentence is correctly framed.

29(D). Option (D) rectifies the error of sentence structure. It places 'filed' after 'has not', which makes it complete.
Correct sentence: The councilor has not filed and will not file his nomination for re-election.

30(C). Articles are words used to determine the standard of nouns.
The definite article 'the' is used before a noun to define it as something specific.
We also use the definite article in front of a noun when we believe the listener/reader knows exactly what we are referring to.

31(C). A person who talks in sleep is called as Somniloquist.
Suffix 'ist' is used to denote a person who is skilled or expert in something.
The word 'Somniloquist' is a Latin word. 'Somni' means sleep and 'loqui' means to talk.
The meanings of remaining words are:
Somnambulist - A person, who walks in sleep.
Oneirocritic –A person who interprets dreams.
Philatelist – A person who collects stamps.

32(C). To smell a rat: to suspect or realize that something is wrong in a particular situation.

33(C). Let this be done by me.

If a sentence is started with Let the passive voice of that sentence also be started with Let.
Rule:
Let +Subject +be + V3 + Other agents.

34(D). Stammer means speak with sudden involuntary pauses and a tendency to repeat the initial letters of words. The word after comma is 'but' which makes it obvious that the person did the opposite of what was supposed.

35(B). 1 is followed by P as it introduces the subject of the sentence as the movie "Avatar". P is followed by R as it consists of the main verb. The next sentence should be Q as it tells us where the movie is doing wonders. S should be the next sentence as it is best preceded by 6. The correct sequence is PRQS.

36(B). 1 is best followed by sentence P because P tells us about some issues. S completes P telling us that the issue is about getting credit for the movie "3 idiots". Sentence Q tells us that it is Chetan Bhagat who is miffed over the issue. The next sentence is R as it shows the action being done by Chetan Bhagat. The correct sequence is PSQR.

37(C). The comparative degree is used before 'than'. Cheaper is the correct answer. In the given sentence there is a comparison between coal and electricity. So, the meaningful sentence is "The electricity is cheaper than coal."

38(A). Few is a quantifier used with plural countable nouns. Little is used with singular uncountable nouns.
Few know about where the soul goes after the death.

39(C). The doctor is suggesting the patient to take things easy for at least next two months.This meaning is implied only by the third sentence.
The other sentences have not been rearranged in a grammatical or meaningful way.

40(A). Few is a quantifier used with plural countable nouns. Little is used with singular uncountable nouns. Work is singular uncountable nouns.
A little work has been done yet. What about remaining work?

41(A). The word 'adjust', according to IPA is transcribed as'/∂'d3∧st/'.
- Phonetic transcription, also known as phonetic script or phonetic notation, is the visual representation of speech sounds or phones by means of symbols.
- The most common type of phonetic transcription uses a phonetic alphabet, such as the International Phonetic Alphabet.

42(D). 'Velar' is the sound formed by the back of the tongue and the soft palate.
A velar consonant is a consonant that is pronounced with the back part of the tongue against the soft palate, also known as the velum, which is the back part of the roof of the mouth.

43(C). Sounds 'f', 'v', 'o', 'r' etc. are fricatives.
- Fricatives, in phonetics, are consonant sounds, such as English 'f' or 'v', produced by bringing the mouth into position to block the passage of the airstream, but not making complete closure, so that air moving through the mouth generates audible friction.
- Fricatives, also known as 'spirants', can be produced with the same positions of the vocal organs as bilabial, labiodental, dental, alveolar, palatal, velar, and uvular consonants.

44(A). When the miscreants saw the police they ran away.
The idiom beat a retreat means to run away from a dangerous or unpleasant situation.
Ex: When we saw the police arriving we beat a hasty retreat.
The phrase 'ran away' is the closest phrase to the idiom 'beat a retreat'.

45(C). The correct answer is- 'up to the required standard'.
Given idiom: Up to the mark means up to the usual standard of performance, quality, etc.
Example: I haven't been feeling up to the mark lately.

46(B). The most appropriate meaning of the given idiom is "at a fast pace".
On the double: very quickly and without any delay.
Example: You'd better get here on the double.

47(A). The most appropriate meaning of the given idiom is "to be the person in charge".
To call the shots means to be the person in charge, to have control over the progress of a situation.
Example: With no boss to call the shots, he drew ideas from all over.

48(A). While there is life, there is hope.
'While there is life there is hope' means that as long as you are alive, you should be hopeful, because it is possible that your situation will improve.

49(C). Figure of speech in above lines is Metonymy.
Metonymy is a figure of speech in which one word or phrase is substituted for another with which it is closely associated; also, the rhetorical strategy of describing something indirectly by referring to things around it. Here 'sceptre (an ornamented staff carried by rulers on ceremonial occasions as a symbol of sovereignty) and crown represent a king. Similarly, a scythe and spade represent a common man or a worker.

50(B). The correct answer is: Personification.
In the given sentence, death has been treated as an apathetic human being, hence personification has been used here.
Personification: the act of giving a human quality or characteristic to something which is not human.

Ques (1-3): Direction: Read the passage given below and answer the questions/complete the statements that follow with the help of given options.

The havoc the October super cyclone caused in Orissa could have been avoided had its mangrove forests not been destroyed to develop shrimp farms. New Scientist magazine, quoting coastal geographers from Cambridge University, recently said: "The (Orissa) coastline was once covered with mangrove forests and these would have dissipated the incoming wave energy."

Indeed, considering the unbridled human activity along the Indian coast, more Orissas can be expected at greater frequency. For, the delicate environment balance has been upset, compounding Nature's abnormalities.

India isn't alone in targeting its coastal areas for economic activates like ports, shrimp farms, oil refineries, luxury hotels and holiday resorts. In a few years, nearly 80 percent of the US population will be living within 50 miles of the coast. In India too, coastal populations are growing.

The emergence of megacities along the sea is seen as the single greatest threat to the world's coastal environment. Today, mangrove forests cover just 15.8 million hectares, and are declining at an assumed rate of 2 per cent every year. In the last few decades, feverish human activity has either destroyed or transformed nearly 50 per cent of the world's total mangrove forest area. Worse, only about one per cent of the global mangrove area is protected.

Mangroves are flowering plants, which grow on tidal coasts between the high and low water marks in clay and silt. They possess unusual "prop and knee" root system which enables them to trap sediments in their roots and provide the seabed a shallow slope. This helps it to absorb the energy of waves and tidal surges, and acts as a shield for the hinterland. The trees themselves form a barrier against wind.

Since mangrove areas are ideal for shrimp fams, they are being 'colonised' and mindlessly destroyed. India is among the top four shrimp exporters, with production growing at 15 per cent a year. But this has extracted its price- in the past 40 years, India is estimated to have lost half its mangrove forests, rendering states like Orissa and Andhra Pradesh vulnerable to the fury of cydones.

1. **Read the following statements.**
   (A) The damage caused by the October cyclone could have been prevented by the mangrove forests.
   (B) Shrimp farms are responsible for the October cyclone.
   (C) The incoming waves could have arrested the October cyclone.
   (a) (A) is true and (B) and (C) are false.
   (b) (A) and (B) are true and (C) is false.
   (c) (A) and (C) are true and (B) is false.
   (d) (A) and (C) are false and (B) is true.

2. **The destruction of the mangrove forests cannot be attributed only to:**
   (a) Waves and tidal surges
   (b) Unbridled human activity
   (c) The development of shrimp farms
   (d) Economic activities

3. **Study the following statements.**
   (A) The mangroves absorb the energy of waves and tidal surges.
   (B) The mangroves form a barrier against clay and silt.
   (a) Both A and B true and B is responsible for A.
   (b) Both A and B are true and B is not responsible for A.

(c) Both A and B are false.
(d) A is true and B is false.

Ques (4-12): Direction : Read the passage given below and answer the questions that follow by choosing the correct/most appropriate options:

Alfred Nobel was a sickly boy in his early years. A weak spine often forced him to rest for days in bed. He was too frail to participate in outdoor games. But as is often seen, the loneliness and moodiness that his condition engendered made him determined to seek comfort in other directions. He decided to develop his mental faculties. He read books voraciously on all subjects - science, literature, history and philosophy. He mastered four foreign languages: Russian, French, German and English.

His determination and ability prompted his father to send him on a world trip to acquire knowledge about business, build right connections, and so on. Accordingly, Alfred set out in 1850 on a two-year tour. He visited Hamburg Copenhagen, Paris, London and the USA. In July 1852 , he joined his father's business and began assisting him in the production of munitions.

The Crimean War (1853-1856) saw the height of the Nobel family's fortunes in Russia. The firm's coffers over-flowed through war orders for armaments. Their speciality was the floating mine, used against enemy ships. Immanuel Nobel had developed a method of igniting gunpowder in these mines with the help of a detonator. It consisted of a glass tube which broke on contact with a ship. This allowed sulphuric acid to pour on a mixture of explosion which in turn ignited the primary charge. But the explosive was not powerful enough to cause serious damage to big warship. This set both the father and the son to seek more powerful explosives.

The end of the Crimean War in 1856 was a severe setback to the Nobles. Munition orders were abruptly called off. A fire destroyed their factory. With creditors clamouring for the return of their money, Immanuel, after a struggle, declared bankruptcy and returned to Sweden in 1859.

4. **What kept Alfred Nobel away from outdoor games?**
   1. His keen interest in reading.
   2. His loneliness and moodiness.
   3. His frail health and sickness.
   4. Lack of facilities for outdoor games.
   (a) 1   (b) 2
   (c) 3   (d) 4

5. **Select the correct option.**
   What prompted Alfred's father to send him on a world trip?
   A. to help him acquire knowledge about business.
   B. to improve his frail health.
   C. to interact with people from different cultures.
   D. to build the right connections to promote their family business.
   1. A and C
   2. C and D
   3. B and D
   4. A and D
   (a) 1   (b) 2
   (c) 3   (d) 4

6. **What accounted for the phenomenal growth of the Nobel family's munition business?**
   1. Immanuel Noble's impeccable business strategies.
   2. Large scale orders for armament's during the Crimean War.
   3. Alfred Nobel's determination and his connections.

4. The Nobel's monopoly in the munition industry.
(a) 1 (b) 2
(c) 3 (d) 4

7. **The chief reason for the Nobel's financial run was:**
1. Poor financial management practices.
2. The end of the Crimean war.
3. A devastating fire which destroyed their factory.
4. Panicky creators clamouring for the return of their money.
(a) 1 (b) 2
(c) 3 (d) 4

8. **Which of the following munitions made the Nobles most popular?**
1. Mortars
2. Heat projectiles
3. The floating mine
4. Missile motors
(a) 1 (b) 2
(c) 3 (d) 4

9. **Which of the following words means the same as the word, 'voraciously' as used in para 1 of the passage?**
1. Greatly
2. Wisely
3. Avidly
4. Aggressively
(a) 1 (b) 2
(c) 3 (d) 4

10. **Which of the following words is opposite is meaning to the word, 'abruptly' as used in para 4 of the passage?**
1. Carefully
2. Gradually
3. Unwisely
4. Gingerly
(a) 1 (b) 2
(c) 3 (d) 4

11. **Which part of speech is the underlined word in the following sentence?**
The end of the Crimean War was a <u>severe</u> setback to the Nobles.
1. Noun
2. Adverb
3. Conjunction
4. Adjective
(a) 1 (b) 2
(c) 3 (d) 4

12. **Which part of the following sentence contains an error?**
They bought/(a) some new furnitures/(b) before shifting/(c) to their new house/(d)
1. (b)
2. (a)
3. (d)
4. (c)
(a) 1 (b) 2
(c) 3 (d) 4

Ques (13-20): Direction: Read the following passage and answer the questions that follow.

The four-year tiger census report, Status of Tigers in India, 2018, released by Prime Minister Narendra Modi shows numbers of the cat have increased across all landscapes.

The Global Tiger Forum, an international collaboration of tiger-bearing countries, has set a goal of doubling the count of wild tigers by 2022. More than 80% of the world's wild tigers are in India, and it's crucial to keep track of their numbers.

The total count in 2018 has risen to 2,967 from 2,226 in 2014 — an increase of 741 individuals an increase of 33%, in four years. This is by far the biggest increase in terms of both numbers and percentage since the four yearly census using camera traps and the capture-mark-recapture method began in 2006. The 2018 figure has a great degree of credibility because, according to the report, as many as 2,461 individual tigers (83% of the total) have actually been photographed by trap cameras. In 2014, only 1,540 individuals (69%) were photographed.

The tiger census is needed because the tiger sits at the peak of the food chain, and its conservation is important to ensure the well-being of the forest ecosystem. The tiger estimation exercise includes habitat assessment and prey estimation. The numbers reflect the success or failure of conservation efforts. This is an especially important indicator in a fast growing economy like India where the pressures of development often run counter to the demands of conservation.

Where has the tiger population increased the most?

The biggest increase has been in Madhya Pradesh — a massive 218 individuals (71%) from 308 in 2014 to 526.

However, since tigers keep moving between states, conservationists prefer to talk about tiger numbers in terms of landscapes.

So, why have the numbers gone up?

The success owes a lot to increased vigilance and conservation efforts by the Forest Department. From 28 in 2006, the number of tiger reserves went up to 50 in 2018, extending protection to larger numbers of tigers over the years. Healthy increases in core area populations eventually lead to migrations to areas outside the core; this is why the 2018 census has found tigers in newer areas. Over the years, there has been increased focus on tigers even in the areas under the territorial and commercial forestry arms of Forest Departments.

The other important reason is increased vigilance, and the fact that organized poaching rackets have been all but crushed. According to Nitin Desai of Wildlife Protection Society of India, there has been no organized poaching by traditional gangs in Central Indian landscapes since 2013.

The increased protection has encouraged the tiger to breed. Tigers are fast breeders when conditions are conducive.

The rehabilitation of villages outside core areas in many parts of the country has led to the availability of more inviolate space for tigers. Also, because estimation exercises have become increasingly more accurate over the years, it is possible that many tigers that eluded enumerators in earlier exercises were counted this time.

13. **The Global Tiger Forum comprises:**
(a) America and the European Union.
(b) All countries of the United Nations.
(c) Countries which have tigers.
(d) National Geographic and World Wildlife Fund.

14. **The year 2022 marks the target date for:**
(a) Doubling the count of India's tiger population.
(b) Tripling the world tiger population.
(c) Tripling India's tiger population.
(d) Doubling the count of world tiger population.

15. **2018 census on the big cat has been the most reliable because-**
(a) It photographed 1540 tigers.
(b) It photographed all living tigers of India.
(c) It photographed 83% of the tigers.

(d) It only uses the capture-mark-recapture method.

16. **Researchers refer to places where tigers are found not by states but by the term:**
    (a) Landscapes
    (b) Deep forests
    (c) Ecosystems
    (d) Green belts

17. **What is the tiger population of Madhya Pradesh?**
    (a) 526
    (b) 741
    (c) 50
    (d) 28

18. **Which of the following statements is not true as per the passage?**
    (a) There are more reliable ways of data collection.
    (b) The tiger reserves have increased to 100 in 2018.
    (c) Poaching gangs have been reduced drastically.
    (d) Forest departments have become more watchful.

19. **What has been the impact of providing inviolate spaces for tigers?**
    (a) The number of villagers killed by man eater tigers has increased.
    (b) Tiger numbers have increased due to safe breeding places.
    (c) The poachers have been caught in these spaces very easily.
    (d) Tigers have moved from Uttar Pradesh to Madhya Pradesh.

20. **Pick out a word that is similar in meaning to:**
    CONDUCIVE
    (a) Helpful
    (b) Reclusive
    (c) Hindering
    (d) Unfavorable

21. **Find out the words which mean the same as 'shell-shocked'.**
    (a) Hellish
    (b) Devil
    (c) Amateur
    (d) Stunned

22. **Find out the words which mean the same as 'relentless'.**
    (a) Determining
    (b) Flexible
    (c) Merciful
    (d) Unforgiving

23. **Fill in the blank with the most appropriate word out of the four alternatives suggested below the question.**
    Ensure your life is a _______ of knowledge and wisdom.
    (a) Guild
    (b) Petulance
    (c) Rogue
    (d) Orating

24. **What is the plural form of "fungus"?**
    (a) Fungi
    (b) Funguses
    (c) Mould
    (d) Rot

25. **Direction: In the given question, a word has been written in four different ways out of which only one is incorrectly spelled. Select the incorrectly spelled word.**
    (a) Wastness
    (b) Vastness
    (c) Wasteness
    (d) Vasteness

26. **Direction: Change the following sentence into assertive sentence:**
    Hurrah! My brother has topped the Civil Services Examination.
    (a) It is a matter of joy that my brother has topped the Civil Services Examination.
    (b) I am happy because my brother topped the Civil Services Examination.
    (c) It was a matter of joy that my brother topped the Civil Services Examination.
    (d) It is a matter of joy that his brother topped the Civil Services Examination.

27. **Direction: Combine the following simple sentences into one sentence:**
    The new chairman assured candidates. Recruitment process will be more transparent.
    (a) The new chairman assured candidates of a more transparent recruitment process
    (b) The new chairman assured candidates for a more transparent recruitment process
    (c) Recruitment process being more transparent, the new chairman assured candidates
    (d) Having assured candidates, recruitment process will be more transparent

28. **Direction: Choose the correct part of speech of the underlined word as used in the following sentence:**
    I'm going to make myself a sandwich and get back to work.
    (a) Reflexive pronoun
    (b) Noun
    (c) Verb
    (d) Adver

29. **What part of speech is the word 'Intelligent'?**
    (a) Noun
    (b) Pronoun
    (c) Adjective
    (d) Adverb

30. **Direction: The question contains a sentence or part thereof followed by four choices. Select from these choices the one that most logically completes the idea contained in the given sentence or part.**
    Since today's practical economic experience suggests savings to be a direct result of higher incomes, not the other way round as we have all believed so far,
    (a) Any additional income will also generate corresponding increase in savings
    (b) There`s a lot of room for India's savings to go north
    (c) India's need for investment funds can be met, at least partially, from incremental incomes
    (d) Capital formation can very well be a closed process

31. **In the following question, a sentence has been given in Direct/Indirect. Out of the Four alternatives suggested, select the one which best expresses the same sentence in Direct/Indirect and mark Your answer.**
    He said,"I cannot help you at present because I am myself in difficulty."
    (a) He said that I cannot help you at present because I myself in difficulty.
    (b) He said that he could not help me at present because he was himself in difficulty.
    (c) He told that he could not help you at present because he was himself in difficulty.
    (d) He asked that he could not help you at present because he was himself in difficulty.

32. **Direction : The question presents a sentence, a part of which is underlined. Beneath the sentence, you will find four ways of phrasing the underlined part. Chose the correct replacement of the underlined phrase.**
    The findings of the inquiry committee, as revealed by the chairman, is very encouraging to people.

(a) is very encouraging

(b) are very encouraging

(c) is being very encouraging

(d) has been very encouraging

33. **Direction:** A sentence with an underlined word is given below. Select the most appropriate antonym for the underlined word from the given options.
In their efforts to reduce crime the government <u>expanded</u> the police force.

(a) Elongated   (b) Contracted

(c) Enlarged   (d) Increased

34. **Direction:** In the following question a part of the sentence is bold. Below are given alternatives to the bold part at (A), (B), and (C) and which may improve the sentence. Choose the correct alternative. In the case of no improvement, your answer is (D).
The Prime Minister called **on** the President.

(a) By   (b) In

(c) To   (d) No Improvement

35. **Direction:** Pick out the most effective word from the given word to fill in the blanks to make the sentence meaningfully complete.
Marry . . . . . . a question to Mohan yesterday.

(a) Was asked   (b) Asked

(c) Had asked   (d) Asking

36. **Direction:** Pick out the most effective word from the choices below to fill in the blanks to make the sentence meaningfully complete.
A cup of water was enough to _____ his thirst.

(a) Satisfy   (b) Appease

(c) Quench   (d) Extinguish

37. **Direction:** In the given question, a part of the sentence is printed in bold. Below the sentence, alternatives to the emboldened part are given as (A), (B) and (C), which may help improve the sentence. Choose the correct alternative out of the given four options. In case the given sentence is correct, your answer will be option (D), i.e., "No correction required".
As we are starting to **run off** time, we have to make your speech short.

(a) Run over   (b) Run away

(c) Run out   (d) No correction required

38. **Direction:** Find the correct sentence from the given options.

(a) By next week, Karan will have been working in TCS for 15 years.

(b) You have been worked here since last year.

(c) I will have been played for a year when I complete the age of 23.

(d) She writes novels since her college time.

39. **Direction:** Pick out the most effective word from the given word to fill in the blanks to make the sentence meaningfully complete.
400 videos ________ already ________ by Angel for English on YouTube.

(a) are, uploaded   (b) have, uploaded

(c) are been, uploaded   (d) have been, uploaded

40. **Direction: Arrange the words to make a meaningful** sentence.
there / are/ four / directions / sub-directions /and / four.

(a) There four directions and four sub-directions are.

(b) There are four directions and four sub-directions.

(c) Four directions and four sub-directions there are.

(d) There are four sub-directions and four directions.

41. **Direction:** Select the most appropriate meaning of the underlined idiom in the given sentence.
The new CEO is in favour of giving plenty of <u>elbow room</u> to the managers.

(a) Tough competition

(b) Huge salaries and perks

(c) Freedom to do what one wants

(d) Leave to go on vacation

42. **Direction:** Select the most appropriate meaning of the underlined idiom in the given sentence.
The embezzlement in the company's accounts has <u>come to light</u>.

(a) been rewarded   (b) been concealed

(c) been revealed   (d) been punished

43. **Direction:** Select the most appropriate meaning of the underlined idiom in the given sentence.
If we <u>lay our heads together</u>, we will surely find a solution.

(a) Work in consultation   (b) Rest for a while

(c) Take a break   (d) Work in isolation

44. **Direction:** Select the most appropriate meaning of the given idiom.
Eat one's words

(a) forgive and forget

(b) become less acceptable

(c) retract what one has said

(d) oppose sternly

45. **Direction:** Select the most appropriate meaning of the given idiom.
One track mind

(a) thinking of another point of view

(b) using a well-known path

(c) always thinking of only one thing

(d) waiting anxiously for something

Ques (46-47): Direction: Point out the figure of speech used in the sentence given below.

46. **We had nothing to do, and we did it very well.**

(a) Antithesis   (b) Paradox

(c) Anticlimax   (d) Litotes

47. **Rivers of blood flowed on the battlefield**

(a) Hyperbole   (b) Alliteration

(c) Simile   (d) Metaphor

48. **Which of these terms refer to the study of speech process?**

(a) Phonology   (b) Phonetic substances

(c) Phonetics   (d) Semantics

49. **Which of these is not a type of phonetics?**

(a) Articulatory   (b) Personal

(c) Acoustic   (d) Auditory

50. **Which of these terms refer to the study of hearing and perception of speech sounds?**
  (a) Articulatory phonetics (b) Acoustic phonetics
  (c) Auditory phonetics (d) Laboratory phonetics

// Smart Answer Sheet //

Correct — Percentage of students who answered correctly.

Skipped — Percentage of students who skipped.

Q.	Ans.	Correct / Skipped	Q.	Ans.	Correct / Skipped	Q.	Ans.	Correct / Skipped
1	B	85.2% / 0.0%	2	A	42.88% / 1.34%	3	D	50.22% / 1.8%
4	C	81.82% / 0.0%	5	D	54.0% / 1.54%	6	B	51.06% / 1.35%
7	B	86.76% / 0.0%	8	C	52.59% / 1.33%	9	C	82.38% / 0.0%
10	B	89.06% / 0.0%	11	D	80.46% / 0.0%	12	A	55.37% / 1.32%
13	C	46.0% / 1.49%	14	D	79.6% / 0.0%	15	C	84.68% / 0.0%
16	A	60.93% / 1.24%	17	A	56.97% / 1.06%	18	B	43.62% / 1.49%
19	B	78.07% / 0.0%	20	A	76.41% / 0.0%	21	D	51.12% / 1.38%
22	D	58.12% / 1.25%	23	A	68.3% / 1.92%	24	A	52.54% / 1.97%
25	D	55.79% / 1.49%	26	A	47.24% / 1.65%	27	A	62.65% / 2.0%
28	A	48.23% / 1.75%	29	C	84.59% / 0.0%	30	B	57.75% / 1.18%
31	B	88.61% / 0.0%	32	B	64.77% / 1.48%	33	B	67.48% / 1.68%
34	D	68.23% / 1.2%	35	B	52.29% / 1.88%	36	C	53.96% / 1.14%
37	A	48.23% / 1.16%	38	A	43.6% / 1.42%	39	D	46.48% / 1.78%
40	B	68.42% / 1.56%	41	C	57.52% / 1.57%	42	C	69.09% / 1.03%
43	A	45.27% / 1.01%	44	C	56.27% / 1.36%	45	C	78.38% / 0.0%
46	B	86.92% / 0.0%	47	A	68.87% / 1.04%	48	C	56.86% / 1.74%
49	B	55.88% / 1.96%	50	C	55.05% / 1.05%			

// Hints and Solutions //

1(B). According to the passage, statement (A) & (B) are true. "The havoc the october super cyclone caused in Orissa could have been avoided had its mangrove forests not been destroyed to develop shrimp forms." The given statement (C) is false.

2(A). As per the passage, the destruction of the mangrove forests cannot be attributed to below given activities.
(A) The development of shrimp farms.
(B) Unbridled human activity
(C) Economic activities
Waves and tidal surges can't be attributed to the destruction of the mangrove forests.

3(D). According to the passage the mangroves trees absorb the energy of waves and tidal surges and acts as a shield for the hinterland. The trees themselves form a barrier against wind.
Therefore, we can clearly identify that statement (A) is true

& (B) is false.

4(C). According to the passage, Alfred Nobel kept away from outdoor games due to his frail health and sickness.

5(D). According to the passage, Alfred's father prompted to help him acquire knowledge about business and build the right connections to promote their family business send him on a world trip.

6(B). According to the passage, large scale orders for armament's during the Crimean War accounted for the phenomenal growth of the Nobel family's munition business.

7(B). According to the passage, the chief reason for the Nobel's financial run was the end of the Crimean war.

8(C). According to the passage, the floating mine was the munition that made the Nobles most popular.

9(C). 'Avidly' words mean the same as the word, 'voraciously' as used in para 1 of the passage. The word "voraciously" means very hungry, having a huge appetite; very eager a voracious reader rate, and "Avidly " means with great interest or enthusiasm therefore synonym of this word is 'Avidly'.

10(B). 'Gradually' word is the opposite meaning of the word, 'abruptly' as used in para 4 of the passage. The word "abruptly" means suddenly and unexpectedly, in a rude or curt manner whereas "Gradually" means in a gradual way; slowly; by degrees.

11(D). Here the underlined word 'severe' is an adjective i.e., a word naming an attribute of a noun, such as sweet, red, or technical.

12(A). The error lies in the usage of 'furnitures' instead of 'furniture'. The correct sentence is "They bought some new furniture before shifting to their new house."

13(C). The Global Tiger Forum comprises countries which have tigers.
According to the passage "The Global Tiger Forum, an international collaboration of tiger-bearing countries ."
The word bearing suggests the countries which have tigers.

14(D). The year 2022 marks the target date for doubling the count of world tiger population.
According to the passage ' 'The Global Tiger Forum, an international collaboration of tiger-bearing countries, has set a goal of doubling the count of wild tigers by 2022.' '

15(C). 2018 census on the big cat has been the most reliable because it photographed 83% of the tigers.
According to the passage '' The 2018 figure has a great degree of credibility because, according to the report, as many as 2,461 individual tigers (83% of the total) have actually been photographed by trap cameras.' '

16(A). Researchers refer to places where tigers are found not by states but by the term landscapes.
According to the passage ' 'However since tigers keep moving between states, conservationists prefer to talk about tiger numbers in terms of landscapes. "

17(A). 526 is the tiger population of Madhya Pradesh.
According to the passage ' 'The biggest increase has been in Madhya Pradesh — a massive 218 individuals (71%) from 308 in 2014 to 526.''

18(B). Statement 'The tiger reserves have increased to 100 in 2018' is not true as per the passage.
According to the passage "The success owes a lot to

increased vigilance and conservation efforts by the Forest Department. The other important reason is increased vigilance and the fact that organized poaching rackets have been all but crushed. Also, because estimation exercises have become increasingly more accurate over the years, it is possible that many tigers that eluded enumerators in earlier exercises were counted this time."

19(B). Tiger numbers have increased due to safe breeding places has been the impact of providing inviolate spaces for tigers.

According to the passage " The increased protection has encouraged the tiger to breed. Tigers are fast breeders when conditions are conducive. The rehabilitation of villages outside core areas in many parts of the country has led to the availability of more inviolate space for tigers."

20(A). 'Helpful' word is similar in meaning to Conducive.

Conducive means making a certain situation or outcome likely or possible.

Example: Darkness is conducive to sleep.

Helpful means giving or rendering aid or assistance; of service .

Example: Your comments were very helpful.

21(D). The given word 'shell-shocked' means to suffer from a shock due to a sudden alarming experience.

Meaning of the given options:
- **Stunned:** to deprive of consciousness or strength by or as if by a blow, fall, etc.
- **Hellish:** terrible; awful.
- **Devil:** the most powerful evil being, according to the Christian, Jewish and Muslim religions.
- **Amateur:** A person who takes part in a sport or an activity for pleasure, not for money as a job.

22(D). The given word 'relentless' means to be harsh and inflexible.

Meaning of the given options:
- **Unforgiving:** Not willing to forgive or excuse people's faults or wrongdoings.
- **Flexible:** Able to bend or move easily without breaking.
- **Determining:** To discover the facts about something.
- **Merciful:** Feeling or showing mercy.

23(A). Ensure your life is a **Guild** of knowledge and wisdom.

The meanings of the given words:-
- Guild: an association of people for mutual aid or the pursuit of a common goal.
- Petulance: the quality of being childishly sulky or bad-tempered.
- Rogue: a dishonest or unprincipled man.
- Orating: make a speech, especially pompously or at length.

24(A). The plural form of fungus is fungi.

25(D). Vasteness is an incorrectly spelled word

Wastness means the state of lying barren or being waste.

Vastness means very great extent or size; immensity." the vastness of the Atlantic Ocean"

Wasteness means the quality or state of being waste.

26(A). The given sentence is an exclamatory sentence.

'Hurrah' is an exclamation which is used to show excitement, pleasure, or approval.

To change the sentence into assertive we follow the steps mentioned below:
- Exclamation 'Hurrah' is replaced with 'It is a matter of

joy', which is followed by 'that'.
- After 'that' remaining statement is put as it was in original sentence.

Following above steps we get the required assertive sentence as following:
- It is a matter of joy that my brother has topped the Civil Services Examination.

27(A). We can combine multiple sentences into a single sentences by using a preposition with noun or gerund.
- He saw the moon. He became glad.
- Combined: On seeing the moon, he became glad.
- I bought a watch. I paid Rs. 500 for this.
- Combined: I bought a watch for Rs. 500.

The given sentences can be combined using this method.
- Note: Assure take preposition 'of' it.

So, the combined sentence will be as following:
- The new chairman assured candidates of a more transparent recruitment process.

28(A). Let us see the meanings of the given options:

Reflexive pronoun: Reflexive pronouns are words like myself, yourself, himself, herself, itself, ourselves, yourselves and themselves.
- They refer back to a person or thing.

Noun: A word that refers to a person, place, thing, event, substance, or quality.

Verb: A word or phrase that describes an action, condition, or experience.

Demonstrative pronoun: A demonstrative pronoun is a pronoun that represents a noun and expresses its position as near or far (including in time).

In this sentence, the word 'myself' is a reflexive pronoun and it is used when the subject of the verb is "I" and the object is the same person.
- Example: I bought myself a new coat.

Therefore, the correct answer is 'Reflexive Pronoun'.

29(C). The word 'Intelligent' is an adjective that means having or showing the ability to understand, learn and think; clever.
- Example: Suma is a very bright and intelligent woman who knows her own mind.

30(B). Since higher incomes lead to more savings, there is a lot of room (with incomes going up) for India's savings to go north (upward). Option (B) is correct.

The word 'corresponding' weaken option (A) as there is no information on the degree of correlation between income and savings.

The other options relate to 'capital' or 'investment' and do not fit better than option (B) (savings) in the context.

31(B). He said that he could not help me at present because he was himself in difficulty.

32(B). 'Are very encouraging' is the correct usage because the subject (findings) is plural and thus, needs a plural verb. So, only (B) satisfies the condition.

33(B). The word 'expanded' means to make greater in size, amount, or number.

The word 'contracted' means decreased in size, number, or range.

From the given words, we can say that the word 'contracted' is the most appropriate antonym for the word 'expanded'.

34(D). No improvement is required.

Sometimes 'on' is confused with 'onto'. The preposition 'on' indicates that something is already in the position. 'Onto' indicates a movement from one place onto the

surface of some type.
The book is on the table. But Pete took the book out of his backpack and put it onto the table.
Could you move those clothes onto the sofa?
"The Prime Minister called on the President".

35(B). Sentence is in past tense with active voice.
So, the following rule has been followed-
Rule:
Subject + V3 + other agents.
Therefore, the sentence is, "Marry asked a question to Mohan yesterday."

36(C). The complete sentence will, "A cup of water was enough to **quench** his thirst."
In the question quench will be use because the meaning of quench is to satisfy one's thirst by drinking.
Then, the meaning of the sentence will be, to satisfy one's thirst by drinking a cup of water was enough.
Meaning of other options-
- Satisfy means to meet the expectations, needs, or desires of someone.
- Appease means to satisfy a demand or a feeling.
- Extinguish means put an end to; destroy.

37(A). The context is saying that the speech needs to be shortened. So, the most appropriate phrasal verb to make the statement contextually correct is 'run over' which means to continue for longer than planned.
The meanings of other phrasal verbs are:
Run off - to run away.
Run away - to leave expectedly.
Run out - to use all of something and not have any left.

38(A). The correct answer is- ' By next week, Karan will have been working in TCS for 15 years.' The Future perfect continuous tense is used to express an action that is in progress and will be in progress at a certain future time
The general structure is- will/shall + have been + V1+ ing.
Thus, the correct answer is- 'By next week, Karan will have been working in TCS for 15 years.'
The Future perfect continuous tense is used to express an action that is in progress and will be in progress at a certain future time.
Example: Will have been playing for a year when I complete the age of 23.

39(D). Sentence is in present perfect tense with passive voice.
Rule:
Subject + have/has + been + V^3 + other agents.
400 videos have been already uploaded by Angel for English on YouTube.

40(B). Follow the order of Verb – other words after starting the sentence with the introductory 'there.' The information about directions must be arranged in descending order. Hence we must mention 'four directions' first and then 'four sub-directions.'

41(C). The new CEO is in favour of giving plenty of freedom to do what one wants to the managers.
Elbow room means the freedom and ability to act as one wants.
Example: I can hardly move. Give me some elbow room.

42(C). The embezzlement in the company's accounts has been revealed.
The idiom come to light means become widely known or evident.
Ex: "no new facts came to light".
The phrase 'come to light' is the closest phrase to the word 'revealed'.

43(A). The correct answer is- 'work in consultation'.
Given idiom: Lay heads together means to work together to come up with an idea or solution.
Example: If the two of you lay your heads together, I'm confident you'll figure out a workable solution.

44(C). The most appropriate meaning of the given idiom is 'retract what one has said'.
Eat one's words: retract what one has said, especially in a humiliating way.
Example: They will eat their words when I win.

45(C). The most appropriate meaning of the given idiom is "always thinking of only one thing".
One-track mind: used in reference to a person whose thoughts are preoccupied with one subject or interest.
Example: My sister has a one-track mind, only thinking about how something can further her career.

46(B). The figure of speech in above this sentence is paradox.
A paradox is a logically self-contradictory statement or a statement that runs contrary to one's expectation. It is a statement that, despite apparently valid reasoning from true premises, leads to a seemingly self-contradictory or a logically unacceptable conclusion.

47(A). The correct answer is: **Hyperbole**
Hyperbole is a figure of speech in which an author or speaker purposely and obviously exaggerates to an extreme. In the given sentence, the speaker is exaggerating that the amount of blood flowing in the battlefield is so much that it resembles a river.

48(C). Phonetics is the study of speech processes. It includes the anatomy, neurology and pathology of speech. It also includes the articulation, classification and perception of speech sounds.

49(B). Phonetics can be divided into three main branches. These are Articulatory phonetics, Accoustic phonetics and Auditory phonetics.

50(C). Auditory phonetics is the study of hearing and perception of speech sounds. Articulatory phonetics deals with the movement of speech organs whereas Acoustic phonetics deals with the physical properties of speech sounds.

Ques (1-7): Direction : Read the passage given below and answer the questions that follow by selecting the correct/most appropriate options.

(1) The monthly report card in school would make some children gloat and others weep. I did neither. I just took it because I saw it as a transaction between my teacher and my father! Reading it always made my father blow up. The teacher must have said something not so nice. But I was unconcerned. I had too much else going on that interested me.

(2) The alarming increase in student suicides today is because we have created a society founded on the premise that life is a race. So you rush to the finishing line! Is it any wonder that so many choose to end their lives? This is the self-destructive model we have created for ourselves.

(3) If our joy is about being better than someone else, it is not success; it is sickness. To reap the benefits of someone else's failure is a tragic way to live.

(4) Each individual is born with a particular kind of genius. Education should create the right atmosphere to allow that genius to flower to its optimal potential.

(5) A student asked, how to live in an increasingly competitive and ambitious world. I told him, whether, knowledge, power, love or fame, you are essentially trying to experience a little more of life than you have now. The man going to the bar and the man going to the temple are seeking the same thing! They are looking for fulfilment, but through different means. Both want an experience of life that is a little more intense and pleasurable than it is currently.

(6) At present, the stimuli are outside. But once you know that the source of both pleasure and pain, agony and ecstasy are within you, why would you outsource it? Why would you export it to alcohol or heaven or to some authority figure?

1. **Which of the following is false?**
    The author was unconcerned about his report card because:
    1. his teacher seemed to be satisfied
    2. he believed it was something between his father and his teacher.
    3. he was occupied with other things which interested him.
    4. the report would make his father flare up.
    (a) 1 (b) 2
    (c) 3 (d) 4

2. **According to the author competition based learning:**
    1. is not appreciated by parents.
    2. is needed by students.
    3. leads to overall development.
    4. is self-destructive.
    (a) 1 (b) 2
    (c) 3 (d) 4

3. **Read the sentences given below.**
    A. We all look for fulfilment in our own way.
    B. The source of both pleasure and pain is within us.
    1. Both A and B are true.
    2. Only A is true.
    3. Both A and B are false.
    4. Only B is true.
    (a) 1 (b) 2
    (c) 3 (d) 4

4. **Which one of the following words is similar in meaning to the word, 'alarming' as used in the passage? (para2)**
    1. disgusting

2. disappointing
3. disheartening
4. disturbing
(a) 1 (b) 2
(c) 3 (d) 4

5. **Which of the following words is most opposite in meaning to the word, "particular' as used in the passage? (para4)**
    1. random
    2. general
    3. peripheral
    4. integral
    (a) 1 (b) 2
    (c) 3 (d) 4

6. **Which part of speech is the underlined word in the following sentence?**
    "It was a transaction <u>between</u> my teacher and my father".
    1. Adjective
    2. Conjunction
    3. Preposition
    4. Pronoun
    (a) 1 (b) 2
    (c) 3 (d) 4

7. **Which part of the sentence given below contains an error?**
    Reading it/ (a), always made/(b), my father/(c), to blow out/(d)
    1. (b)
    2. (a)
    3. (d)
    4. (c)
    (a) 1 (b) 2
    (c) 3 (d) 4

Ques (8-12): Direction : Read the following passage and answer the questions given after it.

In the late 18th century the Industrial Revolution began to transform life in Britain. Until then, most people lived in the countryside and made their living from farming. By the mid-19th century most people in Britain lived in towns and made their living from mining or manufacturing industries.

In 1712 a man named Thomas Newcomen (1663-1729) made primitive steam engines for pumping water from mines. In 1769 James Watt (1736-1819) patented a more efficient steam engine. In 1785 his engine was adapted to driving machinery in a cotton factory. The use of steam engines to drive machines slowly transformed industry.

Meanwhile, during the 1700s Britain built up a great overseas empire. The North American colonies were lost after the War of Independence 1776-1783. On the other hand, after the Seven Years War 1756-1763, Britain captured Canada and India. Britain also took Dominica, Grenada, St. Vincent and Tobago in the West Indies. In 1707 the Act of Union was passed. Scotland was united with England and Wales. England became part of Great Britain.

Owning land was the main form of wealth in the 18th century. Political power and influence were in the hands of rich landowners. At the top were the nobility. Below them were a class of nearly rich landowners called the gentry. In the early 18th century there was another class of landowners called yeomen who were small landowners, described as farmers of the middle class. However, during the century this class became less and less numerous. However other middle class people such as merchants and professional men became richer and more numerous, especially in the towns.

Below them were the great mass of the population, craftsmen and labourers. In the 18 th century probably half the population lived at subsistence or bare survival level.

In the early 18 th century England suffered from gin drinking. It was cheap and it was sold everywhere as you did not need a license to sell it. Many people ruined their health by drinking gin. Sadly, for many poor people drinking gin was their only comfort. The situation improved after 1751 when a tax was imposed on gin.

At the end of the 17 th century it was estimated the population of England and Wales was about 5 1/2 million. The population of Scotland was about 1 million. The population of London was about 600,000. In the mid-18 th century the population of Britain was about 6 1/2 million. In the late 18 th century it grew rapidly and by 1801 it was over 9 million. The population of London was almost 1 million.

During the 18 th century, towns in Britain grew larger. Nevertheless, most towns still had populations of less than 10,000. However, in the late 18 th century new industrial towns in the Midland and the North of England mushroomed. Meanwhile, the population of London grew to nearly 1 million by the end of the century. Other towns were much smaller. The population of Liverpool was about 77,000 in 1800. Birmingham had about 73,000 people and Manchester had about 70,000. Bristol had a population of about 68,000. Sheffield was smaller with 31,000 people and Leeds had about 30,000 people.

8. **By the end of the 18 th century the population of Britain was:**
   (a) around 5 1/2 million   (b) over 9 million
   (c) almost 6 1/2 million   (d) about 1 million

9. **Among the following towns, which had the maximum population?**
   (a) Birmingham   (b) Liverpool
   (c) Manchester   (d) Bristol

10. **Which of the following statements is not true according to the passage?**
   (a) After the War of Independence, Britain had colonies in North America.
   (b) In the mid-19 th century the towns grew and most people were engaged in mining and manufacturing.
   (c) In 18 th century England almost half the population consisted of poor people.
   (d) Before the Industrial Revolution, most of the people in England lived in villages and were engaged in agriculture.

11. **Which of the following was not a colony of Britain in the West Indies?**
   (a) Tobago   (b) Canada
   (c) Dominica   (d) Grenada

12. **Which of the following transformed life in 18 th century England?**
   (a) Making of Great Britain
   (b) The Industrial Revolution
   (c) Invention of the steam engine
   (d) Farming and mining

Ques (13-20): Direction: Much of the information we have today about chimpanzees comes from the groundbreaking, long-term research of the great conservationist, Jane Goodall.

Jane Goodall was born in London, England, on April 3, 1934. On her second birthday, her father gave her a toy chimpanzee named Jubilee. Jubilee was named after a baby chimp in the London Zoo. To this day, Jubilee sits in a chair in Jane's London home. From an early age, Jane was fascinated by animals and animal stories. By the age of 10, she was talking about going to Africa to live among the animals there.

As a young woman, Jane finished school in London, attended secretarial school, and then worked for a documentary filmmaker for a while. When a school friend invited her to visit Kenya, she worked as a waitress until she had earned the fare to travel there by boat. She was 23 years old.

Once in Kenya, she met Dr. Louis Leakey, a famous paleontologist and anthropologist. He was impressed with her thorough knowledge of Africa and its wildlife, and hired her to assist him and his wife on a fossil-hunting expedition to Olduvai Gorge. Dr. Leakey soon realized that Jane was the perfect person to complete a study he had been planning for some time. She expressed her interest in the idea of studying animals by living in the wild with them, rather than studying dead animals through paleontology.

Dr. Leakey and Jane began planning a study of a group of chimpanzees who were living on the shores of Lake Tanganyika in Kenya. At first, the British authorities did not approve their plan. They thought it was too dangerous for a woman to live in the wilds of Africa alone. But Jane's mother, Vanne, agreed to join her so that she would not be alone. Finally, the authorities gave Jane the clearance to go to Africa and begin her study.

In July of 1960, Jane and her mother arrived at Gombe National Park in what was then called Tanganyika and is now called Tanzania. Jane faced many challenges as she began her work. The chimpanzees did not accept her right away, and it took months for them to get used to her presence in their territory. But she was very patient and remained focused on her goal. Little by little, she was able to enter their world. At first, she was able to watch the chimpanzees only from a great distance, using binoculars.

Eventually, she was able to sit among them, touching, patting, and even feeding them. It was an amazing accomplishment for Jane, and a breakthrough in the study of animals in the wild. Jane named all of the chimpanzees that she studied, stating in her journals that she felt they each had a unique personality.

The study started by Jane' Goodall in 1960 is now the longest field study of any animal species in their natural habitat. Research continues to this day in Gombe and is conducted by a team of trained Tanzanians.

13. **What is the passage about?**
   (a) Jane Goodall's fascination for animals
   (b) Study of food habits of animals
   (c) Kenya and Tanzania
   (d) Documentary film-making

14. **An anthropologist is a person who studies:**
   (a) Politics
   (b) Chimpanzees
   (c) Behavior of animals
   (d) Scientific study of humanity, human behavior, human biology, culture, societies and linguistic.

15. **Why did the British, authorities not approve of Dr. Leakey and Jane's plan?**
   (a) Because Dr. Leakey was an anthropologist
   (b) Because it was dangerous for a woman to live alone in the forests of Africa
   (c) Because Jane's mother agreed to join her
   (d) Because Dr. Leakey's wife did not want it

16. **The term 'wilds', in the passage, means:**

(a) Fierce animals

(b) Wild and dangerous animals

(c) Chimpanzees

(d) In an area of a place that is especially remote and in which it is difficult & dangerous to live

17. Jane named all of the chimpanzees she studied because she felt they each had a:

(a) Unique perception

(b) Unique face

(c) Unique personality

(d) Unique habitat

18. Jane's toy chimpanzee, _______, sits in a chair in Jane's London home:

(a) Jubilee

(b) Leakey

(c) Vanne

(d) Tanganyika

19. Why did Dr. Leakey hire Jane to assist him?

(a) Because she was from London

(b) Because of her thorough knowledge of Africa and its wild life

(c) Because she worked for a documentary film-maker

(d) Because she attended a secretarial school

20. The study started by Jane Goodall in 1960 continues till date in the form of research in:

(a) Tanzania

(b) Kenya

(c) London

(d) Gombe

21. **Direction:** In the following question, an idiomatic expression or a proverb is highlighted. Select the alternative which best describes its use in the sentence. **She asked him to join their band tour with no strings attached.**

(a) By following their rules

(b) By signing a document

(c) By tying up the agreement with a string

(d) Without any preconditions

22. In the test, we will _______ your work and then give you detailed feedback.

(a) assess

(b) judge

(c) measure

(d) check

23. **Direction:** In the given question, out of the four alternatives, choose the alternative which best expresses the meaning of the idiom/Phrase.
Zero tolerance

(a) Accuracy is paramount

(b) Non-acceptance of antisocial behaviour

(c) No return without risk

(d) No problem at all

24. Arrange the following in meaningful and logical order.
1. School
2. Office
3. Playschool
4. College
5. Retirement

(a) 3, 1, 4, 2, 5

(b) 1, 3, 4, 2, 5

(c) 4, 2, 5, 1, 3

(d) 3, 1, 2, 4, 5

25. Find out that word, the spelling of which is wrong.

(a) Beetle

(b) Beautician

(c) Bearable

(d) Beautifull

26. **Direction : Change the narration.**
I don't speak French, she said.

(a) She told that she did not speak French.

(b) She said that I did not speak French.

(c) She told that she does not speak French.

(d) She said that she did not speak French.

27. **Direction : Identify the part having an error and mark the suitable option.**
(A) Deep in the mountains, (B) there is less chance for (C) anyone to get a cell-phone connection. (D) No error

(a) (A)

(b) (B)

(c) (C)

(d) (D)

28. **Direction : Select the option that fills in the blanks most suitably in the same order.**
India has many ____ issues: turf battles between ministers; and ____ implementation of various products throughout the country.

(a) pending, vested

(b) vexatious, tardy

(c) outstanding, speedy

(d) contentious, dogged

29. **Direction: Select the most appropriate meaning of the given idiom.**
Always a bridesmaid, never a bride

(a) Someone who fulfills his or her potential

(b) Someone who is born unlucky

(c) Someone who always comes second

(d) Someone who does not deserve to win

30. **Direction: Fill in the blank with a correct preposition.**
A prisoner was accused _______ murder.

(a) of

(b) for

(c) to

(d) off

31. **Direction : A sentence has been split into four parts. One of the parts may have an error of grammar or syntax. Select the part having the error.**

(a) But there are some things

(b) that need to pass over,

(c) to appreciate

(d) the profound skill of the architects.

32. **Direction: In the following question, the whole or a part of the sentence is underlined. Below are given alternatives to the underlined part which may improve the sentence. Choose the correct alternative. In case no improvement is required, choose the 'No Improvement' option.**
The amount multiplies **over** a period of time.

(a) By

(b) Within

(c) In

(d) No Improvement

33. **Direction: In the given question, a part of the sentence contains an error. Find out which part of the sentence has an error and choose the appropriate option. If the sentence is free from error, select the 'No error' option.**
My cousin cannot understand why his teacher says that the Earth move around the sun.

(a) Cannot understand

(b) Teacher says

(c) Move around the

(d) No error

Ques (34-40): Direction: Select the alternative that will improve the underlined part of the sentence. In case there is no improvement select 'No improvement'.

34. Sometimes she has to accept change, if she <u>want to move forward</u>.
    (a) Wanting to move forward
    (b) Wants to move forward
    (c) Wanted to move forward
    (d) No Improvement

35. The old man <u>shouted angry</u> at the cat that had ruined his newspaper.
    (a) Shouted anger
    (b) Shouts angry
    (c) Shouted angrily
    (d) No Improvement

36. My observation is that bringing a vehicle <u>to a suddenly stop</u> may cause a serious accident.
    (a) to a suddenly stoppage
    (b) to a sudden stoppage
    (c) to a sudden stop
    (d) No improvement

37. Ravi's sister <u>exciting</u> beyond words and could not refrain from caressing it.
    (a) are excited
    (b) were excited
    (c) was excited
    (d) No improvement

38. A more developed model of this car <u>may be showing</u> in the showroom soon.
    (a) had shown
    (b) will be shown
    (c) was shown
    (d) is going to show

39. <u>I haven't hardly studied</u> for this examination.
    (a) Hardly I have studies
    (b) I have hardly studied
    (c) No hardly I have studied
    (d) No improvement

40. <u>Is there some</u> maggie in the fridge?
    (a) Is there many
    (b) Is there any
    (c) Is their much
    (d) No improvement

41. Direction: Select the most appropriate meaning of the underlined idiom in the given sentence.
    You must seize the opportunity <u>to make amends</u> for your earlier curtness.
    (a) to correct a mistake
    (b) to make a proposal
    (c) to give a suggestion
    (d) to offer a deal

42. Direction : Select the most appropriate meaning of the given idiom.
    Fight shy of:
    (a) To invite
    (b) To avoid
    (c) To challenge
    (d) To perform

43. Direction : Select the most appropriate meaning of the given idiom.
    Bury the hatchet:
    (a) Dig a grave
    (b) Hide a treasure
    (c) Forget past quarrels
    (d) Sow the seeds

44. Direction : Select the most appropriate meaning of the given idiom.
    Lend an ear
    (a) Be good for a particular thing
    (b) Pay attention to
    (c) Not tell something to others
    (d) Not make trouble

45. Find the correct proverb for the given sentence.
    Her repeated effort has made her a master of the subject.
    (a) Practice makes a man perfect
    (b) Practice makes it better
    (c) Practice is the best medicine
    (d) Hard work makes a man perfect

Ques (46-47): Direction: Point out the figure of speech used in the sentence given below.

46. **The Puritan had been rescued by no common deliverer from the gasp of no common foe.**
    (a) Hyperbole
    (b) Epigram
    (c) Metaphor
    (d) Litotes

47. **The child is the father of the man.**
    (a) Oxymoron
    (b) Epigram
    (c) Antithesis
    (d) Hyperbole

48. **What is the term used for ingressive air-sounds produced?**
    (a) Claps
    (b) Snap
    (c) Clicks
    (d) Beats

49. **Which of these refer to the sound features of a language?**
    (a) Morphemics
    (b) Phonetic substances
    (c) Phonetics
    (d) Syntax

50. **What does the phonetic symbol d represent?**
    (a) Voiced bilabial plosive
    (b) Voiceless palatal plosive
    (c) Voiced alveolor plosive
    (d) Voiced dental fricative

Correct　Percentage of students who answered correctly.

Skipped　Percentage of students who skipped.

Q.	Ans.	Correct / Skipped	Q.	Ans.	Correct / Skipped	Q.	Ans.	Correct / Skipped
1	A	89.33% / 0.0%	2	D	57.68% / 1.9%	3	A	76.46% / 0.0%
4	D	53.26% / 1.81%	5	B	49.88% / 1.56%	6	C	52.85% / 1.08%
7	A	83.27% / 0.0%	8	B	60.35% / 1.6%	9	B	53.54% / 1.17%
10	A	47.16% / 1.58%	11	B	79.63% / 0.0%	12	B	68.48% / 1.1%
13	A	41.22% / 1.7%	14	D	41.81% / 1.71%	15	B	62.76% / 1.93%
16	D	44.05% / 1.75%	17	C	59.52% / 1.84%	18	A	56.42% / 1.88%
19	B	45.7% / 1.11%	20	D	56.05% / 1.7%	21	D	44.51% / 1.6%
22	A	49.56% / 1.56%	23	B	81.97% / 0.0%	24	A	64.67% / 1.58%
25	D	79.05% / 0.0%	26	D	64.44% / 1.46%	27	B	59.48% / 1.59%
28	B	64.8% / 1.14%	29	C	53.12% / 1.74%	30	A	40.53% / 1.18%
31	B	40.55% / 1.17%	32	D	48.23% / 1.69%	33	C	57.51% / 1.13%
34	B	54.77% / 1.04%	35	C	80.35% / 0.0%	36	C	67.21% / 1.69%
37	C	54.33% / 1.83%	38	B	65.31% / 1.83%	39	B	44.74% / 1.8%
40	B	43.61% / 1.66%	41	A	59.6% / 1.97%	42	B	11.42% / 4.44%
43	C	56.12% / 1.67%	44	B	22.64% / 4.43%	45	A	59.89% / 1.55%
46	D	77.43%	47	B	46.02%	48	C	82.15%

		0.0%			1.87%			0.0%
49	B	76.68%	50	C	84.16%			
		0.0%			0.0%			

// Hints and Solutions //

1(A). According to the first paragraph of the passage, 'because I saw it as a transaction between my teacher and my father!' We can deduce that author believed that it was something between his father and his teacher. Option (B) is true.
According to the paragraph 'But I was unconcerned. I had too much else going on that interested me.' We can easily say that he was occupied with other things which interested him. So, option (C) is true.
'Reading it always made my father blow up' here blow up means explode or make something explode, to suddenly get very angry. Conveys the report that would make his father flare-up which means a situation in which something, such as violence, pain, or anger suddenly starts or gets much worse. Flare-up and Blow up are synonyms of each other, So option (D) is also true.
We are left with only one option i.e., Option (A) which is the correct answer as 'his teacher seems to be satisfied' is a false statement.

2(D). According to the passage, "The alarming increase in student suicides today is because we have created a society founded on the premise that life is a race. So you rush to the finishing line! Is it any wonder that so many choose to end their lives? This is the self-destructive model we have created for ourselves".
So, we can say that according to the author competition based learning is self-destructive.

3(A). According to the passage, "The man going to the bar and the man going to the temple are seeking the same thing! They are looking for fulfilment, but through different means. Both want an experience of life that is a little more intense and pleasurable than it is currently."
So, it can be concluded that statement (A) is true.
According to the passage, "At present, the stimuli are outside. But once you know that the source of both pleasure and pain, agony and ecstasy are within you, why would you outsource it?"
So, it can be concluded that statement (B) is true.

4(D). The meaning of the given words:
- Alarming: worrying or disturbing.
- Disturbing: causing anxiety; worrying.
- Disgusting: arousing revulsion or strong indignation.
- Disappointing: failing to fulfil someone's hopes or expectations.
- Disheartening: causing someone to lose determination or confidence; discouraging or dispiriting.

Disturbing is similar in meaning to the word alarming.

5(B). The meaning of the given words:
- Particular: something specific.
- General: involving, applicable to, or affecting the whole.
- Random: made, done, or happening without method or conscious decision.
- Peripheral: relating to or situated on the edge or periphery of something.
- Integral: necessary to make a whole complete; essential or fundamental.

So, from the meanings given above, particular and general are antonyms of each other.

6(C). Word 'between' is a preposition i.e, a word governing, and usually preceding, a noun or pronoun and expressing a relation to another word or element in the clause, as in 'the man on the platform', 'she arrived after dinner', 'what did you do it for ?'.

7(A). Part (b) contains an error.
- The error lies in the usage of 'made' instead of 'makes'.
- When we are talking about something in present tense then we have to use some of the words like every day, month, week, year; always; sometimes; never; frequently etc in the sentence.
- As the given sentence is having always in it that means we are talking about present tense and the verb form of the verb after always depends upon the subject before it. Here, 'it' is there that means the verb form should be v5.

8(B). The theme of the passage is about how industrialization transformed life in Britain . The passage also gives insights into the population statistics of the different parts which make up Great Britain.
In the fifth paragraph of the given comprehension, it is mentioned that in the late 18 [th] century it grew rapidly and by 1801 it was over 9 million.

9(B). In the last passage of the given comprehension. It is stated that the population of Liverpool was about 77,000 in 1800. Birmingham had about 73,000 people and Manchester had about 70,000. Bristol had a population of about 68,000. Sheffield was smaller with 31,000 people and Leeds had about 30,000 people.

10(A). In the third paragraph of the given passage, it is stated that the North American colonies were lost after the War of Independence 1776-1783.
So, the statement ' After the War of Independence, Britain had colonies in North America. ' is wrong statement. Except this all statements are true.

11(B). In the third paragraph of the given passage, it is mentioned that Britain also took Dominica, Grenada, St. Vincent and Tobago in the West Indies.
Canada is not mentioned in the colonies of Britain in West Indies. So, Canada was not a colony of Britain.

12(B). In the opening paragraph, it is mentioned that in the late 18 [th] century the Industrial Revolution began to transform life in Britain.
So, we can say that "the industrial revolution" transformed life in 18 [th] century England.

13(A). The passage is about Jane Goodall's fascination for animals.
- In the introductory para, it was written how Jane was fascinated by animals and animal stories.
- Later, while working with Leakey, she expressed her interest in studying animals by living in the wild with them.
- Later, she continued her study of animals, especially chimpanzees in Tanzania.
- Jane's study is a breakthrough in the study of animals in the wild.
- Thus, the entire passage shows how Jane was fascinated with animals that shaped her life to a greater extent.

14(D). The correct answer is Scientific study of humanity, human behavior, human biology, culture, societies and linguistic.
- An anthropologist refers to a person who studies human, human behaviour, human biology, culture, societies and language.
- The word comes from "Anthropos", which means "humankind", and "-logist", a suffix, refers to a person

15(B). The correct answer is Because it was dangerous for a woman to live alone in the forests of Africa.
- The British, authorities did not approve of Dr Leakey and Jane's plan because it was dangerous for a woman to live alone in the forests of Africa.
- The plan was to study a group of chimpanzees who were living on the shores of Lake Tanganyika in Kenya.
- It was mentioned in the passage, that "the British authorities did not approve their plan. They thought it was too dangerous for a woman to live in the wilds of Africa alone".
- They approved her plan only when Jane's mother decided to join her.

16(D). The correct answer is In an area of a place that is especially remote and in which it is difficult & dangerous to live.
- The term 'wilds', in the passage, means an area of a place that is especially remote and in which it is difficult & dangerous to live.
- The phrase "wilds" refer to places which are far away from human habitat and full of dangers and risk.
- Example- What can be more adventurous than venturing into the wilds of Africa to a person who always looks for adventure?
- Africa was full of such "wilds" as most of the country was covered in forest, and not much had been discovered about the country till that date.
- Living in those areas is very risky, especially for a single woman.

17(C). The correct answer is Unique personality.
Jane named all of the chimpanzees she studied because she felt they each had a unique personality.
- It was mentioned in the passage that, "Jane named all of the chimpanzees that she studied, stating in her journals that she felt they each had a unique personality".
- Unique personality refers to unique character traits or traits that are not common.

18(A). It was mentioned in the passage that, "On her second birthday, her father gave her a toy chimpanzee named Jubilee."
The complete sentence will be, Jane's toy chimpanzee, Jubilee, sits in a chair in Jane's London home.

19(B). The correct answer is Because of her thorough knowledge of Africa and its wild life.
- The complete answer will be, "Dr Leakey hired jane to assist him because of her thorough knowledge of Africa and its wild life."
- Dr. Leakey was impressed of Jane's thorough knowledge of Africa and its wildlife.
- He soon realized that Jane was the perfect person to complete a study he had been planning for some time.
- That is why he hired her.

20(D). The complete answer will be, "The study started by Jane Goodall in 1960 continues to date in the form of research in Gombe."
- Jane started the study on chimpanzees in 1960.
- It is now the longest field study of any animal species in their natural habitat.
- Research is still being done in Gombe.

21(D). 'With no strings attached' means without any rules or demands or restrictions attached.

22(A). In the test, we will **assess** your work and then give you detailed feedback.

23(B). Zero tolerance means absolutely no toleration of even the smallest infraction of a rule. Tolerance cannot be related with accuracy.

24(A). The correct logical order is:
Playschool → school → college → office → retirement
So, 3, 1, 4, 2, 5 is the correct sequence.

25(D). All options are correct except option (D). Beautifull will be Beautiful

26(D). In assertive sentences like this, 'said' remains unchanged and is followed by 'that'. If the reporting verb is in the past tense and the reported speech is in the present, reported speech (with the change of narration) changes to the past. Subject 'I' becomes 'She'.
Thus, ' She said that she did not speak French' is the right answer.

27(B). 'Little' should be used instead of 'less'. The comparative form 'less' is not required in this case. 'Little' means 'next to none'.
Correct sentence: Deep in the mountains, there is little chance for anyone to get a cell phone connection.

28(B). 'Vexatious' issues refer to disturbing issues; 'tardy implementation' refers to delayed implementations.
Complete sentence: India has many vexatious issues: turf battles between ministers; and tardy implementation of various products throughout the country.

29(C). An idiom is a phrase, saying, or a group of words that has a metaphorical (not literal) meaning, which has become accepted in common usage.
Always a bridesmaid never a bride refers to someone who is never the most important person in a situation or always comes second.
Its use in a sentence is as follows: When will I get a promotion? I'm so sick of being always the bridesmaid, never the bride.
This would mean that the doctor would make all possible efforts in order to find a cure.

30(A). 'of' is the correct preposition for the blank because it expresses the relationship between a part and a whole, here it forms a relationship between the prisoner and murder.
Look at the following points-
'for' is wrong because it means in support of or in favour of.
'to' means expressing motion in the direction of.
'off' means away from the place in question.

31(B). Here, the error is in option B. Things don`t need to pass over. We need to pass over them. Thus, passive voice should be used to correct the error. So, the correct phrase will be `that need to be passed over.'

32(D). There is no error in the given sentence, the given sentence is grammatically correct.
The verb is perfectly fitting here, i.e., multiplies, because we are referring to a specified amount here, as article 'the' is used to make it specific.

33(C). Singular subject 'the Earth' will take a singular verb 'moves'.
Correct sentence: My cousin cannot understand why his

teacher says that the Earth moves around the sun.

34(B). The simple present tense is used when an action is happening right now, to state or ask about things in general, or when it happens regularly or unceasingly.
The structure is given below:
Subject + V1 + object.
The verb will take 's/es' if the given noun/pronoun (3rd person) is singular.
Example:
He plays badminton daily.
Certain verbs used only in the simple present tense are given below:
verbs of perception (see, hear, smell, etc.), think, know, has/have, possess, like, want, desire, hate, seem, imagine, etc.
For Examples:
My brother is owning a car. (incorrect)
My brother owns a car. (correct)

35(C). The underlined part is incorrect as angry is an adjective.
We use the adverb form of anger i.e. angrily in order to modify verbs, adjectives, or other adverbs.
For e.g.: The woman looked angry at the blotches on her freshly painted wall. (Wrong)
The woman looked angrily at the blotches on her freshly painted wall. (Correct)
Thus, the underlined phrase 'shouted angry' will be replaced with 'shouted angrily' to make the sentence contextually and grammatically correct.

36(C). The underlined part is wrong because "to a sudden stop" will come in place of "to a suddenly stop".
Sudden is an adjective and suddenly is an adverb. Stop is a noun and adjective qualifies a noun. So, sudden will be used.
Stoppage means break in a journey. So, usage of stoppage is irrelevant here.

37(C). The given sentence is in passive voice and in simple past tense.
The simple past is a verb tense that is used to talk about things that happened or existed before now.
For example: He won a car race.
In the simple past tense, we make passive verb forms by putting 'was/were' before the past participle form of the verb.
So, in the underlined part of the given sentence, 'was excited' will be the most appropriate choice.

38(B). Had shown means something shown in the past.
Will be shown means something is going to be shown in the future.
Was shown means something shown in the past.
Is going to show means something is going to be shown right now or in some interval of time.
As the word 'soon' is used in the sentence, therefore, first and second options are incorrect and the use of verb 'show' in the fourth option is incorrect.

39(B). In the underlined segment, the use of the adverb 'not' is incorrect.
In the given sentence, the adverb 'hardly' is used which means no or not (suggesting surprise at or disagreement with a statement).
Hardly is already negative, therefore, there is no need to use an extra 'not'.
Therefore, the use of the adverb 'not' is superfluous or not necessary in the sentence.

40(B). Usage of 'some': Use 'some' in affirmative sentences when there is neither a lot nor a little.
'Some' can be used with both countable and uncountable nouns.
Example: I've saved some money to spend on vacation this summer.
Usage of 'any': Use "any" in questions to ask if someone has something (interrogative sentences).
'Any' can be used with both countable and uncountable nouns.
Example: Is there any pasta left?
Use 'any' with countable and uncountable nouns in negative sentences to state that something doesn't exist.
Example: We won't have any time for shopping today.
From the above explanations, it is clear that the given sentence is an interrogative sentence.
Therefore, 'Is there any' is the most appropriate answer.

41(A). You must seize the opportunity to correct a mistake for your earlier curtness.
The most appropriate meaning of the given idiom 'To make amends' is 'to correct a mistake'.
To make amends: to do something to correct a mistake that one has made or a bad situation that one has caused.
Example: She tried to make amends by apologizing to him.

42(B). The most appropriate meaning of the given idiom is to avoid.
To invite: For someone to offer one entrance to the place where they live.
To challenge: To question one, perhaps aggressively, on a particular issue, statement, or viewpoint.
To perform: To begin and bring to completion some kind of procedure or activity focused on someone or something.

43(C). The most appropriate meaning of the given idiom is to forget past quarrels.
'To bury the hatchet' means to end a quarrel, make piece and become friends again.
Example: India and Pakistan are being often advised by world bodies to bury the hatchet for their own growth.

44(B). Pay attention to the most appropriate meaning of the given idiom.
Example: Sorry I'm late, I had to lend an ear to Jane. She's been going through a lot lately.
Be no slouch: Be good for a particular thing.
Keep something under wraps: Not tell something to others.
No trouble: Not make trouble.

45(A). The correct proverb is 'practice makes a man perfect'. It means to succeed in life in any particular field or subject, one needs to practice regularly with full commitment and planned strategies.
Example of Use: "I've been working on my tennis serve, and I think I'm getting better."

46(D). The figure of speech in above sentence is Litotes.
Litotes is a figure of speech that employs an understatement by using double negatives or, in other words, a positive statement expressed by negating its opposite expressions. The double negatives are 'no common deliverer' and ' no common foe' in this example.

47(B). The correct answer is: **Epigram.**
The given sentence is trying to express the idea that one's personality is formed in one's childhood. Therefore, it is an epigram as the fact is told in a witty way.
An epigram is a statement which expresses a thought in a witty or funny way.

48(C). Normally, speech sounds are produced on egressive pulmonic air-stream during exhilaration. In few cases, ingressive air sounds are also made. Such speech sounds are called clicks.

49(B). Phonetic substances refer to the sound features of a language, as studied by articulatory, acoustic and auditory phonetics.

50(C). The symbol d refers to Voiced alveolor plosive. The symbol b refers to Voiced bilabial plosive and c refers to Voiceless palatal plosive.

Ques (1-5): Direction: Read the passage and answer the following question.

Child labor is an important topic that is being debated as a serious social issue all around the world. Keeping society aware of this issue will help to avoid such illegal and **inhuman** activity from destroying the lives of many children. Child labor is something that replaces the normal activities of a child, like education, playing, etc., with economic activities. These economic activities may be paid or unpaid work, which benefits the family of the child or the owner the child works for. The age limit is restricted to fourteen years or even seventeen years in case of dangerous work. Children may be forced to do child labor because of poverty and financial problems in their families. Many owners accept child labors since they only need a less amount as salary or even accept non-monetary jobs too. Children are often made to do such hard jobs by their irresponsible parents. They send their kids for domestic work for the money as well as for the food they get through these works. These demanding works often spoil childhood and give a harder way of living to the kid.

Parents allow their children for such jobs because of a lack of awareness too. When they are too poor to take admission to schools and the lack of good schools in their locality may also lead to such activities. Not all forms of jobs done by children are considered child labor, but there are some things to note while categorizing them. Whether the job is done mentally, morally, physically, or socially, does it affects the child in a dangerous way? Does the job done affect their education and other childhood activities like playing? The job they do shouldn't be both tiring and excessive and they are forced to avoid other activities they should be doing at their age. These are the characteristics of Child Labor. In extreme ways, there are owners who treat children like slaves and separate them from their families to do such hard jobs. Whatever the job done, child labor depends on the age of the kid involved, the type of activity, and the hours of work they do per day. In conclusion, children are meant to be enjoying their childhood and should be allowed to educate themselves at an early age. There are many **schemes** introduced by the government to reduce such child labors like providing free education and taking severe actions against those who promote child labor.

1. **Which of the following statements is true in terms of child labor?**
   (a) Children cannot get admission to school and should continue earning money through labor.
   (b) Children are meant to be enjoying their childhood and should not be allowed to do these jobs.
   (c) Children below 17 are more active and can provide better productivity as laborers.
   (d) Since they only need a less amount as salary, they should continue to do these jobs.

2. **What do the government schemes include to reduce child labor?**
   (A). Providing free education.
   (B). Taking severe actions against those who promote child labor.
   (C). Encouraging more wages for child laborers.
   (a) Only (A)   (b) Only (B)
   (c) All except (A)   (d) All except (C)

3. **What are the characteristics to look for to identify child labor?**
   (A). Whether the job affects the child in a dangerous way
   (B). Whether the jobs done affect their education and other childhood activities like playing.
   (C). Whether the jobs are fun and not risky.

(a) Only (A)   (b) Only (B)
(c) All except (B)   (d) All except (C)

4. **Why do parents push their children into doing child labor?**
   (A). Lack of awareness
   (B). Lack of good schools in the area
   (C). Too poor to admit their children to schools
   (a) All except (A)   (b) All except (B)
   (c) All except (C)   (d) All of these

5. **Why do owners prefer child labors?**
   Because -
   (A). They are cute
   (B). They need less salary or wages
   (C). They do not throw tantrums
   (a) Only (A)   (b) Only (B)
   (c) Only (C)   (d) All of the above

Ques (6-12): Direction: Read the passage given below and answer the given question by choosing the correct option:

1. The study of handwriting is known as graphology and it has been practiced for hundreds of years. Professional forensic graphologists have worked on many court cases to use handwriting to link suspects with crimes.

2. Handwriting is particularly important legally in the case of signatures and proving whether signatures are real or forged can be pivotal. Graphologists also work to verify whether autographs are real or fake.

3. Some handwriting analysts also study writing samples to determine personality types and some businesses commission this analysis before hiring new employees. The method is even sometimes used to help couples see if they are compatible. According to graphologists, there is very little you can't tell from a persons' handwriting.

4. From psychological conditions like high blood pressure and schizophrenia to personality traits like dominance and aggression : if you write by hand, graphologists can analyse you.

5. Everything from the size of your letters to how closely you space words can reveal intricate details of your personality. In general, the size of your letters can reveal whether you are shy or outgoing Compared to a standard lined sheet of paper, if you write with tiny letters that do not reach the top line, you are likely to have a timid and introverted personality. If you write with large letters that go over the topline, you are likely to be the opposite : outgoing, confident and attention seeking.

6. Studies suggest that people who space words widely like freedom and independence, whereas those choosing to write with small spaces prefer to be among others and do not like to be alone.

6. **An attention seeking, confident person writes with:**
   (a) cursive letters   (b) large letters
   (c) rounded letters   (d) tiny letters

7. **Read the following statements:**
   A. Graphology has been practised for thousands of years.
   B. A person's handwriting reveals everything about him.
   (a) A is false and B is true.   (b) Both A and B are true.
   (c) Both A and B are false.   (d) A is true and B is false.

8. **Which one of the following words is similar in meaning to the word, 'verify' (Para-2) as used in the passage ?**
   (a) Confirm   (b) Notify
   (c) Discover   (d) Clarify

9. **Which part of speech is the underlined word in the**

following sentence ?
Graphologists can verify whether the autographs are real or fake?
(a) Preposition   (b) Pronoun
(c) Conjunction   (d) Adverb

10. **Which of the following statements is not true?**
Handwriting is used by graphologists to:
(a) verify genuineness of signatures.
(b) help couples to determine their suitability to each other.
(c) predict about a person's future criminal tendency.
(d) nail criminals.

11. **A graphologist can give accurate information about:**
(a) a person's mental health.
(b) setbacks a person is likely to face in future.
(c) a person's chances of success.
(d) a person's popularity graph.

12. **A person who writes with large letters that cross over to the top line is likely to be:**
(a) introverted.   (b) aggressive.
(c) diffident.   (d) outgoing.

Ques (13-20): Direction. Read the passage given below and answer the question/complete the statements that follow by choosing the best options from the given ones.

By absolute standards, people are slow readers. Yet, they differ widely in reading rates. Some **gulp** books by taking in a hundred words or more within a minute; others **plod** along through weeks or more. However, there is nothing to prove that slow readers **retain** and comprehend the reading matter better.

Now, it is a fast that the reading rate can be improved by exercise. Many techniques to teach people to read faster were undertaken, for the first time at Harvard University in the United States after the Second World War, and classes were organised for businessmen wishing to learn fast reading.

A widely held opinion is that when a person reads, his eyes sweep smoothly across the page. Actually during an hour of continuous reading, his eyes remain fixed for an average of 57 minutes, and only move in the remaining three minutes. The greater the number of words the reader can cover during a stop and the better he comprehends them, the faster the reading. Precisely this goal is sought in training people to read fast.

It appears that fast reading should be started at school when children have not yet picked up bad reading habits (especially subvocalising), that is the tendency to form words with their **vocal** chords. It is a well known fact that a drawing, a diagram or a photograph will usually carry more information than a printed text taking up the same area. A person grasps this graphic information all at a time. This ability is usually utilized in technical publications, but not to the full extent yet. Coupled with fast reading, this may raise the rate of information input tens or even hundreds of times.

13. **According to the given comprehension, what is a widely held opinion?**
(a) When a person reads clearly says everything in as he started reading.
(b) When a person reads clearly say everything in a single glance.
(c) When a person reads move his eyes smoothly across the page.
(d) When a person reads move his eyes quickly across the page.

14. **Read the following statements:**

(a) Some people read books very fast.
(b) However, they do not understand all that they have read.
(c) Slow readers have better understanding and retention of the materials that they have read.
Which statement is/are correct?
(a) (a) is true and (b) and (c) are false.
(b) (a) and (b) are true and (c) is false.
(c) (a) is false and (b) and (c) are true.
(d) (a) and (c) are true and (b) is false.

15. **In one hour of continuous reading for how long do a person's eyes remain static?**
(a) 1 minute   (b) 3 minutes
(c) 57 minutes   (d) All the time

16. **The number of words a reader understands is _________ proportional to his reading speed.**
(a) directly   (b) inversely
(c) conversely   (d) reciprocally

17. **Read the following statements.**
(a) Printed materials take up a lot a space.
(b) Graphic information can be used only for technical publication.
Which statement is/are correct?
(a) (a) is wrong and (b) is right.
(b) (a) is right and (b) is wrong.
(c) Both (a) and (b) are right.
(d) Both (a) and (b) are wrong.

18. **Some gulp books 'Gulp' here means that they are:**
(a) Slow readers.   (b) Fast readers.
(c) Moderate readers.   (d) Inconsiderate readers.

19. **In vocal chords vocal is used as a/an:**
(a) Verb   (b) Noun
(c) Adverb   (d) Adjective

20. **In which of the following sentences is the word 'retained' used in the same sense as in slow readers retain ....?**
(a) The police retained control of the situation.
(b) Clay soil can retain water.
(c) He retained a consultant for tax calculations.
(d) He retained his freedom by strictly following the rules

21. **Direction: Complete the following sentence by choosing the appropriate word from the given options:.**
Radha's presentation was the ___ in her class.
(a) better   (b) great
(c) dangerous   (d) best

22. **Find out that word, the spelling of which is correct.**
(a) Adulation   (b) Adlation
(c) Aduletion   (d) Addulation

23. **Direction: Choose the word that can substitute the given sentence.**
A place where money is made.
(a) Mint   (b) Stable
(c) Granary   (d) Cloak room

24. **Direction: In the following question, out of the four alternatives, choose the alternative which best expresses the meaning of the idiom/Phrase.**

Something up one's sleeve

(a) A grand idea   (b) A secret plan

(c) A profitable plan   (d) Something important

25. **Direction: Fill in the blanks with an appropriate word.**
     Gold biscuits have an undeniable ________.

(a) accomplish   (b) arrange

(c) allure   (d) assist

26. **Direction: Select the most appropriate synonym of the given word.**
     PRODIGAL

(a) Modest   (b) Intelligent

(c) Talented (d) Wasteful

27. **Select the wrongly spelt word.**

(a) decibel   (b) decease

(c) decency   (d) decieve

28. **Direction: Select the most appropriate word for the given group of word.**
     A factual written account of important or historical events in the order of their occurrence.

(a) Journal   (b) Chronicle

(c) Chronology (d) Register

29. **Direction: Given below are four jumbled sentences. Select the option that gives their correct order.**
     A. On the other hand, the Saracen chief looked slighter and shorter, but he was also strong.
     B. The Briton was a hugely powerful man with thick brown hair.
     C. They went side by side to the well, where they ate their simple meal and rested.
     D. They were a great contrast to each other.

(a) DCAB   (b) CDAB

(c) BADC   (d) DABC

Ques (30-32): Direction : A part of the sentence is underlined. Below are given alternatives to the improve the sentence. Choose the correct alternative. In case no improvement is needed, your answer is option 'D'.

30. **We spent an hour discussing <u>about his character.</u>**

(a) on his character   (b) of his character

(c) his character   (d) no improvement

31. **He <u>declined</u> all the allegations against him.**

(a) spurned   (b) refused

(c) refuted   (d) no improvement

32. **It is time we <u>leave</u>.**

(a) left   (b) have to leave

(c) would leave (d) no improvement

33. **Direction :** In the following questions, a sentence is given with two blanks. You have to find the pair of words from the given options that fit both the blanks in the given order and make the sentence grammatically and contextually correct.

     Congress leaders stress that this manifesto ______ the needs and ______ of the marginalised sections of society.

(a) covers, inspirations   (b) includes, requirements

(c) addresses, aspirations (d) indicates, qualities

Ques (34-40): Direction: In the following question, out of the four alternatives, select the alternative which will improve the underlined part of the sentence. In case no improvement is needed, select "No improvement".

34. **Each of the students of this class <u>has to submit their</u> assignment before the end of this month.**

(a) has to submit his   (b) have to submit his

(c) have to submit their (d) No improvement

35. **Acclaimed Punjabi singer Sardool Sikander <u>has passed away at</u> Fortis hospital in Mohali in Punjab on Wednesday.**

(a) had passed away at   (b) passed away at

(c) passes away at   (d) No improvement

36. **The trip to Ladakh seemed to be very expensive so <u>I did not went there</u> with my friends.**

(a) I haven't gone there   (b) I do not go there

(c) I did not go there   (d) No improvement

37. **<u>Although he is working</u> in this organization for the last two years, he hasn't done anything remarkable.**

(a) Although he had been working

(b) Although he was working

(c) Although he has been working

(d) No improvement

38. **They built a wall to avoid soil <u>being washed away</u>.**

(a) to be washed away   (b) been washed away

(c) be washed away   (d) No improvement

39. **Strategically the Andaman and Nicobar islands <u>hold phenomenal importance</u> in regional geopolitics.**

(a) holds phenomenal importance

(b) helds phenomenal importance

(c) holds phenomenon importance

(d) No improvement

40. **Mr Sharma along with <u>his wife and son are going</u> for a week-long vacation.**

(a) her wife and son are going

(b) his wife and son were gone

(c) his wife and son is going

(d) No improvement

41. **Direction: Select the most appropriate meaning of the underlined idiom in the given sentence.**
     She felt <u>like a fish out of water</u> at her new job.

(a) Comfortable and relaxed

(b) Angry and hurt

(c) Happy and free

(d) Uncomfortable and restless

42. **Direction: Select the most appropriate meaning of the given idiom.**
     A fair weather friend

(a) an unreliable friend

(b) a dependable friend

(c) a friend turned into an enemy

(d) a jealous friend

43. **Direction: Select the most appropriate meaning of the given idiom.**
     Breath of fresh air

(a) a peaceful and relaxing place

(b) someone with a pleasant voice

(c)   a high-priced and expensive thing

(d)   someone or something new and refreshing

44. Direction : Select the most appropriate meaning of the given idiom.

Cut a sorry figure

(a)   Render an apology

(b)   Make a sculpture

(c)   Create a poor impression

(d)   Break a record

45. Which of the following is not a proverb?

(a)   Where there's smoke, there's fire

(b)   Like father, like son

(c)   No man is an island

(d)   Beat around the bush

Ques (46-47): Direction: Point out the figure of speech used in the sentence given below.

46. The camel is the ship of the desert.

(a)   Pun   (b)   Personfication

(c)   Apostrophe   (d)   Metaphor

47. The bread jumped out of the toaster.

(a)   Idiom   (b)   Metaphor

(c)   Hyperbole   (d)   Personification

48. What is the full form of IPA ?

(a)   Indian Phonetic Alphabet

(b)   International Phonetic Alphabet

(c)   International Phonetic Agreement

(d)   Indian Phonetic Agreement

49. What does the sign / / represent?

(a)   Phonetic transcription   (b)   Centralization

(c)   Voiced bilabial nasal   (d)   Rising- falling pitch

50. /ə'sɪdjʊəs/ is the phonetic transcription of:

(a)   Acidic   (b)   Assimilate

(c)   Assignment   (d)   Assiduous

// Smart Answer Sheet //

Correct Percentage of students who answered correctly.

Skipped Percentage of students who skipped.

Q.	Ans.	Correct	Skipped	Q.	Ans.	Correct	Skipped	Q.	Ans.	Correct	Skipped
1	B	79.31%	0.0%	2	D	78.26%	0.0%	3	D	45.94%	1.03%
4	D	50.39%	1.97%	5	B	62.07%	1.24%	6	B	60.54%	1.48%
7	C	54.01%	1.81%	8	A	42.2%	1.81%	9	C	61.0%	1.99%
10	C	53.26%	1.68%	11	A	58.21%	1.9%	12	D	65.87%	1.2%
13	C	86.89%	0.0%	14	A	63.57%	1.09%	15	C	61.79%	1.32%
16	A	49.61%	1.36%	17	B	43.64%	1.83%	18	B	87.57%	0.0%
19	D	55.75%	1.7%	20	C	54.93%	1.08%	21	D	81.87%	0.0%
22	A	80.61%	0.0%	23	A	54.18%	1.46%	24	B	56.2%	1.27%
25	C	50.87%	1.95%	26	D	77.3%	0.0%	27	D	77.43%	0.0%
28	B	76.16%	0.0%	29	C	87.72%	0.0%	30	C	45.06%	1.07%
31	D	88.76%	0.0%	32	A	51.49%	1.86%	33	C	62.38%	1.67%
34	A	48.72%	1.88%	35	B	68.7%	1.7%	36	C	66.18%	1.71%
37	C	61.01%	1.34%	38	D	83.12%	0.0%	39	A	47.88%	1.52%
40	C	52.98%	1.45%	41	D	66.45%	1.4%	42	A	45.28%	1.47%
43	D	42.26%	1.38%	44	C	57.53%	1.68%	45	D	55.53%	1.04%
46	D	60.85%	1.74%	47	D	66.71%	1.93%	48	B	57.36%	1.33%
49	A	88.7%	0.0%	50	D	54.38%	1.47%				

// Hints and Solutions //

1(B). The passage speaks of child labor as an inhuman aspect. It generally describes the reasons as well as the effects of child labor.

2(D). The passage speaks of child labor as an inhuman aspect. It generally describes the reasons as well as the effects of child labor.

3(D). The passage speaks of child labor as an inhuman aspect. It generally describes the reasons as well as the effects of child labor.

The sentences in the passage clearly mention "...does it affects the child in a dangerous way?" and "Does the job done affect their education and other childhood activities?" The job they do shouldn't be both tiring and excessive that they are forced to avoid other activities they should be doing in their age.

Other than point (C), the rest are mentioned in the passage.

4(D). The passage speaks of child labor as an inhuman aspect. It generally describes the reasons as well as the effects of child labor.

The sentences in the passage clearly mention "Parents allow their children for such jobs because of lack of awareness too. When they are too poor to take admissions in schools and the lack of good schools in their locality may also lead to such activities".

These demanding works often spoil their childhood and give a harder way of living to the kid.

5(B). The passage speaks of child labor as an inhuman aspect. It generally describes the reasons as well as the effects of child labor.

The sentence in the passage clearly mentions "Many owners accept child labors since they only need a less amount as salary or even some accept non-monetary jobs too".

Here, points (B) and (C) are not mentioned in the passage or in the above sentence as well. Therefore, they are invalid.

6(B). From the given lines of the passage it's clearly stated how confident and attention seeking a person writes. He writes with large letters.

7(C). From the given lines of the passage w e can infer from this line that the first statement of the question is false, since it says thousands instead of hundreds. Second statement is tricky as we cannot locate it exactly. However, if we look at the last line of the 3rd point of the passage it states 'there is very little you can't tell from a person's handwriting'. We can conclude from this line that statement A as well as B is false.

8(A). Verify means make sure, confirm or demonstrate that (something) is true, accurate, or justified; Confirm means establish the truth or correctness of (something previously believed or suspected to be the case). Thus, confirm is the most similar in meaning to verify.

9(C). Conjunctions are words that link other words, phrases, or clauses together. 'Or' is a coordinating conjunction used to join two different choices. Thus, 'or' is used as a conjunction in the sentence: Graphologists can verify whether the autographs are real or fake.

10(C). While reading the passage we can see that we cannot locate the statement, 'predict about a person's future criminal tendency.' All the other phrases can be easily found in the given passage. Thus, the correct answer is 'predict about a person's future criminal tendency.'

11(A). The passage consistently refers to the ability of graphology to reveal a person's mental psyche. When we look at the other options we can see that they talk about the future and nowhere in the passage it has been mentioned that Graphology can reveal the future.

12(D). From the given lines of the passage i n the 5th point of the above given passage it's clearly stated what kind of person writes with large letters that cross over to the top line. Thus, the correct answer is 'outgoing'.

13(C). As we can see in the third paragraph of the passage, it is clearly mentioned that " **A widely held opinion is that when a person reads, his eyes sweep smoothly across the page.** Actually, during an hour of continuous reading, his eyes remain fixed for an average of 57 minutes, and only move in the remaining three minutes". Thus, A widely held opinion is that when a person reads move his eyes smoothly across the page.

14(A). As we can see in the first paragraph of the passage, it is clearly mentioned that "Some gulp books by taking in a hundred words or more within a minute ; others plod along through weeks or more". It can be concluded that statement (a) is true.
There is no mention in the passage whether faster readers understand all that they have read or not. So, statement (b) is false.
As we can see in the first paragraph of the passage, it is clearly mentioned that "However, there is nothing to prove that slow readers retain and comprehend the reading matter better ". It can be concluded that statement (c) is false.

15(C). As we can see in the third paragraph of the passage, it is clearly mentioned that "Actually during an hour of continuous reading, his eyes remain fixed for an average of 57 minutes, and only move in the remaining three minutes".
Thus, it can be concluded that in one hour of continuous reading a person's eyes remain static for 57 minutes.

16(A). As we can see in the third paragraph of the passage, it is clearly mentioned that "The greater the number of words the reader can cover during a stop and the better he comprehends them, the faster the reading".
Thus, it can be concluded that the number of words a reader understands is directly proportional to his reading speed.

17(B). As we can see in the fourth paragraph of the passage, it is clearly mentioned that "It is a well-known fact that a drawing, a diagram or a photograph will usually carry more information than a printed text taking up the same area". It can be inferred that statement (a) is true.
We can also see in the fourth paragraph of the passage, it is clearly mentioned that "It is a well-known fact that a drawing, a diagram or a photograph will usually carry more information than a printed text taking up the same area. A person grasps this graphic information all at a time. This ability is usually utilized in technical publications, but not to the full extent yet". So, statement (b) is false as there is no mention in the passage that this technique is only used in technical publications.

18(B). Gulp means swallowing words quickly making them fast readers often audibly.
As we can see in the first paragraph of the passage, it is clearly mentioned that "Some gulp books by taking in a hundred words or more within a minute; others plod along through weeks or more". It means that in short time readers read many words just like consuming words in large amount which make them fast reader.
Thus, it can be concluded that there gulping books mean reading them in a faster manner.

19(D). Here the underlined word ' vocal ' is an adjective i.e., a word naming an attribute of a noun, such as sweet, red, or technical.
Vocal means relating to the human voice.
For example:- Foley has been particularly vocal in his criticism of the government.

20(C). Retain means continue to have (something); keep possession of; absorb and continue to hold (a substance).
For examples:
- It was amazing how Alex could retain his composure. (to maintain someone's mental stability)
- A landlord may retain part of your deposit if you break the lease. (to keep or hold one's possession on something)

Thus, it can be concluded that retain can be used in different senses but in the passage, we are talking about the retention power of the readers and how well they are comprehending things after reading them .

21(D). The correct sentence with the appropriate word from the given options is: Radha's presentation was best in her class.
Superlative adjectives are used to describe an object which is at the upper or lower limit of a quality (the tallest, the smallest, the fastest, the highest). They are used in sentences where a subject is compared to a group of objects.
In the given sentence, 'best' is the superlative form of good, with the comparative form being 'better'.
In the given sentence, Radha is being compared to her whole class as a group. Thus the superlative degree best is used.

22(A). All options are incorrect except option (A). Adulation is only correctly spelled.

23(A). A place where money is made called mint.
A place for horses is called stable.
A place for grains is called granary.
A place for luggage at railway station is called cloak room.

24(B). Something up one's sleeve: To have a secret plan, idea, or advantage that can be utilized if and when it is required.

25(C). Gold biscuits have an undeniable **Allure** .
Allure is used for something which has a quality of being

powerfully attractive.
So, the correct answer is Gold biscuits have an undeniable allure.

26(D). The word 'Prodigal' means given to spending money freely or foolishly.
The synonyms of the word 'Prodigal' are "wasteful, extravagant, squandering".
From the synonym of the given word, we can say that the word 'wasteful' is the same in meaning.
The word 'wasteful' means given to spending money freely or foolishly.

27(D). Decieve': There is no such word in English or we can say that there is some spelling mistake in this word, correct spelling is 'Deceive'.
'Decibel' is a unit used to measure the intensity of a sound or the power level of an electrical signal.
'Decease' means a person's death.
'Decency' means behaviour that conforms to accepted standards of morality or respectability.

28(B). 'Chronicle' is a factual written account of important or historical events in the order of their occurrence.
'Journal' is a newspaper or magazine that deals with a particular subject or professional activity.
'Chronology' is the study of historical records to establish the dates of past events.
'Register' is an official list or record of names or items.

29(C). The correct answer is "BADC".
The sentence 'B' is independent of any other sentences as it is giving general information about "The Briton". Hence, 'B' is the first part.
The phrase "On the other hand" mentioned in the sentence 'A' is introducing a contrasting sentence with the sentence 'B'. Hence, 'A' follows 'B'.
The sentence 'D' is showing the quality of contrast between the sentence 'B' and 'A'. Hence, 'D' follows 'A'.
The sentence 'C' is the concluding sentence.

30(C). In the given sentence, the use of 'about' (Preposition) is superfluous (unnecessary).
When we talk about some verbs, we do not use prepositions to succeed them, in some cases, one of which is this sentence.
Thus, 'his character' is the right usage.

31(D). Declined means politely refuse (an invitation or offer).
Spurned means reject with disdain or contempt.
Refused means indicate or show that one is not willing to do something.
Refuted means prove (a statement or theory) to be wrong or false; disprove.
Thus, the correct word to be used here is 'declined'.
Therefore the sentence is grammatically correct, no improvement is required.

32(A). The sentence structure will be as follows :
It is time + Subject (we) + Past Verb (left) → Refers to the present moment
Thus, 'left' is the right usage.

33(C). Congress leaders stress that this manifesto **addresses** the needs and **aspirations** of the marginalised sections of society.
First word of all the options could fit the first blank grammatically as well as contextually, but the second word makes a difference here.
In option A, 'inspirations' seems contextually incorrect.
In option B, 'requirements' is redundant as it means the same as "needs".
In option C, 'aspirations' absolutely fits the context as well grammar. Aspiration is different from 'need' in a way that "need" refers to the necessities of an individual whereas 'aspiration" is more about luxurious desires of an individual.

34(A). The usage of 'their' is wrong in the given sentence.
If 'of' is used after 'each, every, one, etc.' the noun or pronoun that comes immediately after 'of' will be in plural form but the noun or pronoun that comes in the latter part of the sentence will be in the singular form.
E.g. Each of them has brought his own meal.
According to the rule and example that are given above, 'has to submit his' will be used in the underlined part of the given sentence.

35(B). The given sentence is in the past indefinite tense.
The past indefinite tense is used to denote the actions that happened in past.
When a past time like yesterday, last month, name of any specific day, etc. is given, the sentence must be in the past indefinite tense.
E.g. I visited the Taj Mahal on Sunday.
In the past indefinite tense, V2 is used.
In the given sentence, past time i.e. Wednesday has been mentioned. So, the sentence should be in the past indefinite tense.
According to the rule and example that are given above, 'passed away at' will be used in the underlined part of the sentence.

36(C). The use of 'went' with the helping verb 'did' is wrong.
The given sentence is in the past indefinite tense and in the past indefinite tense the helping verb 'did' is used in the negative and interrogative sentences.
Generally, V2 is used in the past indefinite tense but if the sentence is negative or interrogative 'did + V1' is used.
Examples,
I completed my graduation year.
I did not go to the office yesterday.
According to the rule and example that are given above, 'I did not go there will be used in the underlined part of the sentence.

37(C). The given sentence is in the present perfect continuous tense.
The structure used in the present perfect continuous tense-
subject+ has/have + been + V1 + ing + object + for/since + time.
Example,
He has been running for the last two hours.
According to the rule and example that are given above, 'Although he has been working' will be used in the underlined part of the sentence.

38(D). There are some verbs that are followed by V1 + ing.
Some examples of these verbs are: enjoy, love, hate, like, admit, deny, finish, avoid, etc.
Examples,
I try to avoid going shopping on Sundays.
I haven't finished writing my new novel.
According to the rule and examples that are given above, 'being washed away' is correct in the given sentence.

39(A). According to subject-verb agreement, the subject and verb in a sentence must agree with each other.
If the subject is singular, the verb should also be singular and vice-versa.
Examples,

The dogs are chasing a cat.

The prime minister delivers a speech.

According to the rule and examples that are given above, 'hold phenomenal importance' will be used in the underlined part of the given sentence.

40(C). If two nouns are joined by 'along with, in addition to, as well as, together with, and not, etc.' the verb will agree with the first subject.

Examples,

The captain along with other players is going to England for the next match.

Rajan as well as his cousins is working in a multi-national company.

According to the rule and examples that are given above, "his wife and son is going" will be used in the underlined part of the sentence.

41(D). In the given sentence 'like a fish out of water is an idiomatic expression. Its meaning of it is as follows:

Like a fish out of water- to feel awkward because you are in a situation that you have not experienced before or because you are very different from the people around you.

Example: I felt like a fish out of water in my new school.

Uncomfortable and restless- not able to sit, lie, etc., in a pleasant and worried, anxious, uneasy, not restful.

42(A). The most appropriate meaning of the given idiom is "an unreliable friend".

A fair-weather friend is used to refer a friend who is not reliable in difficult times.

Example: I am looking for a loyal friend, not a fair-weather friend.

43(D). The most appropriate meaning of the given idiom "someone or something new and refreshing".

Breath of fresh air means someone or something that makes a situation feel new, different, and exciting.

Example, The beautiful new paint colour is a breath of fresh air for the office.

All the other options except option (D) is irrelevant.

44(C). Create a poor impression is the most appropriate meaning of the given idiom.

Cut a sorry figure: Create a poor impression

Create a poor impression meaning: Produce a strong effect

on one. This phrase is often qualified with an adjective such as bad, worse, or the like.

My apologies: excuses or regrets

Make a sculpture: an individual piece of such work

Break a record: to do something that is better, faster etc than anything that has been done before

45(D). The phrase 'beat around the bush' is not a proverb, as it is an idiom. It means to delay or avoid talking about something difficult or unpleasant.

Example Sentence:

Will you please stop beating about the bush and get to the point?

46(D). The correct answer is **Metaphor.**

In the given sentence 'the camel' is described as 'the ship of desert' as it is believed that the camel and the ship have some similar characteristics. So, it is a metaphor.

A metaphor is a figure of speech which is used to describe a person or an object by directly mentioning another thing or object.

47(D). The correct answer is Personification.

In the line given in the question, the bread which is a non-living thing is jumping. So, we can say that the bread is being taken as a living being as jumping is an act performed by living beings only.

Personification is a figure of speech where non-living objects are described to seem like people.

Hence, the correct option is (B).

48(B). IPA is International Phonetic Alphabet which provides a uniform international medium for studying and transcribing sounds of all languages of the world. In case of English, it assists in creating international intelligibility in pronunciation.

49(A). Phonetic transcription is represented by / / . Centralization is represented by ". Voiced bilabial nasal is represented by m .

50(D). Phonetic transcription, also known as phonetic script or phonetic notation, is the visual representation of speech sounds or phones by means of symbols. The most common type of phonetic transcription uses a phonetic alphabet, such as the International Phonetic Alphabet.

Ques (1-7): Direction : Read the passage given below and answer the question that follow by choosing the correct / most appropriate option.

1. Sindhutai was born on 14 th November 1948 in the cattle grazing family in Maharashtra's Wardha district. Her father was keen to educate her but mother was not. At the age of ten she was married to a man twenty years her senior. Post marriage she faced a difficult life but she did not lose hope. In her new home she fought against the exploitation of local women, who collected cow dung, by the forest department and landlords. This only made things more difficult for her.

2. At the young age of twenty, when nine-months pregnant, she was beaten badly and left to die by her husband. She gave birth to a baby girl Mamta in that semi-conscious state and struggled to stay alive. Sindhutai took to begging on the streets and railway platforms to survive. Because she feared being picked up by men at night she often spent the night at cemeteries. Such was her condition that people called her a ghost since she was seen at night in the cemeteries.

3. In this constant tussle to survive, she found herself in Chikaldara, situated in the Amravati district of Maharashtra. Here, due to a tiger preservation project, 84 tribal villages were evacuated. Amidst the confusion, a project officer impounded 32 cows of Adivasi villagers and one of the cows died. Sindhutai decided to fight for the proper rehabilitation of the helpless tribal villagers. Her efforts were acknowledged by the Minister of Forests and he made appropriate arrangements for alternative relocation.

4. It was during these tiring times that she realized how difficult it would be for abandoned children or orphans and decided to do something for them. Her first adopted child was Deepak, whom she found on a railway track. Quite soon she had adopted sixteen children.

5. So Sindhutai started taking care of children in return for some food. Looking after these kids soon became the mission of her life. She set up four NGOs to accomplish her mission.

6. This way Sindhu became Sindhutai or Mai or mother of orphans.

1. **Sindhutai directed her ire at the forest department and landlords as:**
   1. the landlords fundamentally deprived the tribals of their land.
   2. they forced women to do all kinds of menial jobs for them
   3. they charged exorbitant interest on loan to the poor.
   4. the forest officials exploited local women who collected cow dung.
   (a) 1   (b) 2
   (c) 3   (d) 4

2. **In which sense was Sindhutai a saviour for the adivasis of Chikaldara?**
   1. She united them against their oppressors.
   2. She got the tribals whose land was acquired by the government, rehabilitated.
   3. She persuaded them to give up the superstitious beliefs and think rationally.
   4. She worked for the economic and educational empowerment of the adivasis.
   (a) 1   (b) 2
   (c) 3   (d) 4

3. **What earned Sindhu the title of Sindhutai or Sindhumai?**
   1. her work for the adivasis
   2. her invaluable work for the orphans
   3. her leadership quality

4. **her empowerment of the poor adivasis**
   (a) 1   (b) 2
   (c) 3   (d) 4

4. **Which of the following words is similar meaning to the word, 'Constant' as used in para 3 of the passage?**
   1. reasoning
   2. tough
   3. continuing
   4. perturbing
   (a) 1   (b) 2
   (c) 3   (d) 4

5. **Which of the following words is the most opposite in meaning to the word 'abandoned' as used in the para 4 of the passage?**
   1. preferred
   2. accomplished
   3. protected
   4. promoted
   (a) 1   (b) 2
   (c) 3   (d) 4

6. **Which part of speech is the underlined word in the following sentence?**
   Her first adopted child was Deepak.
   1. Noun
   2. Adjective
   3. Pronoun
   4. Adverb
   (a) 1   (b) 2
   (c) 3   (d) 4

7. **Which part of the following sentence contains an error?**
   The price/(a), of this car/(b), is higher/(c), than yours/(d)
   1. (b)
   2. (c)
   3. (d)
   4. (a)
   (a) 1   (b) 2
   (c) 3   (d) 4

Ques (8-16): Direction: Read the passage given below and answer the questions that follow by selecting the correct/most appropriate options.

Man who is believed to have evolved from apes is a curious mixture of varied motives. He is not only the subject of needs but is also their creator. He not only seeks to satisfy his needs but also caters to his desire for beauty and grace. He is eager to satisfy his passion for more and more knowledge. Although in a general way, the maxim 'necessity is the mother of invention' is true, it is by no means the whole truth. Man is something much greater than an intelligent being using his intellect to make newer inventions from time to time. He has within him a spirit which is ever exhorting him to cut down his needs and learn to be happy with what he has. The real purpose underlying this maxim lies in its utility in the worldly sense. It tells us to be up and doing, not to be passive in our attitude to life. It asks us not to remain slaves of old habits and ways of life. We must face new situations with a creative mind. Every new difficulty, every new problem, which confronts us in life, can be tackled successfully with the spirit of inventiveness.

8. **Which one of the following is not the whole truth according to the passage?**

(a) Man has a desire for beauty and grace.
(b) Necessity is the mother of invention.
(c) Man desires to cut down his needs and wants.
(d) Man learns to be happy with what he has.

9. **What does the maxim mentioned in the passage teach us?**
(a) To be worldly in the strict sense of the term
(b) To be slave of our needs and wants
(c) To endeavor constantly to face every new situation in a new way with creative mind
(d) To be active in life and do something to help mankind

10. **What does the spirit within man tell him to do?**
(a) To be a mixture of varied motives
(b) To evaluate the situations intelligently
(c) To cut down his desires and passions
(d) To acquire more and more wealth and comforts

11. **Which of the following statements is/are true in the context of the passage?**
I. Man should be passive in his attitude to life.
II. Spirit of inventiveness may not stand in good stead in solving every new problem.
III. Man has a passion for more and more knowledge.
(a) Only I
(b) Only I and II
(c) Only III
(d) Only II and III

12. **Which one of the following is similar in meaning to the word 'maxim' as used in the passage?**
(a) Principle
(b) Direction
(c) Value
(d) Observation

13. **Which one of the following is not the characteristic of man as per the passage?**
(a) Man has many needs and motives.
(b) Man creates many needs for himself.
(c) Man seeks to satisfy his needs.
(d) Man desires to have more and more comforts and money.

14. **Which one of the following statements is not true as per the passage?**
(a) Spirit of inventiveness will stand in good stead.
(b) Man is the subject of various wants.
(c) Man creates new needs because they are sometimes good or beautiful.
(d) Man's inner spirit tells him to be on the lookout for newer and higher wants.

15. **Choose the word which is opposite in meaning to the word 'seeks' as used in the passage.**
(a) Deplores
(b) Avoids
(c) Vanishes
(d) Approaches

16. **Which one of the following is similar in meaning to the word exhorting as used in the passage?**
(a) Urging
(b) Supporting
(c) Demanding
(d) Clarifying

Ques (17-20): Direction: Read the passage given below carefully and answer the question the follow by selecting the correct/most appropriate option:
1. There is something we all want to do, although few of us readily admit it : Get rid of guests.
2. For nine months in the year, only my closest friends come to see me. Then, when temperatures start soaring in the plains, long-lost acquaintances suddenly remember that l exist, and people whom I am barely able to recognize appear at the front door, willing to have me put them up for periods ranging from six days to six weeks.
3. Occasionally, I am the master of the situation I inform them that the cottage is already bursting, that people are sleeping on the floor. If the hopefuls start looking around for signs of these uncomfortable guests, I remark that they have all gone out for a picnic.
4. The other day I received visitors who proved to be more thick-skinned than most. The man was a friend of a friend of an acquaintance of mine. I had never seen him before. But on the strength of this distant relationship, he had brought his family along.
5. I tried the usual ploy but it didn't work. The man and his family were perfectly willing to share the floor with any others who might be staying with me.
6. So I made my next move. 'I must warn you about the scorpions', I said. The scorpion-scare is effective with most people. But I was dealing with professionals. The man set his son rolling up the carpet. 'Sometimes centipedes fall from the ceiling', I said desperately.
7. We were now interrupted by someone knocking on the front door. It was the postman with a rejected manuscript, his arrival inspired me to greater inventiveness.
8. 'I'm terribly sorry', I said, staring hard at a rejection slip. 'I'm afraid I have to leave immediately. A paper wants me to interview the Maharishi. I hope you won't mind. Would you like the name of a good hotel ?'
9. 'Oh, don't worry about us', said the woman expansively. 'We'll look after the house while you are away.

17. **The postman delivered to the author:**
(a) his rejected manuscript alongwith a cheque.
(b) his rejected manuscript alongwith a rejection slip.
(c) a letter commissioning him to write a new novel.
(d) a letter inviting him to interview the Maharishi.

18. **Which one of the following words is similar in meaning to the word, 'readily' (Para 1) as used in the passage?**
(a) easily
(b) efficiently
(c) plainly
(d) frankly

19. **Which one of the following words is opposite in meaning to the word, 'soaring' (Para 2) as used in the passage?**
(a) exasperating
(b) falling
(c) deteriorating
(d) hovering

20. **Which part of the following sentence contains an error ?**
(a) Both Raghunath as well as Ravish
(b) have given their consent
(c) to the new proposal
(a) (a)
(b) (c)
(c) (b)
(d) (d)

21. **In the following question, out of the four alternatives, select the alternative which best expresses the meaning of the Idiom/Phrase.**
To carry weight
(a) To carry burden
(b) Carry the day
(c) Be important
(d) Carry through

22. **In the following question, out of the four alternatives, select the alternative which best expresses the meaning of the Idiom/Phrase.**
To be fair and square

(a) Worthy   (b) Honest

(c) Successful   (d) Obedient

23. **Choose an option, which can be substituted for a given word/sentence/phrase out of given options.**
One who loves mankind is called

(a) Optimist   (b) Philanthropist

(c) Optometrist   (d) Truant

24. **Choose an option, which can be substituted for a given word/sentence/phrase out of given options.**
A remedy for all diseases is

(a) Medicine   (b) Medical

(c) Panacea   (d) None of these

25. **Choose the word with correct spelling.**

(a) Endure   (b) Climaxe

(c) Comand   (d) Analoug

26. **Select the answer choice that identifies the noun in the sentence.**
To seize a foreign embassy and its inhabitants is flagrant disregard for diplomatic neutrality.

(a) Seize   (b) Its

(c) Flagrant   (d) Neutrality

27. **In the following the question choose the word which best expresses the meaning of the given word.**
CORPULENT

(a) Lean   (b) Gaunt

(c) Emaciated   (d) Obese

28. **Choose the correct alternative which can be substituted for the below given word/sentence.**
Commencement of words with the same letter

(a) Pun   (b) Alliteration

(c) Transferred epithet   (d) Oxymoron

Ques (29-31): Direction : A sentence is shown below in three parts. Identify the part which contains the grammatical error (if any). If the sentence has no error, then select 'No error'.

29. **Everyone (A) except she have (B) traveled by air.(C)**

(a) (A)   (b) (B)

(c) (C)   (d) No error

30. **Our summer (A)/ vacation is between (B)/ 10th May to 10th June. (C)**

(a) (A)   (b) (B)

(c) (C)   (d) No error

31. **One of the greatest responsibilities of a scientist (A)/ is that his discoveries and inventions are (B)/ utilized to the overall development of the nation. (C)**

(a) (A)   (b) (B)

(c) (C)   (d) No error

Ques (32-33): Direction: The following sentence is divided in to four parts. Any of the parts may contain an error. Select the part that has an error.

32. **Her mother died (a)/ of influenza but her father (b)/ also though very weak, (c)/ is out of danger (d).**

(a) (a)   (b) (b)

(c) (c)   (d) (d)

33. **If I am you (a)/ I would have seen (b)/ to it that (c)/ I won the lottery (d).**

(a) (a)   (b) (b)

(c) (c)   (d) (d)

Ques (34-39): Direction: Select the alternative that will improve the underlined part of the sentence. In case there is no improvement select 'No improvement'.

34. **The movie Uri tells the story of a surgical strike by the Indian army <u>towards militants in POK</u> .**

(a) For militants in POK   (b) Over militants at POK

(c) Against militants in POK   (d) No improvement

35. **<u>I, your brother and you</u> will be partners in the business.**

(a) I, you and your brother   (b) You, your brother and I

(c) You, I and your brother   (d) No improvement

36. **Everybody who was present in the conference room must be sorry for <u>what they did</u> during the meeting.**

(a) what he did   (b) what made them did

(c) what were they doing   (d) No improvement

37. **You are requested to <u>take out</u> your shoes before entering.**

(a) take off   (b) take on

(c) put off   (d) No correction

38. **The patient had died before the ambulance <u>had come</u> .**

(a) Have come   (b) Come

(c) Came   (d) Had came

39. **Our meals usually have at least one item <u>make of some kinds</u> of grain.**

(a) No substitution required   (b) making of any kinds

(c) made of some kind   (d) makes of kind

40. **Direction: In the following sentence, a part of the sentence is underlined. Below are given alternatives to the underlined part, which may improve the sentence. Choose the correct alternative. In case no improvement is needed, choose the option 'No improvement.'**
He has visited many places all over the city looking at the perfect location to set up his factory.
A. Looking after
B. Looking for
C. Looking out

(a) Only A   (b) Only B

(c) Only C   (d) No Improvement

41. **Direction : Select the most appropriate meaning of the given idiom.**
all in all

(a) having all authority   (b) first in line

(c) completely lost   (d) every person

42. **Direction : Select the most appropriate meaning of the given idiom.**
Not make head or tail

(a) very boring and not at all fun

(b) not able to understand anything

(c) not find something interesting

(d) very unusual and strange

43. **Direction : Select the most appropriate meaning of the given idiom.**
On tenterhooks

(a) Anxious and tense   (b) Happy and joyous

(c) Alert and enthusiastic   (d) Neutral and undecided

44. **Direction : Select the most appropriate meaning of the given idiom.**
On cloud nine
(a) Extremely happy and excited
(b) Very far away from home
(c) Knowledgeable and wise
(d) Crazy and foolish

45. **Choose the correct meaning of the proverb.**
To save one's face
(a) to oppose
(b) to hide oneself
(c) to evade disgrace
(d) to say plainly

46. **Find out the figure of speech in the following sentence.**
From the cradle to the grave.
(a) Litotes
(b) Transferred Epithet
(c) Metonymy
(d) Synecdoche

47. **In which figure of speech as, so, like words are used?**
(a) Fable
(b) Allegory
(c) Metaphor
(d) Simile

48. **/tʃɔː/ is the phonetic transcription of:**
(a) Chorus
(b) Charge
(c) Cheer
(d) Chore

49. **Choose the correct phonetic transcription and the primary stress mark: photography**
(a) /fəutə'graːf /
(b) /fə'təugraːfl /
(c) /fə'tɒgrəfi/
(d) /fotograːfl /

50. **Choose the correct symbol for the underlined consonant/ vowel sound:-**
ch eerful
(a) th
(b) θ
(c) ch
(d) tʃ

// Smart Answer Sheet //

		Correct
		Skipped

Correct — Percentage of students who answered correctly.

Skipped — Percentage of students who skipped.

Q.	Ans.	Correct / Skipped	Q.	Ans.	Correct / Skipped	Q.	Ans.	Correct / Skipped
1	D	78.14% / 0.0%	2	B	54.66% / 1.33%	3	B	53.67% / 1.62%
4	C	66.36% / 1.07%	5	C	50.82% / 1.61%	6	B	62.1% / 1.69%
7	C	64.96% / 1.85%	8	B	68.47% / 1.06%	9	C	62.09% / 1.73%
10	C	82.21% / 0.0%	11	C	69.89% / 1.42%	12	A	50.01% / 1.82%
13	D	43.45% / 1.89%	14	D	48.48% / 1.43%	15	B	47.25% / 1.91%
16	A	58.19% / 1.38%	17	B	49.14% / 1.51%	18	A	65.27% / 1.48%
19	B	52.75% / 1.1%	20	A	62.02% / 1.85%	21	C	41.23% / 1.58%
22	B	89.49% / 0.0%	23	B	52.4% / 1.62%	24	C	59.2% / 1.48%
25	A	46.83% / 1.06%	26	D	55.3% / 1.13%	27	D	55.55% / 1.48%
28	B	42.37% / 1.83%	29	B	20.89% / 3.3%	30	C	77.0% / 0.0%
31	C	60.84% / 1.26%	32	C	81.87% / 0.0%	33	A	83.29% / 0.0%
34	C	43.76% / 1.07%	35	B	59.59% / 1.63%	36	A	54.11% / 1.89%
37	A	65.42% / 1.57%	38	C	85.14% / 0.0%	39	C	41.61% / 1.42%
40	B	53.36% / 1.75%	41	A	87.88% / 0.0%	42	B	54.39% / 1.45%
43	A	58.58% / 1.08%	44	A	52.22% / 1.9%	45	C	23.21% / 4.73%
46	C	31.23% / 4.39%	47	D	64.56% / 1.95%	48	D	89.52% / 0.0%
49	C	57.01% / 1.15%	50	D	57.61% / 1.07%			

// Hints and Solutions //

1(D). According to the passage, " In her new home, she fought against the exploitation of local women, who collected cow dung, by the forest department and landlords. This only made things more difficult for her."
Upon the perusal of the above lines, it can be concluded that Sindhutai directed her anger at the forest department and landlords as they exploited the local women who collected cow dung.

2(B). According to the passage, " In this constant tussle to survive, she found herself in Chikaldara, situated in the Amravati district of Maharashtra. Here, due to a tiger preservation project, 84 tribal villages were evacuated. Amidst the confusion, a project officer impounded 32 cows of Adivasi villagers and one of the cows died. Sindhutai decided to fight for the proper rehabilitation of the helpless tribal villagers."
Upon the perusal of the above lines, it is clear that Sindhutai got the tribals whose villages were evacuated and she decided to fight for the rehabilitation of the tribal villagers.

3(B). According to the passage, "So Sindhutai started taking care of children in return for some food. Looking after these kids soon became the mission of her life. She set up four NGOs to accomplish her mission."
According to the passage, "This way Sindhu became Sindhutai or Mai or mother of orphans."
So, it is concluded that her invaluable work for the orphans earned Sindhu the title of Sindhutai or Sindhumai.

4(C). The meaning of the given words:
- Constant: occurring continuously over a period of time, a situation that doesn't change.
- Continuing: without a break in continuity; ongoing.
- Reasoning: the process of thinking about something and making a judgement or decision.
- Tough: difficult or causing problems.
- Perturbing: to make somebody worried or upset.
From the above meaning, it is evident that continuing is the same meaning as the word constant.

5(C). The meaning of the given words:
- Abandoned: left completely and no longer used or wanted.
- Protected: to keep somebody/something safe, to defend.
- Preferred: better than another or others; tend to choose.
- Accomplished: highly skilled at something, achieve or complete successfully.
- Promoted: to encourage something, to help something to happen or develop, to advertise.
From the above meaning, it is evident that Protected is the opposite meaning of the word Abandoned.

6(B). Adjective: It is a part of speech that modifies a noun or noun phrase. Example: What a stubborn man Sudeep is?

So, in the sentence "adopted" is a past participle known as an adjective that modifies the noun "child".

7(C). Part (d) contains an error.
We use the comparative degree to compare one person, thing, or group with another person, etc.
In the question, we are comparing the "price of this car" with the "price of your car or yours" so we have to use "that of" otherwise there will be confusion about whether we are comparing "the price of this car with another car " or only comparing "one car with another car".
So, we are talking about the "price of one car with another car" so we have to either replace "yours" with "that of yours or that of your car" to make the sentence grammatically correct.
Correct sentence: The price of this car is higher than that of yours.

8(B). Necessity is the mother of invention. is not the whole truth according to the passage.

9(C). To endeavor constantly to face every new situation in a new way with creative mind the maxim mentioned in the passage teach us.

10(C). To cut down his desires and passions the spirit within man tell him to do.

11(C). According to these lines of the passage, ' He is eager to satisfy his passion for more and more knowledge.' statement III is true.

12(A). The word which is similar in meaning to maxim is principle.

13(D). 'He is not only the subject of needs but is also their creator. Man who is believed to have evolved from apes is a curious mixture of varied motives.'

14(D). Man's inner spirit tells him to be on the lookout for newer and higher wants statements is not true as per the passage.

15(B). Seeks means to attempt or desire to obtain or achieve something. Avoids means keep away from or stop oneself from doing something.

16(A). Urging means to try earnestly or persistently to persuade someone to do something. Exhorting means strongly encourage or urge someone to do something.

17(B). From the given lines of the passage it is evident that the postman had brought the author's rejected manuscript along with the rejection slip.

18(A). From the given lines of the passage we can understand that 'readily' means without delay or difficulty or easily.

19(B). From the given lines of the passage we can deduce that 'soaring' means to increase rapidly above the usual level. On the other hand, Falling means to move from a higher to a lower level, typically rapidly and without control; If something is falling, it is becoming lower in size, amount, or strength. Therefore Falling is the opposite of soaring.

20(A). In the given statement, the error is in the usage of the conjunctions. The correct sentence will be: 'Both Raghunath and Ravish have given their consent to the new proposal.'

21(C). The idiom "to carry weight" means be important; effective or strong.

22(B). The idiom "fair and square" means being very accurate or honest.

23(B). One who loves mankind is called a philanthropist.
A person who is inclined to be hopeful and to expect good outcomes is called an optimist.
A healthcare professional who provides primary vision care ranging from sight testing and correction to the diagnosis, treatment and management of vision changes is called an optometrist.
A child who stays away from school without permission is called a truant.

24(C). A remedy for all diseases is called a panacea.
The art, science, and practice of caring for a patient and managing the diagnosis are called medicine.
A n examination of the body by a doctor to check your state of health is called medical.

25(A). Endure- to suffer something painful or uncomfortable, usually without complaining

26(D). Neutrality is a noun. Seize (A) is a verb. Its (B) is a possessive pronoun modifying the noun inhabitants. Flagrant (C) is an adjective modifying the noun disregard.

27(D). Obese- having excessive body fat
Corpulent-having a large bulky body
Lean- to move the top part of your body and head forwards
Gaut- very thin because of hunger, illness, etc.
Emaciated- extremely thin and weak because of illness

28(B). Alliteration: The occurrence of the same letter or sound at the beginning of adjacent or closely connected words.
Pun: A joke exploiting the different possible meanings of a word or the fact that there are words which sound alike but have different meanings.
Transferred epithet: A transferred epithet often involves shifting a modifier from the animate to the inanimate, as in the phrases.
Oxymoron: A figure of speech in which apparently contradictory terms appear in conjunction.

29(B). Here the error is in the third option. "She have" will be replaced with "her has",
1) Objective case (her) is used after "except"
2) Singular verb is used for the subject "everyone"

30(C). The sentence is grammatically incorrect, and the error lies in part (C). When in any sentence 'between' is used it is followed by 'and' and not 'to' whereas 'from' is usually followed by the preposition 'to'. Thus, 'to' should be replaced with 'and' in order to make the sentence grammatically sound.

31(C). Part (C) has the grammatically incorrect part. The preposition that should come after "utilized" is "for". The phrase "utilize for" means to make use of someone or something for some particular purpose or function.

32(C). The word 'also' should be deleted because it would mean that he also died.

33(A). It should be "if I were you" because for an impossible wish, 'were' should be used.

34(C). The sentence uses the incorrect preposition 'towards'.
As it talks about the 'strike' by Indian army; the preposition should show this opposition/ conflict between two parties.
Let's look at how the given prepositions are used:
Towards: expressing the relation between behaviour and the thing at which it is directed. Example: He was always warm towards her.
For: indicating the purpose of something. Example: The

flowers are for you.
Over: showing the trajectory or duration of something. Example: The people were scattered all over the mountain.
Against: in opposition to. Example: It is the job of the police to fight against crime.

35(B). We have to use the correct order of pronouns in the sentence.
First-person pronoun is always used at the last.
The second person pronouns come first.

36(A). The underlined part is incorrect because "he" will come in place of "they".
He/ him/ his/ himself is used with common gender pronouns like everyone, everybody, someone, somebody, anyone, anybody, etc.

37(A). Put off: Postpone; delay; arrange a later date.
"The meeting has been put off until next week because of the strike."
Take out: Remove or cause to disappear
Try this. It should take out the stain.
Take off: Leave the ground (a plane), Remove something
May I take off my jacket? It's warm in here.
The plane took off at 7 o'clock
Take on: Hire or engage staff
Business is good so the company is taking on extra staff.
Here in the sentence, It is clear that there is a request to remove the shoes before entering.

38(C). We know that when two actions occur in the past, one after the other, then, the first action is expressed in the past perfect tense and the second action is expressed in the simple past tense.
For Example:
The patient had died before the doctor came.
He came after she had gone.
In the given sentence, the action of the patient's death occurred earlier, thus, it will be expressed in the past perfect tense (had died).
The action of the arrival of the ambulance occurred later, therefore, it will be expressed in simple past tense (came). Therefore, the simple past tense 'came' should be used in place of the past perfect tense 'had came'.

39(C). The erroneous Part 'make of some kinds' should be 'made of some kind'.
We use "made of" when we talk about the basic material or qualities of something. It has a meaning similar to 'composed of'.
Example: She wore a beautiful necklace made of silver.
Here, 'grain' is uncountable that is why a singular form that is 'kind' will be used.

40(B). The sentence implies that the person (subject) is in search of a location for his factory setup. Therefore, the only participle that goes well with the context of the sentence is 'looking for'.
Look out (Phrasal Verb): be vigilant and take notice.
Look after (Phrasal Verb): take care of
Look forward to (Phrasal Verb): await eagerly
Look for (Phrasal Verb): to hope to get something that you want or need
The correct sentence is: He has Looking for many places all over the city looking at the perfect location to set up his factory.

41(A). All in all - Having all authority
Example: All in all, I think you've done very well.
The first line of: It is the first or most important thing.
Be lost in space: Completely lost.
Each and every one: Each individual person or thing that comprises a group or whole.

42(B). "not able to understand anything" is the most appropriate meaning of the given idiom.
The idiom "Not make head or tail" is related to the random decision-making process.
It means you are unable to understand something (or someone) mainly because it's puzzling or unclear.

43(A). Anxious and tense is the most appropriate meaning of the given idiom.
On tenterhooks: in a state of suspense or agitation because of uncertainty about a future event.
Example: he was on tenterhooks waiting for the director's decision

44(A). "Extremely happy and excited" is the most appropriate meaning of the given idiom.
On cloud nine: To be extremely happy and excited, a feeling of well-being or elation. If you say that someone is on cloud nine, you are emphasizing that they are very happy.
Example: I was on cloud nine once I had completed it.

45(C). The correct meaning of the proverb "To save one's face" is "to evade disgrace".
To save one's face: To try to regain favorable standing after something embarrassing has happened.
Sentence: To avoid having other people lose respect for oneself. He tried to save face by working overtime.

46(C). The figure of speech in "From the cradle to the grave" is "Metonymy".
From the cradle to the grave (= from infancy to death).
Metonymy literally means a change of name. In metonymy an object is denoted by the name of something which is generally associated with it.

47(D). In Simile, as, so, like words are used.
A simile is a figure of speech that compares two things that are different from each other but have similar qualities. These are generally formed through the usage of the words 'as' or 'like'.

48(D). Phonetic transcription, also known as phonetic script or phonetic notation, is the visual representation of speech sounds or phones by means of symbols. The most common type of phonetic transcription uses a phonetic alphabet, such as the International Phonetic Alphabet.

49(C). The word photography has four syllables. The main stress is on the second syllable. Phonetic transcription of photography is /fə'tɒgrəfi/.

50(D). The symbol tʃ shows the sound of ch such as in church, chair. Phonetic transcription of cheerful is 'tʃɪəful. The word cheerful has 2 syllables.

Ques (1-7): Direction: Read the given passage and answer the questions that follow by selecting the most appropriate option.

"Get well soon!" Shanta said, handing Partha a yellow balloon. She was his third visitor. That's because she was his class teacher's daughter, and her mother made her visit him. The other two, Rahul and Syed, weren't really his friends, although they often ganged up with him against other kids to take away their lunch pocket money. Partha knew he wouldn't have long to live. He could feel it, deep inside. Seeing his aunty crying after talking with the doctor confirmed it. His time had come. He didn't tell his visitors, though. They would either pity him, or be happy to get rid of him. Once Shanta left, he ripped a page off from his notebook and wrote-

"Dear God, I know I messed up and nobody likes me. Please give me a second chance. I can show you what a good friend I can be."

He drew a map showing the way from the school to the hospital, walked shakily to the window, and let the balloon fly away, carrying his message towards God.

The balloon was heading straight to a telephone pole, but a gentle breeze blew it away just in time. It crossed the park and disappeared out of view.

The next day, a boy he had never met. before came to visit him. "I find balloon," he said. "You are lonely?"

He just nodded, too startled to talk.

"I lonely too. My family come from Afghanistan and I no speak English good." He smiled. "I bring gift to you." He handed him a small bag of fruits. "I pray for friend, and God give me friend."

Normally, he would have made fun of his broken English and his long, baggy brown kurta, but he knew better. He smiled and offered him the first orange.

1. Partha felt lonely because _______ visited him when he was at the hospital.
- (a) his class teacher
- (b) only Syed and Rahul from his class
- (c) he had no friends at school, so no one
- (d) shanta

2. An antonym for the word 'shakily' in the passage is:
- (a) unsure
- (b) unsteadily
- (c) firmly
- (d) rickety

3. Partha's feeling of loneliness soon turned to:
- (a) irritation
- (b) sympathy
- (c) self-pity
- (d) anger

4. Partha would not go back to school to meet his schoolmates and teachers because:
- (a) his parents wanted to change his school
- (b) he did not have long to live
- (c) he hated his school as he had no friends
- (d) his doctors did not let him

5. The message in the passage is:
- (a) loneliness is inevitable
- (b) about faith in God
- (c) all actions have consequences
- (d) friendship is rare

6. The change in Partha's attitude is evident when he:
- (a) accepted the fruits from a stranger, although he disliked oranges
- (b) refrained from poking fun at the Afghan boy and shared the fruits

- (c) was unmoved even when his aunt was crying
- (d) sent a letter to God written on a balloon

7. A phrase that can replace the words 'ganged up' is:
- (a) joined in opposition
- (b) formed a group
- (c) supported together
- (d) became friends

Ques (8-13): Direction : Read the passage given and answer the questions that follow by selecting the most appropriate options :

Madam Cama's Paris home became a shelter for world revolutionaries. Even Lenin, the father of Russian revolution visited her house and exchanged views. Savarkar got all encouragement in writing the history of the First Indian War of Independence from Cama. She helped its printing in Holland as no English publisher came forward to publish it. It was a banned book but found its way to India. Smuggled ingeniously under "Don Quixote" covers ! She became the publisher of "Vande Mataram", a revolutionary magazine and its distributor, an extremely difficult task in the days of British espionage. Another magazine "Madan's Talwar" was also started in memory of Madan Lal Dhingra who laid down his life for the country. Both the magazines were outlawed in India and England. Madam Cama somehow found ways to send them to Indian revolutionaries.

Madam Cama also fought for the cause of women. Speaking at National Conference at Cairo, Egypt in 1910, she asked, "Where is the other half of the Egypt ? I see only men who represent half the country !" She stressed the role of women in building a nation.

When the First World War broke out in 1914, Madam Cama took an anti-British stand and tried her best to make the Indian people aware of the exploitative nature of British imperialism.

The British had banned her entry into India, being afraid of her revolutionary past and staunch nationalistic outlook. But the lioness was getting old and 35 years of fighting on foreign-land had taken its toll. She decided to return to her motherland. Her health was worsening. After reaching Bombay, she was hospitalized and died on 13th of August, 1936.

8. Not only did Madam Cama participate in India's struggle for freedom, she also:
- (a) worked for the upliftment of the poor.
- (b) opened schools in slums.
- (c) created awareness of the importance of cleanliness among women.
- (d) championed the cause of women.

9. The author's attitude to Madam Cama can be described as:
- (a) hostile
- (b) laudatory
- (c) critical
- (d) contradictory

10. The word which is opposite in meaning to 'famous':
- (a) unpopular
- (b) undesirable
- (c) mysterious
- (d) known

11. 'Madam Cama fought for the cause of women.' Tense of the above sentence has been correctly changed into past perfect in:
- (a) Madam Cama had fought for the cause of women.
- (b) Madam Cama has been fighting for the cause of women.
- (c) Madam Cama is fighting for the cause of women.
- (d) Madam Cama had been fighting for the cause of women.

12. Which part of speech is the underlined word in the sentence given below ?
'I see only men <u>who</u> represent half of the country.'

(a) Adjective   (b) Pronoun
(c) Adverb   (d) Noun

13. How did the book, 'The First Indian War of Independence' find its way to India' ? The book was:
(a) couriered
(b) mailed
(c) smuggled
(d) sent through a secret agent

Ques (14-20): Direction: Read the following passage and answer the questions that follow.

According to a new American study headed by Dr. Willis, it has been found that people who exercise in the morning seem to lose more weight than people completing the same workouts later in the day.

These findings help shed light on the vexing issue of why some people shed considerable weight with exercise and others almost none. The study adds to the growing body of science suggesting that the timing of various activities, including exercise, could affect how those activities affect us.

The relationship between exercise and body weight is somewhat befuddling. Multiple past studies show that a majority of people who take up exercise to lose weight drop fewer pounds than would be expected, given how many calories they are burning during their workouts. Some gain weight. But a few respond quite well, shedding pound after pound with the same exercise regimen that prompts others to add inches.

The Midwest Trial 2, was conducted in the University of Kansas, U.S. on how regular, supervised exercise influences body weight.

The trial involved 100 overweight, previously inactive young men and women who were made to work out five times a week at a physiology lab, jogging or otherwise sweating until they had burned up to 600 calories per session.

After 10 months of this regimen, almost everyone had dropped pounds. But the extent of their losses fluctuated wildly, even though everyone was doing the same, supervised workout. A team of researchers started brainstorming what could be responsible for the enormous variability in the weight loss.

They hit upon activity timing. They decided to do a Follow -up study of the Mid West Trial 2. In this new study, the Mid West Trial 2 Follow up study the researchers now studied a team of participants who could visit the gym whenever they wished between 7 a.m. and 7 p.m. They also tracked everyone's calorie intakes and daily movement habits throughout the 10 months. They knew, too, whether and by how much people's weights had changed.

Now, they checked weight change against exercise schedules and quickly noticed a consistent pattern.

Those people who usually worked out before noon had lost more weight, on average, than the men and women who typically exercised after 3 p.m.

The researchers uncovered a few other, possibly relevant differences between the morning and late-day exercisers. The early-exercise group tended to be slightly more active throughout the day, taking more steps in total than those who worked out later. They also ate less.

These factors may cumulatively have contributed to the striking differences in how many pounds people lost, Dr. Willis says.

Thus it seems that people who worked out before noon lost more weight, on average, than those who typically exercised after 3 p.m. But Dr. Willis also points out that most of those who worked out later in the day did lose weight, even if not as much as the larkish exercisers, and almost certainly became healthier. "I would not want anyone to think that it's not worth exercising if you can't do it first thing in the morning," he says. "Any exercise, at any time of day, is going to be better than none."

14. Find one word in the passage which means the same as 'confusing'.
(a) Brainstorming   (b) Vexing
(c) Striking   (d) Befuddling

15. The Mid West Trail 2 was a:
(a) U.S based study on 100 participants who exercised 3 times a week and burnt 300 calories.
(b) Canadian study on 500 participants who exercised 6 times a week and burnt 600 calories.
(c) A European study on 100 participants who exercised 7 times a week and burnt 800 calories.
(d) U.S based study on 100 participants who exercised 5 times a week and burnt 600 calories.

16. What would Dr. Willis say to someone who has given up exercising because they cannot do so in the morning?
(a) Evening is the worst time to exercise
(b) Exercise only with a trainer
(c) Any exercise is better than none.
(d) Exercise is good only in the morning.

17. The Mid West Trail 2 duration was-
(a) 18 months   (b) 6 months
(c) 10 months   (d) 12 months

18. Select the option which is not true.
The successful weight losers in the Mid West Trial 2 Follow-up study __________.
(a) ate less   (b) slept more
(c) remained active.   (d) walked more.

19. Select the correct option.
By 'larkish exercisers' the writer refers to people who-
(a) like to sing in the morning.
(b) love to see the lark in the morning.
(c) exercise in the morning.
(d) like to exercise late with the larks.

20. Find one word which means the same as the following.
A set of rules about food and diet that someone follows.
(a) Fundamental   (b) Regimen
(c) Regiment   (d) Catalogue

21. Find out the words which mean the same as 'overhauled'.
(a) Damaging   (b) Modernize
(c) Hurting   (d) Injuring

22. Direction: Complete the following sentence by choosing the appropriate word from the given options.
One must ____ one's dream with all determination.
(a) Direct   (b) Complete
(c) Follow   (d) Peruse

23. What is the feminine gender of "milkman"?
(a) Milkery   (b) Milkee
(c) Milkmaid   (d) Milkgirl

24. What is the plural form of "loaf"?
(a) Loafes   (b) Loafas
(c) Loaves   (d) Loafs

25. In the given question, four words are given out of which one word is correctly spelt. Choose the correctly spelt word.

(a) Consecrate   (b) Concestrate

(c) Consecrete   (d) Connsectrate

Ques (26-28): Direction: In each of the questions given below, a sentence is given with two blanks. From the given options, choose the one that gives the correct combination of words that fit in the blanks.

26. Though a rate cut was a _________ conclusion ahead of the monetary policy announcement, the _________ was of either a 25 or 50 basis points one.

     (a) accustomed, experience   (b) foregone, expectation

     (c) forest, explanation   (d) earnest, exposition

27. Arguably, the _________ for fiscal concessions is limited given the overall revenue scenario, but the government can certainly push for further _________ to incentivise investment.

     (a) spectacular, terminal   (b) space, reforms

     (c) surety, radio   (d) function, yield

28. In a country as _________ as India, it is impossible to ensure that vegetarian and non-vegetarian preferences are _________ into delivery logistics.

     (a) reverse, faced   (b) reticent, feared

     (c) diverse, factored   (d) recess, fused

Ques (29-30): Direction: Select the most effective pair from the given pairs of words to fill in the blanks to make the sentence meaningfully complete.

29. One of the ______ reasons we fight wars is that people don't take ______ interest in politics.

     (a) good, any   (b) major, many

     (c) major, enough   (d) two, very

30. Komodo dragons are _____ lizards which can weigh more than humans and are somewhat _____.

     (a) small, innocuous   (b) venomous, tiny

     (c) docile, timid   (d) gigantic, venomous

Ques (31-33): Direction: Choose the correct form of the verb/ tense from the given sets of options to fill in the blank space in the sentence.

31. When we reached the theatre the play _____ already _____.

     (a) was/began   (b) has/begin

     (c) had been/ begun   (d) had/begun

32. When she _____ back the answer script, she saw she _____ several mistakes.

     (a) was getting, made   (b) had got, made

     (c) got, had made   (d) got, made

33. My friends ____ for me for a long time before they _____ to leave without me.

     (a) were waiting, deciding

     (b) waited, decide

     (c) had waited, decided

     (d) has been waiting, were deciding

34. In the following question, some part of the sentence may have errors. Find out which part of the sentence has an error and select the appropriate option. If a sentence is free from error, select 'No Error'.

     He has decided to visit Mumbai (1)/ with a view to explore the new (3)/ opportunities lying in front of him. (3)/ No error

     (a) 1   (b) 2

     (c) 3   (d) No Error

35. In the following question, some part of the sentence may have errors. Find out which part of the sentence has an error and select the appropriate option. If a sentence is free from error, select 'No Error'.

     I expected that you would (1)/ score much better (2)/ marks but unfortunately you didn't. (3)/ No error

     (a) 1   (b) 2

     (c) 3   (d) No Error

36. In the following question, some part of the sentence may have errors. Find out which part of the sentence has an error and select the appropriate option. If a sentence is free from error, select 'No Error'.

     My husband told me that he (1)/ will be coming to Singapore (2)/ next year for the new project. (3)/ No error

     (a) 1   (b) 2

     (c) 3   (d) No Error

37. A sentence is given below in jumbled order. Arrange the sentence in the right order to form a meaningful and coherent sentence.

     Seeking help

     P) always easy

     Q) is not

     R) for everyone

     (a) PQR   (b) QPR

     (c) RPQ   (d) QRP

38. A sentence is given below in jumbled order. Arrange the sentence in the right order to form a meaningful and coherent sentence.

     I will sign

     P) the cheque

     Q) the work

     R) when you finish

     (a) PQR   (b) PRQ

     (c) RPQ   (d) QPR

Ques (39-40): Direction: In question, a part of the sentence is made bold. Below are given alternatives to the bold part at (A), (B), (C) and (D) which may improve the sentence. Choose the correct alternative. In case no replacement is needed, mark (E) as your answer.

39. **Mr. Tharoor's urban manners charm friends and enemies alike.**

     (a) urban manners charming friends

     (b) urbane manners charming friends

     (c) urban mannerisms charm friends

     (d) urbane manners charm friends

40. **Religious bigots look away on anyone who does not conform to their beliefs.**

     (a) bigots look down on   (b) bigots look behind on

     (c) bigots look in front of   (d) No correction required

41. **Direction:** Given below is an idiom/phrase which is followed by four alternative meanings to each. Choose the correct option which is the most appropriate meaning.

     Like a shag on a rock

     (a) Completely alone   (b) Completely idle

     (c) Complete silence   (d) Complete happy

42. **Direction: Choose the correct meaning of the given idiom.**
"Once in a blue moon"
(a) Night time
(b) An incident that happens extremely rarely
(c) An incident that happens very frequently
(d) Moonless night

43. **Direction: Select the most appropriate meaning of the underlined idiom in the given sentence.**
My neighbour's son is very mischievous and always getting in everyone's hair.
(a) Throwing things at them
(b) Pulling their hair
(c) Entertaining them
(d) Annoying them

44. **Direction: Choose the option which best expresses the meaning of the idiom/phrase given below.**
"Run out of steam"
(a) To run out of an engine
(b) To lose enthusiasm and stop doing something
(c) To run the engine by steam
(d) A very loud and noisy rain storm

45. **Choose the correct meaning of the given proverb:**
"To make hay while the Sun shines"
(a) To make good use of an opportunity
(b) To put out the cut grass for drying up
(c) To create a mayhem during daytime
(d) Be fearful of nights and darkness

Ques (46-47): Direction: "The wind lies asleep in the arms of the dawn
Like a child that has cried all night."

46. **The second line is an example of:**
(a) Simile
(b) Metaphor
(c) Personification
(d) Alliteration

47. **'Metaphor' is defined as:**
(a) far fetched simile
(b) implied simile
(c) covert simile
(d) explicit simile

48. **Choose the correct symbol for the underlined consonant/ vowel sound:-**
mo th er
(a) ð
(b) γ
(c) th
(d) d

49. **The number of vowel and consonant sounds in English is indicated respectively by:**
(a) 22, 22
(b) 5, 39
(c) 10, 34
(d) 20, 24

50. **Direction : Identify the word with a different sound represented by two underlined letters at the final level in one of the following words.**
(a) Chur ch
(b) Ea ch
(c) Rea ch
(d) Epo ch

// Smart Answer Sheet //

Correct — Percentage of students who answered correctly.

Skipped — Percentage of students who skipped.

Q.	Ans.	Correct / Skipped	Q.	Ans.	Correct / Skipped	Q.	Ans.	Correct / Skipped
1	C	57.25% / 1.24%	2	C	43.98% / 1.88%	3	C	52.48% / 1.91%
4	B	64.98% / 1.1%	5	D	82.55% / 0.0%	6	B	63.97% / 1.22%
7	B	67.37% / 1.9%	8	D	67.84% / 1.31%	9	B	44.07% / 1.05%
10	A	46.13% / 1.75%	11	A	57.88% / 1.9%	12	B	26.58% / 4.43%
13	C	46.04% / 1.01%	14	D	48.74% / 1.29%	15	D	42.51% / 1.74%
16	C	53.53% / 1.6%	17	C	58.55% / 1.75%	18	B	63.99% / 1.94%
19	C	63.12% / 1.26%	20	B	76.7% / 0.0%	21	B	42.53% / 1.17%
22	C	66.18% / 1.52%	23	C	43.22% / 1.59%	24	C	77.17% / 0.0%
25	A	41.22% / 1.16%	26	B	68.63% / 1.26%	27	B	66.19% / 1.15%
28	C	51.88% / 1.93%	29	C	52.95% / 1.06%	30	D	27.0% / 4.9%
31	D	43.4% / 1.66%	32	C	24.75% / 4.25%	33	C	40.76% / 1.75%
34	B	76.74% / 0.0%	35	A	65.41% / 1.86%	36	B	76.08% / 0.0%
37	B	87.34% / 0.0%	38	B	78.95% / 0.0%	39	D	53.64% / 1.31%
40	B	53.01% / 1.91%	41	A	22.24% / 3.88%	42	B	17.71% / 3.47%
43	D	14.55% / 4.9%	44	B	25.9% / 4.73%	45	A	42.48% / 1.35%
46	A	86.96% / 0.0%	47	D	52.68% / 1.09%	48	A	69.08% / 1.45%
49	D	58.33% / 1.36%	50	D	79.11% / 0.0%			

// Hints and Solutions //

1(C). Partha felt lonely because he had no friends at school, so no one visited him when he was at the hospital. Refer to the line: "Dear God, I know I messed up and nobody likes me. Please give me a second chance. I can show you what a good friend I can be." He drew a map showing the way from the school to the hospital, walked shakily to the window, and let the balloon fly away, carrying his message towards God.

2(C). An antonym for the word 'shakily' in the passage is "firmly". "Shakily" means in a way that involves someone shaking because of being weak, ill. "Firmly" means in a solid or strong way.

3(C). Partha's feeling of loneliness soon turned to self-pity. "Self-pity" means excessive, self-absorbed unhappiness over one's own troubles. Refer to the lines: Seeing his aunty crying after talking with the doctor confirmed it. His time had come. He didn't tell his visitors, though. They would either pity him, or be happy to get rid of him.

4(B). Partha would not go back to school to meet his schoolmates and teachers because he did not have long to live. Refer to the line: Partha knew's he wouldn't have long to live. He could feel it, deep inside. Seeing his aunty crying after talking with the doctor confirmed it. His time had come. He didn't tell his visitors, though. They would either pity him, or be happy to get rid of him.

5(D). The message in the passage is friendship is rare. The writer has no friends. He moreover, accepts the fact that he had not been a good friend to anyone. Later on, when he sends that message in a balloon and it reaches a boy who comes to meet him, he realizes that friendship is rare and if one has got friends, he is so lucky as true friendship is so rare.

6(B). The change in Partha's attitude is evident when he refrained from poking fun at the Afghan boy and shared the fruits. Refer to the line: Normally, he would have made fun of his broken English and his long, baggy brown kurta, but he knew better. He smiled and offered him the first orange.

7(B). A phrase that can replace the words 'ganged up' is 'formed a group'. 'Ganged up' means to unite as a group against someone or formed a group. Refer to the lines: The other two, Rahul and Syed, weren't really his friends, although they often ganged up with him against other kids to take away their lunch pocket money.

8(D). From the given passage we can infer that Not only did Madam Cama participate in India's struggle for freedom, she also championed the cause of women.

9(B). From the given passage we can infer that the author's attitude to Madam Cama can be described as laudatory.

10(A). The word which is opposite in meaning to 'famous' is 'unpopular'. Famous means- known about by many people. Unpopular means- not liked by many people.

11(A). The past perfect tense of 'Madam Cama fought for the cause of women.' is "Madam Cama had fought for the cause of women." Sentence structure: had + past participle. Example: They had forgotten the answer.

12(B). The part of speech in the underlined word in 'I see only men who represent half of the country.' is Pronoun.

13(C). From the given passage we can infer that How did the book, 'The First Indian War of Independence' find its way to India' ? The book was smuggled.

14(D). Befuddling word in the passage which means the same as 'confusing'.
Befuddling means cause to become unable to think clearly. Example: I was in a befuddling state this morning.

15(D). The Mid West Trail 2 was a U.S based study on 100 participants who exercised 5 times a week and burnt 600 calories.
According to passage, "The Midwest Trial 2, was conducted in the University of Kansas, U.S. on how regular, supervised exercise influences body weight. The trial involved 100 overweight, previously inactive young men and women who were made to work out five times a week at a physiology lab, jogging or otherwise sweating until they had burned up to 600 calories per session."

16(C). Any exercise is better than none would Dr. Willis say to someone who has given up exercising because they cannot do so in the morning.
Dr. Willis said that "I would not want anyone to think that it's not worth exercising if you can't do it first thing in the morning," he says. "Any exercise, at any time of day, is going to be better than none."

17(C). The Mid West Trial 2 duration was 10 months.
According to passage, "After 10 months of this regimen, almost everyone had dropped pounds. But the extent of their losses fluctuated wildly, even though everyone was doing the same, supervised workout. A team of researchers started brainstorming what could be responsible for the enormous variability in weight loss."
So, clearly duration was 10 months.

18(B). The successful weight losers in the Mid West Trial 2 Follow-up study slept more .
According to passage, "The early-exercise group tended to be slightly more active throughout the day, taking more steps in total than those who worked out later. They also ate less ."

19(C). By 'larkish exercisers' the writer refers to people who exercise in the morning.
According to passage, "But Dr. Willis also points out that most of those who worked out later in the day did lose weight, even if not as much as the larkish exercisers, and almost certainly became healthier."

20(B). Regimen one word which means the same as a set of rules about food and diet that someone follows.

21(B). The given word 'overhauled' means to redo or restore something.
Meaning of the given options:
- **Modernize:** To make something suitable for use today using new methods, styles, etc.
- **Damaging:** Harm, hurt, impair, injure, and mar.
- **Hurting:** To cause somebody/yourself physical pain or injury.
- **Injuring:** to harm or hurt yourself or somebody else physically, especially in an accident.

22(C). The correct sentence with the appropriate word from the given option is : One must follow one's dream with all determination.

23(C). The feminine gender of milkman is milkmaid.

24(C). The plural form of loaf is loaves.

25(A). The correctly spelt word is **Consecrate** .
Consecrate means to state formally in a special ceremony that a place or an object can be used for religious purposes.

26(B). According to the context of the sentence it is regarding the decision taken by the RBI to cut the policy rate in order to control the economy of the country. It is said that the rate cut was anyway going to happen but at the same time the expectation was only for a 25 or 50 bps cut by the apex bank. The RBI has taken some other decision and has taken the market by surprise. Among the given words, we can use the pair in B since both the words are correct according to the given context of the blanks in the sentence. In other cases, the words will not fit in the given blanks.

27(B). According to the given context, it is regarding the fact that the revenue scenario of the country is not going to ensure that further fiscal concessions will be possible but one thing that can be done is to incentivize the investment by the government. That will be the best way forward for our economy. Among the given words in options, the pair in Option B will fit in both the blanks in the given sentence whereas the rest are not correct as per the context of the sentence.

28(C). Correct sentence: In a country as <u>diverse</u> as India, it is impossible to ensure that vegetarian and non-vegetarian preferences are <u>factored</u> into delivery logistics.
According to the given context of the sentence it is regarding the fact that the vegetarian and non-veg food items cannot be delivered separately in India and the reason given is that India is a very diverse country with so many people with so many choices. There are various types of people and they are so different. Among the given options, the pair of words in Option C will fit in both the blanks to imply that India is a diverse country and the choice of food items by people cannot be factored in delivery logistics by the online food delivery companies.

Other words in the options are not correct as per the context of the sentence and can be eliminated from consideration.

29(C). Complete Sentence: One of the major reasons why we have wars is that people don't take enough interest in politics.'
We could have used 'two' if there was a surety of only two reasons being given. Thus, we're left with 'major' which makes sense for the first blank.
For part two of the sentence, we have two options many and enough.
We cannot use 'many' because 'interest' is an uncountable noun and 'many' is used for plural countable nouns.
Hence we'll use 'enough' because it is used for uncountable nouns and is making the sentence meaningfully complete.

30(D). Correct Sentence: Komodo dragons are gigantic lizards which can weigh more than humans and are somewhat venomous.
Since Komodo dragons can weigh more than humans, they must be huge.
Hence, for the first blank, 'gigantic' is the best choice for it is a synonym of huge.
And for the second blank, we have venomous which means something which is poisonous.

31(D). When we reached the theatre the play had already begun.
Past perfect tense describes an action which is completed before a certain moment in the past.
It is also used when two actions happened in the past, and one is linked to the other in terms of time.
In case of two clauses, if the simple past tense is used in the dependent clause, then the past perfect tense is used in the independent clause.
In the given sentence, the dependent clause, 'When we reached the theatre' is in simple past tense.
So,the independent clause should be in past perfect tense.
This is expressed by the form 'had' + third form of the verb (begun).

32(C). When she got back the answer script, she saw she had made several mistakes.
When there are two actions to be expressed happened one after another in the past:
The first action should follow the past perfect tense. (Sub + had + V3)
The second one should follow the past indefinite tense. (Sub + V2)
In the given sentence there are two actions being described:
getting back the answer script and making mistakes.
It can be easily understood that first he would have made mistakes. After that he could have found them.
Therefore, action happened later (getting back the answer script) should use 'got (V2)' while the first one should use 'had made (had + V3)'.

33(C). My friends had waited for me for a long time before they decided to leave without me.
The given sentence has two clauses - the independent clause (my friends ... long time) and the dependent clause (before ... without me).
We commonly use before with the past simple tense. It suggests that the second event happened soon after the first one.
Thus, the second blank will use the verb 'decided'.
If 'decided' is used in the second blank, then 'had waited' (past perfect) is used for the first blank.
The past perfect tense is for talking about something that happened before something else, which makes 'had waited' the correct phrase for the first blank.

34(B). We always use gerund (V+ing) form with the structure like "with the view to". Therefore, it should be "exploring" instead of "explore" in part (2) of the sentence. The correct sentence is-
He has decided to visit Mumbai with a view to exploring the new opportunities lying in front of him.

35(A). The Past Perfect tense is used with words like hope, expect, intend etc to indicate hope, expectation, intension etc. The correct sentence is-
I had expected that you would score much better marks but unfortunately you didn't.

36(B). Since the reporting verb is in the past tense, therefore reporting speech will also be in the past tense. Hence 'would be coming' will come instead of 'will be coming'. So, the correct sentence is-
My husband told me that he would be coming to Singapore next year for the new project.

37(B). As the starting statement talks about the seeking help, the next statement would be carrying a verb, so, Q follows. P follows Q as it describes that taking help is not that easy. R will be the concluding statement as it states that it is not easy for everyone. Thus, the correct option is QPR as only that arrangement would make a coherent paragraph.
The correct formation would be, 'Seeking help is not always easy for everyone'.

38(B). As the work can't be signed, so P follows the opening statement as it talks about the signing of the cheque. The next statement will be the condition on which the cheque will get signed. So, R follows P. The concluding statement would be Q as it talked about the work that is yet to be finished. Thus, the correct option is PRQ as only that arrangement would make a coherent paragraph.
The correct formation would be, 'I will sign the check when you finish the work'.

39(D). The word 'urban' means 'relating to or characteristic of a town or city' and is unsuitable in this sentence. The correct word to be used here is 'urbane' which means 'courteous and refined in manner'. Hence 'urbane' should be used in place of 'urban' to make the sentence grammatically correct.
Among the given choices, only option D replaces the given bold part most appropriately.
The sentence after replacement becomes:
Mr. Tharoor's **urbane manners charm friends** and enemies alike.

40(B). Usage of the phrasal verb 'look away' which means 'avert one's gaze' is inappropriate in this sentence.
'Look down on' which means 'to consider someone or something lesser or inferior in some way' would be suitable in this context.
E.g.: She looks down on anyone who hasn't had a university education.
Hence 'look down on' should be used in place of 'look away on' to make the sentence grammatically and contextually correct.
Among the given choices, only option B replaces the given bold part most appropriately.
The sentence after replacement becomes:
Religious **bigots look down** upon anyone who does not conform to their beliefs.

41(A). The most appropriate meaning of the given idiom/phrase

'Like a shag on a rock' is 'Completely alone'.
Like a shag on a rock means someone who is lonely or completely isolated.
For example: Even at parties around lots of people, I still tend to feel **like a shag on a rock** .
By the given meaning and example we can say that 'completely alone' is the appropriate meaning.

42(B). Once in a blue moon: Not very often/An incident that happens extremely rarely. **For example:** My sister lives in Alaska, so I only see her once in a blue moon.

43(D). Getting in everyone's hair - to annoy everyone, usually by being present all the time.
For Example: My sister has a habit of getting in everyone's hair whenever there is an important discussion.

44(B). The meaning of the given idiom 'run out of steam' is 'to lose one's energy, motivation, or enthusiasm to continue doing something.'
Examples:
- After spending hours working on this project, I'm running out of steam.
- Toward the end of the lecture, he seemed to run out of steam.

45(A). "To make hay while the sun shines" is a proverb that means to take advantage of a good opportunity when it presents itself. The phrase is often used to encourage people to act quickly and make the most of their opportunities, as the opportunity may not last forever.

46(A). 'Simile' is a figure of speech.
'A simile' is a comparison between two unlike things using the words 'like' or 'as'.
For example:
- As slippery as an eel.
- Like peas in a pod.

47(D). 'Metaphor' is defined as explicit simile.
- A simile is a figure of speech that directly compares two unlike things.
- To make the comparison, similes most often use the connecting words "like" or "as", but can also use other words that indicate an explicit comparison.
- 'Explicit' means not hiding anything, clear, making something easy to understand.
- The wind lying asleep in the dawn has been explicitly i.e., in a detailed manner compared to the child who has been crying all night.

48(A). The word mother has two syllables. The symbol ð is normally spelled with the letters 'th' as seen in the words 'whether', 'either' and 'they'. Phonetic transcription (also known as phonetic script or phonetic notation) is the visual representation of speech sounds (or phones) by means of symbols.

49(D). The English letter a,e,i,o,u are called vowel, because these represents such sounds. There are 20 vowel sound in English, divided into 3 types of vowel sounds. Consonants is a sound we make which is not a vowel.

50(D). Phonetics is the study and classification of speech sounds. The sound of 'ch' is different in the pronunciation of 'epoch'. Here, 'ch' is pronounced with the 'k' sound.

Ques (1-5): Directions : Read the passage given below and answer the questions by choosing the most appropriate option.

Fifteen years ago, brothers Nadeem Shehzad and Mohammad Saud rescued an injured black kite and took it to a veterinary hospital. The hospital refused to treat the bird saying that they did not treat birds of prey. When the brothers found another wounded kite, they decided to take matters into their own hands. They took advice from veterinarians and the Internet, and set up an operation theatre in their bedroom. This was followed by an open-air ward on their terrace. Adults and children alike from nearby localities began bringing the injured birds they found. Both Nadeem and Mohammad have always loved birds and animals and are saddened by the meagre facilities available to injured animals. Today the brothers have learned to treat such birds and they have 28 injured birds recovering on their rooftop. "We've taught ourselves to treat fairly complicated injuries," said Shehzad. In fact, the brothers are the only people in Delhi who stitch back torn wings. Their patients often fly off even before the stitches are fully healed! "During Independence week, kite flying is a national pastime. However, the glass-coated kite string (manjha) is so sharp that it cuts through wings and bones of birds. It is dangerous for the pigeons, crows, owls, kites and other birds that get entangled in it! Often kite fliers don't realize that by leaving strings of cut kites on trees, wires and buildings - they're creating death traps for birds.

"We also want to learn micro-surgery to join broken arteries and veins. And we're studying techniques of joining bones," said Shehzad, "Then almost all the birds we treat will be able to fly free!"

1. **The report is about:**
    (a) two birds sellers.
    (b) two brothers who treat injured birds.
    (c) two brothers who fly kites.
    (d) two brothers who are veterinarians.

2. **The boys were prompted to treat injured birds on their own because:**
    (a) of their love for birds.
    (b) of their love for surgeries.
    (c) a hospital refused to treat an injured kite.
    (d) there was no hospital for birds.

3. **Who helps the brothers locate injured birds?**
    (a) Hospital staff
    (b) Children who fly kites
    (c) Information on the Internet
    (d) Adults and children from nearby areas

4. **What does the term 'meagre facilities' refer to?**
    (a) Good facilities   (b) Poor quality facilities
    (c) Minimum facilities   (d) Useful facilities

5. **What makes Nadeem and Mohammad special in Delhi?**
    (a) They are experts in kite flying.
    (b) They are the only people who stitch back torn wings.
    (c) They have always loved birds and animals.
    (d) They make kites with soft and harmless strings.

Ques (6-12): Direction : Read the passage given below and answer the following questions.

The culture of Rajasthan is as unique and as colourful as its rich historical past. Rajasthani culture reflects the colourful history of the state. One can find the essence of the culture in its folk dances, traditional cuisines, peoples in Rajasthan and in their everyday life. Being a princely state, Rajasthan is known for its royal grandeur and royalties. It attracts tourists from all over the world with its beautiful traditions, culture, people, history, and monuments. The Rangeelo Rajasthan swears by its historic cities, rustic forts, bustling markets and rich culture that makes the city a regal place to visit in India. Be it the vibrant attires, the traditional dance forms or the language, every tiny atom of the state makes Rajasthan a culturally diverse place. Often hailed as the "Land of Kings", Rajasthan exhibits its royal palaces, fortified Havelis and forts that sing a saga of the bygone years.

If you ever visit this desert state then don't forget to have an insight into the folk music, dance, art and craft of Rajasthan, which will make you fall in love with this place. Rajasthan is truly a state with splendid colourful culture. Opposite to named as 'the land of Kings' or 'the country of Rajputs', Rajasthan culture follows some of the oldest tribes – Bhils, Minas, Meos, Banjaras, Gadia, and Lohars. Culture in Rajasthan is vibrant and includes mesmerizing music, yummy n spicy cuisines and above all unmatchable Dances. In music, the Panihari style is very much famous among visitors apart from the Ghevar dish and the Ghoomar dance of Rajasthan. The euphonious folk music of Rajasthan can even make the desert blossom. These songs are sung as ballads each reciting a different story. They are mellifluous and compelling, having intense lyrics that are usually sung during special occasions and festivals.

6. **What was the status of the education sector prior to 1990?**
    (a) It was run by the state
    (b) It was opened up for the private sector
    (c) It was led by the society
    (d) It was led by the educated manpower

7. **How many people are being victimized to human trafficking in India?**
    (a) A few millions   (b) 400 million
    (c) 26 million   (d) 4000 million

8. **Which of the following crimes is worse according to the given passage?**
    (a) leaving people with no money and shelter
    (b) luring women into fake marriages
    (c) children being subjected to forced slavery
    (d) false promises made regarding job opportunities

9. **What benefits of living in a free country are actually compromised by the victims of human trafficking?**
    (a) living below the poverty line
    (b) money and shelter
    (c) safety and security
    (d) forced labour and commercial sexual exploitation

10. **What does human trafficking deprive people of?**
    (a) Right to property
    (b) Right to freedom
    (c) Right to return to their own country
    (d) Right to servitude as factory workers

11. **How are people tricked into being victims of human trafficking?**
    (a) Through false claims made about job opportunities
    (b) By intimidation or psychological blackmail
    (c) By luring into fake marriages
    (d) All the above

12. The euphonious folk songs of Rajasthan are sung as:
    (a) chants   (b) saga
    (c) ballad   (d) mellifluous

Ques (13-20): Direction: After reading the passage choose the best answer to the given question based on what is stated or implied in the passage and in any accompanying graphics (such as a table or graph).

Questions 11-21 are based on the following passages.

Passage 1

Heaven has appointed to one sex the superior, and to the other the subordinate station, and this without any reference to the character or conduct of either. It is therefore as much for the dignity as it is
5 for the interest of females, in all respects to conform to the duties of this relation. . . . But while woman holds a subordinate relation in society to the other sex, it is not because it was designed that her duties or her influence should be any the less important, or
10 all-pervading. But it was designed that the mode of gaining influence and of exercising power should be altogether different and peculiar....
A man may act on society by the collision of intellect, in public debate; he may urge his measures
15 by a sense of shame, by fear and by personal interest; he may coerce by the combination of public sentiment; he may drive by physical force, and he does not outstep the boundaries of his sphere. But all the power, and all the conquests that are lawful to
20 woman, are those only which appeal to the kindly, generous, peaceful and benevolent principles. Woman is to win every thing by peace and love; by making herself so much respected, esteemed and loved, that to yield to her opinions and to gratify her
25 wishes, will be the free-will offering of the heart. But this is to be all accomplished in the domestic and social circle. There let every woman become so cultivated and refined in intellect, that her taste and judgment will be respected; so benevolent in feeling
30 and action; that her motives will be reverenced;—so unassuming and unambitious, that collision and competition will be banished;—so "gentle and easy to be entreated," as that every heart will repose in her presence; then, the fathers, the husbands, and the
35 sons, will find an influence thrown around them, to which they will yield not only willingly but proudly....
A woman may seek the aid of co-operation and combination among her own sex, to assist her in her
40 appropriate offices of piety, charity, maternal and domestic duty; but whatever, in any measure, throws a woman into the attitude of a combatant, either for herself or others—whatever binds her in a party conflict—whatever obliges her in any way to exert
45 coercive influences, throws her out of her appropriate sphere. If these general principles are correct, they are entirely opposed to the plan of arraying females in any Abolition movement.

Passage 2

The investigation of the rights of the slave has led
50 me to a better understanding of my own. I have found the Anti-Slavery cause to be the high school of morals in our land—the school in which human rights are more fully investigated, and better understood and taught, than in any other. Here a
55 great fundamental principle is uplifted and illuminated, and from this central light, rays innumerable stream all around.

Human beings have rights, because they are moral beings: the rights of all men grow out of their moral
60 nature; and as all men have the same moral nature, they have essentially the same rights. These rights may be wrested from the slave, but they cannot be alienated: his title to himself is as perfect now, as is that of Lyman Beecher:1 it is stamped on his moral
65 being, and is, like it, imperishable. Now if rights are founded in the nature of our moral being, then the mere circumstance of sex does not give to man higher rights and responsibilities, than to woman. To suppose that it does, would be to deny the
70 self-evident truth, that the "physical constitution is the mere instrument of the moral nature." To suppose that it does, would be to break up utterly the relations, of the two natures, and to reverse their functions, exalting the animal nature into a monarch,
75 and humbling the moral into a slave; making the former a proprietor, and the latter its property. When human beings are regarded as moral beings, sex, instead of being enthroned upon the summit, administering upon rights and
80 responsibilities, sinks into insignificance and nothingness. My doctrine then is, that whatever it is morally right for man to do, it is morally right for woman to do. Our duties originate, not from difference of sex, but from the diversity of our
85 relations in life, the various gifts and talents committed to our care, and the different eras in which we live.

13. Which choice best states the relationship between the two passages?
    (a) Passage 2 illustrates the practical difficulties of a proposal made in Passage 1
    (b) Passage 2 takes issue with the primary argument of Passage 1
    (c) Passage 2 provides a historical context for the perspective offered in Passage 1
    (d) Passage 2 elaborates upon several ideas implied in Passage 1

14. Based on the passages, both authors would agree with which of the following claims?
    (a) Women have moral duties and responsibilities
    (b) Men often work selflessly for political change
    (c) The ethical obligations of women are often undervalued
    (d) Political activism is as important for women as it is for men

15. As used in line 2 , "station" most nearly means:
    (a) region   (b) studio
    (c) district   (d) rank

16. In Passage 2 , Grimké makes which point about human rights?
    (a) They are viewed differently in various cultures around the world
    (b) They retain their moral authority regardless of whether they are recognized by law
    (c) They are sometimes at odds with moral responsibilities
    (d) They have become more advanced and refined throughout history

17. As used in line 12 , "peculiar" most nearly means:
    (a) eccentric   (b) surprising

(c) distinctive   (d) infrequent

18. **Which choice provides the best evidence for the answer to the previous question?**
    (a) Lines 58-61 ("Human... same rights")
    (b) Lines 61-65 ("These... imperishable")
    (c) Lines 71-76 ("To suppose... property")
    (d) Lines 77-81 ("When... nothingness

19. **What is Grimké's central claim in Passage 2 ?**
    (a) The rights of individuals are not determined by race or gender
    (b) Men and women must learn to work together to improve society
    (c) Moral rights are the most important distinction between human beings and animals
    (d) Men and women should have equal opportunities to flourish

20. **Beecher would most likely have reacted to lines 65-68 ("Now... woman") of Passage 2 with:**
    (a) sympathy, because she feels that human beings owe each other a debt to work together in the world
    (b) agreement, because she feels that human responsibilities are a natural product of human rights
    (c) dismay, because she feels that women actually have a more difficult role to play in society than men do
    (d) disagreement, because she feels that the natures of men and women are fundamentally different

Ques (21-23): Direction: In the following question, a part of a sentence is given in bold, it is then followed by alternatives that try to explain the meaning of the idiom/phrase given in bold. Choose the alternative which explains the meaning of the phrase correctly without altering the meaning of the sentence given a question.

21. **Being an introvert, he will only eat his heart out.**
    (a) eat too much   (b) keep brooding
    (c) invite trouble   (d) suffer silently

22. **He is not worth his salt if he fails at his juncture.**
    (a) quite worthless   (b) very proud of himself
    (c) quite strange   (d) very strange

23. **She exhibited remarkable sangfroid during the crisis.**
    (a) temper   (b) irritation
    (c) composure   (d) anger

24. **Direction: Fill in the blank with the correct tense.**
    If the play ______ on time, we wouldn't have missed the train.
    (a) had finished   (b) finished
    (c) had been finishing   (d) will finish

25. **Direction: Fill in the blank with the correct article.**
    I explored the relationship between __ attendances and students' scores on standardized tests.
    (a) a   (b) an
    (c) the   (d) No article

Ques (26-28): Direction: Select the correct active form of the given sentence.

26. **This passage has been cleaned by Bhanu with his vacuum cleaner.**
    (a) Bhanu has cleaned this passage with his vacuum cleaner.
    (b) Bhanu has cleaned his vacuum cleaner with this passage.
    (c) Bhanu was cleaning this passage with his vacuum cleaner.
    (d) Bhanu had cleaned this passage with his vacuum cleaner.

27. **A book has been sent to me by my father on my birthday.**
    (a) My father has sent me a book on my birthday.
    (b) My father is sending me a book on my birthday.
    (c) A book has sent my father on my birthday.
    (d) My father will send me a book on my birthday.

28. **Superstitions are still believed in.**
    (a) People still believed in superstitions.
    (b) People are still believing in superstitions.
    (c) People still can believe in superstitions.
    (d) People still believe in superstitions.

29. **Direction : Select the one which best expresses the same sentence in passive/active voice.**
    His pocket has been picked.
    (a) They have his pocket picked.
    (b) Picking has been done to his pocket.
    (c) He has picked the pocket.
    (d) Someone has picked his pocket.

30. **Direction: A sentence has been split into four parts. One of the parts may have an error of grammar or syntax. Select the part having the error.**
    (a) A perpendicular tower added a satisfying feature
    (b) to the whole cluster of courts,
    (c) but the feature was toned down
    (d) by the action of weather.

Ques (31-33): Direction: In the following question the sentence has an underlined part that can be improved by replacing the part with one among the four options given below. Choose the correct option and if you think no improvements can be made, then select (D) as your answer.

31. **The main point of <u>her speech</u> was well understood.**
    (a) That she spoke   (b) Made when she spoke
    (c) Made by her speech   (d) No improvement

32. **Is there any <u>place</u> for her to sit?**
    (a) Space   (b) Room
    (c) Area   (d) No improvement

33. **If you come across my book anywhere, bring it to me, <u>can you</u>?**
    (a) Don't you?   (b) Will you?
    (c) Isn't it?   (d) No improvement

34. **Direction: In the following sentence, a part of the sentence is underlined. Below are given alternatives to the underlined part, which may improve the sentence. Choose the correct alternative. In case no improvement is needed, choose the option 'No improvement.'**
    Amy has a great voice but whenever she's singing in public she feels shy and holds on.
    A. Holds back
    B. Holds off
    C. Holds out
    (a) Only A   (b) Only B

(c) Only C   (d) No Improvement

35. Direction: In the following sentence, a part of the sentence is underlined. Below are given alternatives to the underlined part, which may improve the sentence. Choose the correct alternative. In case no improvement is needed, choose the option 'No improvement.'
The government can't pin out the exact location where the leak came from.
A. Pin up
B. Pin down
C. Pin on

(a) Only A   (b) Only B
(c) Only C   (d) No Improvement

36. Which of these is not a type of assertive sentence?
(a) Affirmative   (b) Informal
(c) Negative   (d) Emphatic

37. Choose the correct statement:
(a) It is dirty, throw it.   (b) It is dirty, throw it away.
(c) It is dirty, give it.   (d) It is dirty, give it away.

38. Choose the correct statement:
(a) He tore the letter in anger.
(b) He tore up the letter in anger.
(c) He teared the letter in anger.
(d) He teared up the letter in anger.

39. In the following question, some part of the sentence may have errors. Find out which part of the sentence has an error and select the appropriate option. If the sentence is free from error, select 'No error'.
I purchased (A)/ this ball yesterday (B)/ and have given it to my friend. (C)/ No error (D)
(a) A   (b) B
(c) C   (d) No Error

40. In the following question, some part of the sentence may have errors. Find out which part of the sentence has an error and select the appropriate option. If the sentence is free from error, select 'No error'.
The actress (A)/ with all her fans (B)/ are sent to the theatre. (C)/ No error (D)
(a) A   (b) B
(c) C   (d) No Error

41. Direction: Choose the correct meaning of the idiom.
Ways and means
(a) A technique
(b) Methods of achieving something
(c) Norms and regulations of doing something
(d) Improving one's way of doing

42. Direction: Select the most appropriate meaning of the underlined idiom in the given sentence.
Information technology has developed <u>by leaps and bounds.</u>
(a) very gradually   (b) at a rapid pace
(c) in far off places   (d) through unfair means

43. Direction: In the following question, four alternatives are given for the meaning of the given idiom/Phrase. Choose the alternative which best expresses the meaning of the Idiom/Phrase.
Put a spoke in one's wheel
(a) Tried to cause an accident
(b) Helped in the execution of the plan
(c) Thwarted in the execution of the plan
(d) Destroyed the plan

44. Direction: In the following question, four alternatives are given for the meaning of the given idiom/ Phrase. Choose the alternative which best expresses the meaning of the Idiom/Phrase.
A henpecked husband <u>plays second fiddle</u> to his wife.
(a) Pleases
(b) Fondles with
(c) Humour
(d) Plays a subordinate role to

45. Direction: In the following question, out of the four alternatives, choose the alternative which best expresses the meaning of the Idiom/Phrase.
At close quarters
(a) close examinations   (b) live near to each other
(c) live far to each other   (d) in love

Ques (46-47): Direction: Point out the figure of speech used in the sentence given below.

46. Brave Macbeth, with his brandished steel, carved out his passage.
(a) Metaphor   (b) Litotes
(c) Climax   (d) Synecdoche

47. 'Necessity is the mother of invention.'
(a) Imagery   (b) Personification
(c) Apostrophe   (d) None of the above

48. Choose the appropriate option
'raɪs' is the phonetic transcription of -
(a) rise   (b) rice
(c) raise   (d) risk

49. The word 'accelerate' is transcribed as -
(a) ək'seləreɪt   (b) ək'seləraɪt
(c) ik'seləreɪt   (d) ək'seləɪət

50. The correct transcription of the word 'hurt' is:
(a) /huːrt/   (b) /hɜurt/
(c) /hɜːrt/   (d) /hɜːut/

// Smart Answer Sheet //

Correct — Percentage of students who answered correctly.

Skipped — Percentage of students who skipped.

Q.	Ans.	Correct / Skipped	Q.	Ans.	Correct / Skipped	Q.	Ans.	Correct / Skipped
1	B	77.78% / 0.0%	2	C	51.7% / 1.27%	3	D	54.5% / 1.19%
4	B	47.61% / 1.23%	5	B	46.93% / 1.75%	6	A	63.48% / 1.22%
7	A	16.17% / 3.21%	8	C	44.91% / 1.88%	9	C	80.99% / 0.0%
10	B	66.67% / 1.1%	11	D	15.05% / 4.73%	12	C	61.98% / 1.1%
13	B	46.81% / 1.8%	14	A	41.11% / 1.92%	15	D	64.88% / 1.59%
16	B	67.51% / 1.9%	17	C	11.89% / 4.8%	18	B	78.19% / 0.0%

No.	Ans	%	No.	Ans	%	No.	Ans	%
19	A	76.56% / 0.0%	20	D	28.97% / 4.54%	21	D	60.09% / 1.81%
22	A	54.75% / 1.03%	23	C	51.73% / 1.55%	24	A	88.37% / 0.0%
25	D	40.74% / 1.52%	26	A	59.5% / 1.1%	27	A	69.84% / 1.12%
28	D	54.4% / 1.22%	29	D	88.16% / 0.0%	30	C	49.79% / 1.97%
31	D	68.68% / 1.04%	32	A	53.95% / 1.31%	33	B	52.55% / 1.7%
34	A	54.28% / 1.67%	35	B	15.33% / 3.09%	36	B	65.19% / 1.07%
37	B	62.58% / 1.42%	38	B	61.68% / 1.09%	39	C	81.58% / 0.0%
40	C	86.4% / 0.0%	41	B	46.76% / 1.04%	42	B	54.76% / 1.02%
43	C	29.41% / 4.89%	44	D	16.29% / 3.79%	45	A	82.1% / 0.0%
46	D	85.71% / 0.0%	47	B	59.64% / 1.44%	48	B	87.0% / 0.0%
49	A	61.99% / 1.93%	50	C	83.81% / 0.0%			

// Hints and Solutions //

1(B). The report is about two brothers who treat injured birds.

2(C). The boys were prompted to treat injured birds on their own because a hospital refused to treat an injured kite.

3(D). Adults and children from nearby areas helps the brothers locate injured birds.

4(B). The term 'meagre facilities' refer to Poor quality facilities.

5(B). They are the only people who stitch back torn wings makes Nadeem and Mohammad special in Delhi.

6(A). The correct answer is 'it was run by the state'.
When we read the passage carefully, it can be clearly sensed that the passage is talking about the importance of education and its system.
Let's refer to the passage, "Before 1990 when the education sector was State-led which was thought good but the limited resources' allocation to education had limited its growth projects." 'lead/led' means 'be in charge or command of.'

7(A). The correct answer is 'a few millions'.
When we read the passage carefully, it can be clearly sensed that the passage is talking about human trafficking.
Let's refer to the passage, "India has become a source, destination and transit country for men, woman, and children trafficked for forced labour and commercial sexual exploitation. India has become a transit hub for human trafficking with estimated millions, victim to human trafficking."
It means that with an estimated million victims of human trafficking, India has become a transit point for human trafficking.
The exact number of victims of human trafficking in India is not given in the passage.

8(C). The correct answer is 'children being subjected to forced slavery'.
When we read the passage carefully, it can be clearly sensed that the passage is talking about human trafficking.
In the last line of the paragraph, it is given that "Children are subject to involuntary servitude as factory workers, domestic servants, beggars, agricultural workers and many times they are also sexually abused by their owners. No

crime can be worse than this."
The word 'servitude' means 'the state of being a slave'.
From the above lines, it can be inferred that crime against children is the worse according to the passage.

9(C). The correct answer is 'safety and security.
When we read the passage carefully, it can be clearly sensed that the passage is talking about human trafficking.
Let's refer to the passage, "The impact of human trafficking is chilling; and although the brunt of it is faced by the victims, the nation suffers as a whole. Safety and security, the privileges of living in a free country are compromised."
From the given lines, it can be understood that the benefits of living in a free country, such as safety and protection, are compromised by the victims of human trafficking.

10(B). The correct answer is 'right to freedom'.
When we read the passage carefully, it can be clearly sensed that the passage is talking about human trafficking.
The word 'deprive' means 'prevent (a person or place) from having or using something.'
Let's refer to the passage, "Human trafficking is a multi-faceted threat. It robs people of their right to freedom."
The given lines mean that Human trafficking prevents citizens from having their right to freedom.

11(D). The correct answer is 'All the above'.
When we read the passage carefully, it can be clearly sensed that the passage is talking about human trafficking.
Let's refer to the passage, "Most human trafficking victims are actually duped into the trade by the false promises made regarding job opportunities. Many women from third world countries are lured into this trade with the bait of false marriages. Many of the victims are forced either directly with violence or indirectly with psychological blackmail into the trade."
The word 'intimidation' means 'frighten someone, especially in order to make them do what one wants.'
From the given lines, it can be understood that all the options represent how humans are tricked into being victims of human trafficking.

12(C). The correct answer is 'ballad'.
When we read the passage carefully, it can be clearly sensed that the given passage is talking about the rich culture of Rajasthan.
Let's refer to the passage, "The euphonious folk music of Rajasthan can even make the desert blossom. These songs are sung as ballad each reciting a different story."
It means that Rajasthan's melodious folk music is sung as ballads, each telling a different story.

13(B). In Passage 1, Beecher asserts that men and women naturally have different positions in society: "Heaven has appointed to one sex the superior, and to the other the subordinate station" (lines 1-2). She goes on to argue that a woman should act within her subordinate role to influence men but should not "exert coercive influences" that would put her "out of her appropriate sphere" (lines 44-46). In Passage 2, Grimké takes issue with the idea that men and women have different rights and roles. She asserts that as moral beings all people have the same inherent rights and states that "the mere circumstance of sex does not give to man higher rights and responsibilities, than to woman" (lines 66-68).

14(A). While Beecher and Grimké clearly disagree regarding a woman's role in society, the passages suggest that both authors share the belief that women do have moral duties and responsibilities in society. In Passage 1, Beecher writes that "while woman holds a subordinate relation in society to the other sex, it is not because it was designed that her duties or her influence should be any the less important, or all-pervading" (lines 6-10). She suggests that women do have an obligation to use their influence to bring about beneficial changes in society. In Passage 2, Grimké asserts that all people "are moral beings" (lines 58-59) and that both men and women have "rights and responsibilities" (line 68). She concludes that "whatever it is morally right for man to do, it is morally right for woman to do" (lines 81-83).

15(D). Regarding the dynamic of men and women in society, Beecher says that one sex is given "the subordinate station" while the other is given the "superior" station (lines 1-2). In the context of how one gender exists in comparison to the other, the word "station" suggests a standing or rank.

16(B). In Passage 2, Grimké makes the point that human rights are not fleeting or changeable but things that remain, regardless of the circumstances, because they are tied to humans' moral nature. She emphasizes that human rights exist even if societal laws attempt to contradict or override them, citing slavery as an example: "These rights may be wrested from the slave, but they cannot be alienated: his title to himself is as perfect now, as is that of Lyman Beecher: it is stamped on his moral being, and is, like it, imperishable" (lines 61-65).

17(C). When describing how men and women can influence society, Beecher says the ways they can do so "should be altogether different and peculiar" (lines 11-12). In the context of the "altogether different" ways men and women can influence society, the word "peculiar" implies being unique or distinctive.

18(B). The previous question asks what point Grimké makes about human rights in Passage 2, with the answer being that they exist and have moral authority whether or not they are established by societal law. This is supported in lines 61-65: "These rights may be wrested from the slave, but they cannot be alienated: his title to himself is as perfect now, as is that of Lyman Beecher: it is stamped on his moral being, and is, like it, imperishable."

19(A). In Passage 2, Grimké makes the main point that people have rights because they are human, not because of their gender or race. This is clear in lines 58-60, when Grimké states that "human beings have rights, because they are moral beings: the rights of all men grow out of their moral nature" and lines 65-68, when Grimké writes, "Now if rights are founded in the nature of our moral being, then the mere circumstance of sex does not give to man higher rights and responsibilities, than to woman."

20(D). In lines 65-68 of Passage 2, Grimké writes, "Now if rights are founded in the nature of our moral being, then the mere circumstance of sex does not give to man higher rights and responsibilities, than to woman." In other words, gender does not make men's rights and duties superior to women's. Beecher, on the other hand, begins Passage 1 by stating that "heaven has appointed to one sex the superior, and to the other the subordinate station," suggesting that men and women have fundamentally different natures. Therefore, Beecher most likely would have disagreed with Grimké's assertion.

21(D). Being an introvert, he will only **suffer silently** .
Eat his heart out means to suffer from excessive longing for someone or something unattainable.
Example: "I could have stayed in London eating my heart out for you"

22(A). He is **quite worthless** if he fails at his juncture.
Worth one's salt refers to worth (in productivity) what it costs to keep or support one.
Example: We decided that you are worth your salt, and you can stay on as an office clerk.
Whereas not worth his salt refers to inefficient or worthless.

23(C). She exhibited remarkable **composure** during the crisis.
Sangfroid refers to composure or coolness shown in danger or under trying circumstances.

24(A). The given sentence is a conditional sentence.
Conditional sentences usually consist of two clauses- a conditional clause (or if clause) and the main clause (or a result clause) the result clause in the main clause is dependent on the condition in the conditional clause.
Hence, according to the table, the given sentence is the third conditional so we will follow the structure i.e. 'If + past perfect.... subject + would + have + V $_3$ '.

25(D). According to grammar, No article is used when a plural countable noun is generic or nonspecific. Here, generic means 'referring to a class or group; not specific.
In the given sentence, 'attendance and scores' are plural countable nouns hence we can't use the indefinite or the definite article before them.
Let's see an example-
I bought new pens and pencils at the store. (general, not specific ones).

26(A). The instructions given below should be followed while changing a passive voice to an active voice.
* Find the subject and object of the sentence and exchange their places; make changes in their cases as well if subject and object are pronouns.
* Remove the preposition 'by' before the agent.
* Change has + been of the passive voice into 'have' according to the subject to make it an active voice.
* At last line up the remaining part.
So, the final sentence is: Bhanu has cleaned this passage with his vacuum cleaner.

27(A). The instructions given below should be followed while changing a passive voice to an active voice.
* Find the subject and object of the sentence and exchange their places; make changes in their cases as well if subject and object are pronouns.
* Remove the preposition 'by' before the agent.
* Change has + been of the passive voice into 'have' according to the subject to make it an active voice.
* At last line up the remaining part.
So, the final sentence is: My father has sent me a book on my birthday.

28(D). The given sentence is in Passive Voice. As per the question we have to change it into Active Voice.
The structure of the given sentence is as follows:
* Subject + V1 + Object. (Active Voice)
* Subject (Objective Case) + is/am/are + V3 + Object (Subjective Case). (Passive Voice)
Example:
* Aastha teaches English. (Active Voice)
* English is taught by Aastha. (Passive Voice)
The subject of the given sentence is 'Superstitions'.
The object of the given sentence is 'People (Hidden object)'.
The subject will be put in place of the object and the object will be put in place of the subject.

'are believed' will be changed into 'believe'.
Correct Sentence: People still believe in superstitions.

29(D). Someone has picked his pocket.
Whenever the subject is missing in the passive voice, we provide it while changing into the active voice. Indefinite pronoun 'someone' is the correct subject supplied. 'His pocket' will become the object in passive voice.

30(C). Use past perfect (passive) `had been` in place of (past indefinite) `was` because the earlier action in past takes the past perfect tense.
Correct sentence: A perpendicular tower added a satisfying feature to the whole cluster of courts, but the feature had been toned down by the action of the weather.

31(D). There is no grammatical error in the sentence.
Hence, the correct option is (B).

32(A). The correct sentence would be "Is there any space for her to sit?"

33(B). The grammatically correct sentence would be "If you come across my book anywhere, bring it to me, will you?"

34(A). Hold back means to stop yourself from doing or saying something.
Hold out means to not give in, continue to resist
Hold off means to stop someone from taking extreme steps.
Hold on means to wait.
Therefore 'Holds back' should be used in place of 'Holds on' to make the sentence grammatically and contextually correct.
The correct sentence is: Amy has a great voice but whenever she's singing in public she feels shy and holds back.

35(B). Usage of the phrasal verb 'pin out' which means a diagram showing the arrangement of pins on an integrated circuit and their functions is inappropriate in this sentence.
The phrasal verb 'pin down' means to discover exact details about something.
The phrasal verb 'pin-up' means to fix something to a wall, or other vertical surfaces, with a pin.
The phrasal verb 'pin on' means to attach the blame to someone.
Therefore, 'pin down' should be used in place of 'pinout' to make the sentence grammatically and contextually correct.
The correct sentence is: The government can't pin down the exact location where the leak came from.

36(B). An assertive sentence can be classified into three types. They are : Affirmative sentence, negative sentence and emphatic sentence.

37(B). The correct statement is: It is dirty, throw it away. Throw it means to throw to someone. Throw it away means get rid of something.

38(B). The correct statement is: He tore up the letter in anger. To tear means to divide along a straight or irregular line. To tear up means to destroy by tearing to pieces.

39(C). The error is in part (C) of the sentence. The use of verb "purchased" and the word "yesterday" makes it clear that the given sentence is in past tense. Therefore, it is grammatically incorrect to use present verb "have given" in part (C) of the sentence. Thus, The correct sentence is- I purchased this ball yesterday and gave it to my friend.

40(C). If the subject is joined by 'as well as', 'with', 'along with', 'together with' etc. the verb will agree with the first subject. Here, the first subject is "the actress" which is singular; hence, the verb used should also be singular. Hence, replace 'are' with 'is'. So, the correct sentence is- The actress with all her fans is sent to the theatre.

41(B). Ways and means - 'Methods of achieving something', the methods by which something is accomplished or attained, especially in relation to finances
For example: We're here to discuss the goals of the project, not the ways and means.

42(B). The correct answer is- at a rapid pace.
Given Idiom: By leaps and bounds means rapidly or in fast progress.
Example - Her French is improving by leaps and bounds

43(C). Put a spoke in somebody's wheel: to prevent somebody from putting their plans into operation.
His letter really put a spoke in our wheel. The best option is thwarted in the execution of the plan.

44(D). Play second fiddle = Play a subordinate role to
Play a subordinate role to someone or something; be treated as less important than someone or something.

45(A). At close quarters means close examinations.
For example: Real friends never leave us alone in close quarters.

46(D). The figure of above in this statement is Synecdoche.
Synecdoche is a figure of speech in which a part is made to Choice. It is a figure of speech in which a part is made to represent the whole or vice versa. Here 'brandished steel' may represent the sword Macbeth holds or it may be the steel like body of Macbeth or it may be the steel like will power of Macbeth.

47(B). The correct answer is Personification.
Necessity is the mother of invention is a very famous proverb that uses the figure of speech Personification.
Personification: The attribution of human nature or human characteristics to something that is non-human.
Imagery: Visually descriptive; figurative language in literature.
Apostrophe: When a character in a literary work speaks to an object, an idea, or someone who doesn't exist as if it is a living person

48(B). Phonetic transcription of word:-
Rice - /raɪs/

49(A). Phonetic Symbols: These symbols are used to describe the phonemes (sounds). It enables learners to understand and speak the language they are learning. In particular the International Phonetic Alphabet (IPA), each phonetic symbol is associated with a particular sound.

50(C). Transcription of the word 'hurt' is /hɜːrt/, here, it can be seen that 'u' in the word 'hurt' is represented as 'ɜː' because the phonetic symbol 'ɜː' is used whenever there is a sound of 'er', 'ur', or 'ir'—E.g., bird, work, etc.

Ques (1-7): Direction : Read the given passage and answer the questions that follow.

Military rhetoric (China had been accused of standing with Pakistan days after the militant attacks in Kashmir in September) incited Baba Ramdev to demand an economic blockade; and on the ground, fervent nationalists and devoted followers got the ball rolling.

Scattered across the country, families, and individuals started to shun Chinese goods, even as opportunistic fringe elements got into the act. Since some Chinese products in the past have been found to be contaminated (baby food, lead in toys), they are also an easy target for hoaxes. Two weeks ago, Kerala was aflutter over reports that "fake" plastic eggs from China were being sold in supermarkets.

Social media has witnessed active campaigns seeking a boycott of Chinese-made products this Diwali in India. The boycotts urge Indians to shun Chinese-made products and buy Indian-made products instead. However, this unfeasible prospect of a boycott of Chinese goods has started hurting Indian retailers and wholesalers. In the light of recent tension between India and Pakistan, China has aligned itself openly with Pakistan drawing the ire of the common Indians. A large section has taken to social media and also spreading the call for a boycott by word of mouth. Wholesalers in India's largest wholesale market Sadar Bazaar have already claimed that they are seeing a drop of at least 20 percent in Chinese made products and the Confederation of All India Traders recently predicted that the traders expect they will suffer at least 30 percent loss due to the boycott of Chinese-made products. Also, boycotting Chinese-made products on Diwali is also not a solution as after that, and for every non-festive purchase, all products are in some way Chinese made.

Prime Minister Narendra Modi has pushed for greater business integration with China at the BRICS Summit even though the 'corner Pakistan' plan didn't take off at the summit. It makes sense to push trade with China when you consider that early in 2016 India-China trade deficit was reported well above $44 billion. This is a grave concern for the Indian economy and to achieve a sustained balance of trade, both the countries had even signed a five-year cooperation agreement to achieve this balance.

India and China have shared a love-hate relationship since the mid-20th century. However, India's boycott won't even put a dent on the Chinese economy. It is, however, a self-blow. The need and promise of economic prosperity keep the India-China trade relation amicable, stable, and somewhat peaceful.

Boycott of products at a time when long-term plans have not yet fully yielded results causes a negative impact at home. Without suitable Indian alternatives, boycotting Chinese products hurts the earnings of the Indian trader who has invested his money in them and now is unable to sell them off to earn the money back. If these boycotts are to take place, they need to be taken at the root. However, almost every product used in our daily life has some prominent element that is Chinese. This demand just proves to be unfeasible, impulsive, and not well-thought-out. In other words, the threat is more a bark than a bite.

1. What fake thing made the state of Kerala panic?

   (a) Fake baby food   (b) Fake plastic eggs

   (c) Lead in toys   (d) Fake plastic rice

2. Who has predicted the 30% loss for traders due to the boycott of Chinese made products?

   (a) Confederation of All India sellers

   (b) Confederation of All India Trade Unions

   (c) Confederation of All India Factory Workers

   (d) Confederation of All India Traders

3. What does the author mean when they state 'more a bark than a bite' ?

   (a) Something not as unpleasant as thought

   (b) The barking of a dog

   (c) The onset of rabies

   (d) The unpleasant aspects of life

4. Why do Indians have a general distrust for Chinese products?

   (a) In the past, Chinese products have been found to be fake or contaminated.

   (b) Chinese products are substandard compared to Indian products.

   (c) India lost China once in a war and hence the general distrust.

   (d) Chinese products are very costly.

5. According to the passage, what kind of relationship does India and China share?

   (a) A mutually exclusive relationship

   (b) A love-hate relationship

   (c) A certain relationship

   (d) A peaceful relationship

6. What was the India-China trade deficit in early 2016?

   (a) $44 million   (b) Above $44 million

   (c) Above $44 billion   (d) Below $44 million

7. Which plan did not take off at the BRICS Summit?

   (a) Boycott Pakistan   (b) Follow Pakistan

   (c) Corner Pakistan   (d) Ignore Pakistan

Ques (8-13): Direction: Read the passage given below and answer the questions that follow by choosing the correct/most appropriate options.

1. I think it was really my love of walking that first took me to the hills, and then kept me there for two decades. It had become increasingly difficult for me to walk about in Delhi, and I resented this, because I had been walking about in Delhi before most of my readers were born. As a youth I walked from Connaught Place to Humayun Tomb, and from Paharganj to Pusa and although as the years passed I still covered these distances occasionally, It was no longer a pleasurable activity. Rather it become an obstacle race, an exercise in survival.

2. Now whenever I visit Delhi, I do not even try covering long distances. Even crossing a road is something of a feat for me. Usually I wedge myself between two well- built women and cross over in their company. No Maruti owner would risk damage to his car by colliding with me.

3. But being a compulsive walker, I stay out of Delhi as much as possible and do most of walking in the hills. Even hill stations are congested these days, but as I live on the outskirts of one, I have no difficulty in marching off for a few miles with only myself and a circling eagle for company. Here too, motor roads have multiplied But it is possible to leave them at will, taking any old path that leads through fields of maize or mustard, or through oak and rhododendron forest, until a village is reached.

4. Here there is always hospitality if you are not the arrogant or fastidious sort. And occasionally you might come across a mountain stream where you can rest on a bed of ferns. And if there is no stream, you will eventually find a spring, perhaps a mere trickle of water but welcome all the same. Some springs dried up last year when the rains failed. Let us hope for the sake of bird and beast and thirsty trekker that it rains this winter.

8. **What accounts for the long stay of the writer in the hills?**
    (a) The salubrious hilly climate
    (b) His love of mountain streams and forests
    (c) The serenity of the hills
    (d) His love of walking

9. **The author does not enjoy walking about in Delhi because:**
    (a) It is no longer a friendly city
    (b) As become very congested
    (c) There is a lot of noise due to industrial activities
    (d) High level of pollution in Delhi dampens the mood.

10. **The last paragraphs reveals nature's:**
    (a) Mystery
    (b) Creativity
    (c) Beauty
    (d) Liberality

11. **How is a nature lover rewarded when he reaches a village a few miles from the hill?**
    (a) He enjoys perfect peace and serenity.
    (b) He enjoy the sight of farmers engaged in their usual activities.
    (c) He hears the chirping of birds.
    (d) He comes across a mountain stream or a spring.

12. **Which of the following word is similar in the meaning to the word, 'occasionally' as used in the passage (para 1)?**
    (a) Sometimes
    (b) Rarely
    (c) Frequently
    (d) Often

13. **Which of the following words is opposite in meaning to the word, 'difficulty' as used in the passage (para 3)?**
    (a) Eagerness
    (b) Simplicity
    (c) Clarity
    (d) Ease

Ques (14-20): Directions: Read the passage given below carefully and answer the questions that follow by selecting the correct/most appropriate options:

Water is the core of life; hence water must be central to our spiritual thinking. Water is not only most of earth, but also most of life. Therefore water conservation must be our deepest concern.

The Himalayan mountain range is among the highest, youngest and most fragile ecosystem of the planet. The Himalayas have given us some of the great river systems of the earth including the Indus, Ganga, Brahmaputra, Nu Salween, Yangtze and the Mekong. The Himalayas are also called the 'Third Pole', for they contain the largest mass of ice and snow outside the earth's polar region, the north and south poles. There is a permanent snowline above 5,000 metres. Some of the glaciers in the region are the longest outside the two poles.

The Himalayas serve as water towers, providing water on a sustained basis to more than 1,000 million people and millions of hectares of land in South Asia. The greenery, benevolent climate, highly productive ecosystems, food production and overall happiness in South Asia are in fact, attributable to the bounty of the Himalayas. They are not only beautiful; they are life-givers. Little wonder that they are venerated as the abode of gods.

To keep the Third Pole preserved through assured conservation is one of the greatest challenges for the contemporary world. Himalayan mountains are a common but fragile natural resource. As mountain ecosystems have enormous bearing on the earth's systems, their special care, regeneration and conservation of their pristine resources would only bring more happiness, peace and prosperity to large parts of the world. In Agenda 21, Chapter 13 of the United Nations, the importance of mountains is underlined : "mountain environments are essential to the survival of global ecosystems."

The Himalayas in the state of Uttarakhand are especially rich in water resources. This area is home to dozens of perennial streams and numerous other rain-fed rivers along with innumerable rivulets, waterfalls and ponds, etc.

14. **Which of the following has not been mentioned in the passage ?**
    (a) The Himalayas provide us with highly productive ecosystems
    (b) The Himalayas provide water to more than 1000 million people
    (c) The Himalayas irrigate millions of hectares of land
    (d) The Himalayas form the back bone of our tourism industry

15. **Which of the following is false ?**
    (a) The Himalayan mountains are a fragile resource
    (b) Climate change has little effect on the Himalayas
    (c) They bring prosperity to large parts of the world
    (d) They have some of the longest glaciers

16. **What is not so special about the Himalayas in the state of Uttarakhand? The Himalayan state has:**
    (a) many perennial streams
    (b) huge mineral deposits
    (c) many rain fed rivers
    (d) numerous waterfalls and ponds

17. **Which one of the following words is most similar in meaning to the word, 'bounty'?**
    (a) generosity
    (b) assets
    (c) sympathy
    (d) abundance

18. **Which word is opposite in meaning to the word, 'benevolent'?**
    (a) malevolent
    (b) rude
    (c) untruthful
    (d) indecent

19. **Which part of speech is the underlined word in the following sentence ? The area is home to dozens of perennial streams.**
    (a) Noun
    (b) Adverb
    (c) Adjective
    (d) Pronoun

20. **In the context of the passage which of the following is true ? Water should be central to our thinking because:**
    (a) We cannot survive without water
    (b) It is a life-line for our farmers
    (c) It is considered holy by most religions
    (d) It is the core of life

21. **Choose the correctly spelt word.**
    (a) Acquaintence
    (b) Acquantance
    (c) Acquaintance
    (d) Acquentence

22. **In the following question, four words are given out of which one word is incorrectly spelt. Select the incorrectly spelt word.**
    (a) Levity
    (b) Partisan
    (c) Nemeses
    (d) Votary

23. **Direction: Choose the correct alternative which can be substituted for the given sentence.**
    A person who talks in sleep is called as

(a) Philatelist   (b) Somnambulist
(c) Somniloquist   (d) Oneirocritic

24. **Direction: Choose the correct alternative which can be substituted for the given sentence.**
    Place for ammunition and weapons is called as:
    (a) Asylum   (b) Arsenal
    (c) Archives   (d) Acoustics

25. **Find the correct spelling:**
    (a) Accesary   (b) Acessarry
    (c) Acessary   (d) Accessary

Ques (26-28): Direction: Fill in the blanks with an appropriates word.

26. **The old man may not live_____ the winter.**
    (a) in   (b) through
    (c) up to   (d) by

27. **When the morning ______ the murder was discovered.**
    (a) came   (b) happened
    (c) arrived   (d) occurred

28. **Our sir teaches Mathematics _____ English.**
    (a) across   (b) besides
    (c) beside   (d) both

Ques (29-30): Directions: In the following question a sentence is given with two blanks. You have to choose the correct pair of words that fill the blanks correctly in terms of grammar and context.

29. **Trump put Pakistan on notice for ______ terrorist organizations to destabilize neighbouring countries and ______ the country.**
    (a) discouraging, admired   (b) demoting, attacked
    (c) sheltering, acclaimed   (d) encouraging, warned

30. **Widening the tax-payer base has a redistributive effect in ______ inequality and is the biggest _____ of free-market economies.**
    (a) abridging, flaw   (b) addressing, quality
    (c) perceiving, radical   (d) bridging, leveller

Ques (31-33): Direction : In the question given below there are two statements, each statement consists of two blanks. You have to choose the option which provides the correct set of words that fits both the blanks in both the statements appropriately and in the same order making them meaningful and grammatically correct.

31. **The Programme ______ is radical because the exercise envisages a serious re-imagination of government and governance, and ______ cooperative federalism.**
    (a) perceived, lightens   (b) conceived, deepens
    (c) born, jokes   (d) conceptualized, satire

32. **The minister interacted with the local residents and ______ their feedback on the developmental policies as he wanted to know why the district, which was a knowledge hub earlier, was presently ______ in crucial indicators of development.**
    (a) sought, lagging   (b) sort, moving
    (c) wanted, crawling   (d) required, running

33. **The company has extensively invested resources to ensure the delivery of goods goes on ______ and also to develop an ______ service that incorporates various**

distribution channels in line with investors' preference.
    (a) suddenly, exclusive   (b) smooth, excluded
    (c) brokenly, included   (d) seamlessly, inclusive

Ques (34-38): Direction: In question, a part of the sentence is made bold. Below are given alternatives to the bold part at (A), (B), (C) and (D) which may improve the sentence. Choose the correct alternative. In case no replacement is needed, mark (E) as your answer.

34. **One is advised to check the voracity of news articles before forwarding them on whatsapp and other social media.**
    (a) to check the voracity of news
    (b) checking the veracity of news
    (c) to check the veracity of news
    (d) to check the voracity of new

35. **One should lay out one's doubts and insecurities before entering the examination hall.**
    (a) One should lay outside   (b) One should lay aside
    (c) One should lay inside   (d) One should lay behind

36. **The idea of a single bad bank where the NPAs of all PSBs may be transferred as a white bullet to clean up PSB balance sheets must be rejected.**
    (a) transferring as a white bullet
    (b) transferred as a black bullet
    (c) transferred as a silver bullet
    (d) transferred as a platinum bullet

37. **The Indian banking system is beleaguered with non-performing assets .**
    (a) in non-performing assets
    (b) for non-performing assets
    (c) from non-performing assets
    (d) No correction required

38. **The dog made over the biker but was soon left behind in the empty street.**
    (a) dog made before the biker
    (b) dog made after the biker
    (c) dog made out the biker
    (d) dog made onto the biker

Ques (39-40): Direction: In the following question, out of the four alternatives, select the alternative which will improve the underlined part of the sentence. In case no improvement is needed, select "No improvement".

39. **Neither you nor your <u>friends knows how to </u>behave with elders.**
    (a) friend know how to   (b) friends know how to
    (c) friend knows how   (d) No improvement

40. **A recent study showed that mice that lack the FOXO3 gene <u>in their brain is </u>unable to cope with stressful conditions in the brain.**
    (a) in his brain is   (b) in its brain is
    (c) in their brain are   (d) No improvement

41. **Direction: Choose the correct alternative which appropriately describes the given idioms and phrases.**
    Big ticket
    (a) Very less   (b) Very costly
    (c) Very easy   (d) Not much

42. **Direction: Which of the given options best describes the meaning of the phrase.**
    "To stew in one's own juice"?
    (a) To eat healthy food
    (b) To suffer the results of one's own actions
    (c) To eat unhealthy food
    (d) To suffer the results of other's actions

43. **Direction: Select the most appropriate meaning of the underlined idiom in the given sentence.**
    Dowry is a <u>burning question</u> of the day.
    (a) A widely debated issue
    (b) A dying issue
    (c) A relevant problem
    (d) An irrelevant issue

44. **Direction: Choose the option which best expresses the meaning of the idiom/phrase given below.**
    "Let sleeping dogs lie"
    (a) To get someone drunk
    (b) A fair competition where no side has an advantage
    (c) To make a dog sleep
    (d) To avoid restarting a conflict

45. **Direction: Choose the alternative which best expresses the meaning of the given idiom / phrase.**
    Elbow room
    (a) Opportunity for freedom of action
    (b) Special room for the guest
    (c) To give enough space to move or work in
    (d) To add a new room to the house

46. **As unstable as:**
    (a) water
    (b) mule
    (c) mercury
    (d) air

47. **Choose the correct figure of speech in the following sentence**
    'Fair is foul and foul is fair'
    (a) Hyperbole
    (b) Oxymoron
    (c) Metaphor
    (d) Simile

48. **The letter 'o' in the word, 'about' is pronounced like letter, 'o' in the word:**
    (a) Go
    (b) Boy
    (c) Got
    (d) Now

49. **Direction: Choose the correct phonetic symbol for the underlined sound of the word: <u>Water</u>**
    (a) /wotʃ /
    (b) /west/
    (c) /wɔːtə(r)/
    (d) /wɒʃrʊː/

50. **Choose the option with correct primary stress on the given words:**
    Tempestuous -
    (a) ˈtempestʃuəs
    (b) temˈpestʃuəs
    (c) tempesˈtʃuəs
    (d) tempestʃuˈəs

Correct — Percentage of students who answered correctly.

Skipped — Percentage of students who skipped.

Q.	Ans.	Correct / Skipped	Q.	Ans.	Correct / Skipped	Q.	Ans.	Correct / Skipped
1	B	84.77% / 0.0%	2	D	43.68% / 1.71%	3	A	78.2% / 0.0%
4	A	82.93% / 0.0%	5	B	82.98% / 0.0%	6	C	81.88% / 0.0%
7	C	86.16% / 0.0%	8	D	79.97% / 0.0%	9	B	81.9% / 0.0%
10	B	78.66% / 0.0%	11	D	58.37% / 1.63%	12	A	89.45% / 0.0%
13	D	89.22% / 0.0%	14	D	42.23% / 1.91%	15	B	56.07% / 1.38%
16	B	58.0% / 1.83%	17	A	45.92% / 1.73%	18	A	40.72% / 1.73%
19	C	57.43% / 1.15%	20	D	82.7% / 0.0%	21	C	78.42% / 0.0%
22	C	66.79% / 1.55%	23	C	49.39% / 1.0%	24	B	87.74% / 0.0%
25	D	62.86% / 1.05%	26	B	77.05% / 0.0%	27	A	65.16% / 1.12%
28	B	66.41% / 1.92%	29	D	46.77% / 1.32%	30	D	48.07% / 1.39%
31	B	62.97% / 1.8%	32	A	56.25% / 1.52%	33	D	52.0% / 1.02%
34	C	40.62% / 1.65%	35	B	63.05% / 1.35%	36	C	10.72% / 3.72%
37	D	82.46% / 0.0%	38	B	28.9% / 3.31%	39	B	41.76% / 1.18%
40	C	24.74% / 3.79%	41	B	41.31% / 1.92%	42	B	46.19% / 1.52%
43	A	77.67% / 0.0%	44	D	77.46% / 0.0%	45	C	12.38% / 3.35%
46	C	83.53% / 0.0%	47	B	17.89% / 3.2%	48	D	87.53% / 0.0%
49	D	49.22% / 1.04%	50	B	48.97% / 1.54%			

// Hints and Solutions //

1(B). According to the passage, "Two weeks ago, Kerala was aflutter over reports that "fake" plastic eggs from China were being sold in supermarkets."

2(D). According to the passage, "the Confederation of All India Traders recently predicted that the traders expect they will suffer at least 30 percent loss due to the boycott of Chinese-made products."
So, it is concluded that confederation of All India Traders has predicted the 30% loss for traders due to the boycott of Chinese made products.

3(A). The idiomatic expression 'more a bark than a bite' which means something that is not as dangerous as one has attempted to present.
For Example - Don't worry about John's threats—he has more bark than bite.

4(A). According to the passage, "Scattered across the country, families, and individuals started to shun Chinese goods, even as opportunistic fringe elements got into the act. Since some Chinese products in the past have been found to be contaminated (baby food, lead in toys), they are also an easy target for hoaxes. Two weeks ago, Kerala was aflutter over reports that "fake" plastic eggs from China were being sold

in supermarkets."
So, it is concluded that Indians have a general distrust for Chinese products because in the past, Chinese products have been found to be fake or contaminated.

5(B). According to the passage, " India and China have shared a love-hate relationship since the mid-20th century."

6(C). According to the passage, " It makes sense to push trade with China when you consider that early in 2016 India-China trade deficit was reported well above $44 billion."

7(C). According to the passage, "Prime Minister Narendra Modi has pushed for greater business integration with China at the BRICS Summit even though the 'corner Pakistan' plan didn't take off at the summit."
So, it is concluded that Corner Pakistan plan did not take off at the BRICS Summit.

8(D). The accounts for the long stay of the writer in the hills is his love of walking.

9(B). The author does not enjoy walking about in Delhi because it has become very congested.

10(B). The last paragraphs reveals nature's creativity. Refer to the words like mountain streams, bed of ferns, spring with trickle of water.

11(D). He hears the chirping of birds is a nature lover rewarded when he reaches a village a few miles from the hill.

12(A). Sometimes is similar in the meaning to the word, 'occasionally' as used in the passage (para 1). Sometimes: At times, not on regular basis, Occasionally: Sometimes, not regularly.

13(D). Ease is opposite in meaning to the word, 'difficulty' as used in the passage (para 3). Ease: Absence of difficulty.

14(D). "The Himalayas form the back bone of our tourism industry" is not mentioned in the passage.

15(B). "Climate change has little effect on the Himalayas" is false.

16(B). It is mentioned that "The Himalayas in the state of Uttarakhand are especially rich in water resources. This area is home to dozens of perennial streams and numerous other rain-fed rivers along with innumerable rivulets, waterfalls and ponds, etc." It can be deduced that Himalayas are rich in water resources and not in mineral resources.

17(A). Bounty means generosity whereas g enerosity means the quality of being kind and generous. So generosity is the similar in meaning to the word, 'bounty'

18(A). Benevolent means well meaning and kindly whereas m alevolent means having or showing a wish to do evil to others. So the malevolent is the opposite in meaning to the word, 'benevolent.'

19(C). In the given sentence "The area is home to dozens of perennial streams", perennial word is Adjective. Here, Perennial word describe Noun (streams).

20(D). It is mentioned that "Water is the core of life; hence water must be central to our spiritual thinking."

21(C). Option (C) is the correct answer because "acquaintance" is the correct spelling of the word that means knowledge or experience of something, it also means a person one knows slightly, but who is not a close friend. Thus, it is the correct answer.
Other options are incorrect spellings of the word.

22(C). The incorrect spelling among the above-given options is 'nemeses'. Its correct spelling is 'nemesis'.
Let's find out the meanings of the given words:-
Nemesis: the inescapable agent of someone's or something's downfall.
Levity: the treatment of a serious matter with humour or lack of due respect.
Partisan: a strong supporter of a party, cause, or person.
Votary: a person, such as a monk or a nun, who has made vows of dedication to religious service.

23(C). A person who talks in sleep is called a Somniloquist.
Suffix 'ist' is used to denote a person who is skilled or expert in something.
The word 'Somniloquist' is a Latin word. 'Somni' means sleep and 'loqui' means to talk.

24(B). The place for ammunition and weapons is called Arsenal. The meanings of other words are:
- Asylum – Hospital for mad people
- Archives – Place of collecting public/government/ historical records.
- Acoustics – Science of sound

25(D). The correct spelling is Accessary.
Please note that do not get confused between Accesssary and Accessory.

26(B). The old man may not live through the winter. Through can be used as a preposition, an adverb, and an adjective. It has several meanings, including "from one side to the other" "from beginning to end" and "during an entire period".

27(A). When the morning came the murder was discovered. "Came" is the simple past tense. As such "I come" becomes "I came" if you are talking about coming in the past.

28(B). Besides means in addition to or apart from. Beside means at the side of or next to. Other two option i.e., across and both doesn't make sense if put in the sentence. The correct word will be Besides.

29(D). Option (D) – Both the words fit the blank absolutely well, as "encouragement" of terrorism by Pakistan leads to destabilizing environment in neighboring countries, for which Trump "warned" Pakistan.
Option (A) – 'Discouraging' terrorism and then "destabilization" of neighboring countries are contrary to each other.
Option (B) – If terrorism is 'demoted' by Pakistan then there is no point for US to "attack" Pakistan because Pakistan was on back-foot due to its terrorism friendly image.
Option (C) – 'Acclaimed' means to praise, which is contradictory to the "notice" being issued by Trump.

30(D). Option (D) is correct as by narrowing the income parity, one can level the things, thus both the words are complimentary to each other and make a meaningful and grammatically correct sentence.
Option (A) is incorrect as abridging the income gap cannot be a flaw for an economy, thus flaw does not suit the second blank.
Option (B) is incorrect as mere addressing the inequality can't be the biggest quality of an economy, thus both the words are not complimenting each other.
Option (C) is incorrect as perceiving does not suit the context.

31(B). The Programme **conceived** is radical because the exercise envisages a serious re-imagination of government and governance, and **deepens** cooperative federalism.

In the first blank, the only options that fit in are option (B) and (D)- conceived and conceptualized. However, satire meaning spoof does not make sense in either of the statements as the second blank. Deepens on the other hand is a perfect fit.

Thus, option (B) is the best fit here.

32(A). The minister interacted with the local residents and **sought** their feedback on the developmental policies as he wanted to know why the district, which was a knowledge hub earlier, was presently **lagging** in crucial indicators of development.

The correct phrase is sought after which means something in demand. The only option that fits in here is option (A). Also, the second word also fits in well here and conveys the meaning that the movement has been less than expected.

33(D). The company has extensively invested resources to ensure the delivery of goods goes on **seamlessly** and also to develop an inclusive service that incorporates various distribution channels in line with investors' preference.

Option (A): Suddenly does not fit in both while exclusive does not fit in the second statement.

Option (B): Both words are incorrect.

Option (C): Brokenly is the opposite of what is needed.

Option (D) is correct with both words fitting in well.

34(C). The word 'voracity' means 'the quality of craving or consuming large quantities of food' and is unsuitable in this sentence. The correct word to be used here is 'veracity' which means 'truthfulness or accuracy'. Hence 'veracity' should be used in place of 'voracity' to make the sentence grammatically correct.

Among the given choices, only option C replaces the given bold part most appropriately.

The sentence after replacement becomes:

One is advised **to check the veracity of news** articles before forwarding them on whatsapp and other social media.

35(B). Usage of the phrasal verb 'lay out' which means 'One should lay aside' is inappropriate in this sentence.

'Lay aside' which means 'put away' would be suitable in the context.

E.g.: They agreed to lay aside their differences for the good of their families.

Hence 'lay aside' should be used in place of 'lay out' to make the sentence grammatically and contextually correct.

Among the given choices, only option B replaces the given bold part most appropriately.

The sentence after replacement becomes:

One should lay aside one's doubts and insecurities before entering the examination hall.

36(C). The term 'white bullet' does not make any sense. The correct expression is silver bullet'.

Silver bullet (Noun):

Meaning: A simple and seemingly magical solution to a complicated problem.

E.g.: There is no silver bullet that can prevent flooding entirely.

Hence 'silver bullet' should be used in place of 'white bullet' to make the sentence grammatically correct.

Among the given choices, only option C replaces the given bold part most appropriately.

The sentence after replacement becomes:

The idea of a single bad bank where the NPAs of all PSBs may be transferred as a silver bullet to clean up PSB balance sheets must be rejected.

37(D). The original sentence is absolutely correct and hence the bold part needs no replacement.

38(B). Usage of the phrasal verb 'make over' which means 'to officially make someone else the owner of something ' is inappropriate in this sentence.

'Make after' which means 'to begin chasing someone or something' would be suitable in this context.

E.g.: I made after the bus, but there was no way I could catch it.

Hence 'made after' should be used in place of 'made over' to make the sentence grammatically and contextually correct.

Among the given choices, only option B replaces the given bold part most appropriately.

The sentence after replacement becomes:

The **dog made after the biker** but was soon left behind in the empty street.

39(B). If two subjects are joined by 'either...or, neither....nor, but also, nor, or, etc.', the verb will agree with the nearest subject.

Examples,

Either you or your friends are responsible for this loss.

Neither Prabhat nor his parents have arrived yet.

According to the rule and examples that are given above, "friends know how to" will be used in the underlined part of the sentence.

40(C). According to the subject-verb agreement, the verb and pronouns must agree with the main subject of the sentence.

If the subject is singular, the verb will be singular and vice-versa.

Example,

The quality of the fruits of your farm is very good.

As the main subject is 'mice' which is plural of 'mouse', "in their brain are" will be used in the underlined part of the sentence.

41(B). Big ticket means 'v ery costly '.

For example: We've never had much money, so a brand new furniture set is something of a big-ticket item for us.

42(B). To stew in one's own juice: Be left to suffer the consequences of one's own actions.

For example:

- Let him stew in his own juices for a while.
- He's run into debt again, but this time we're leaving him to stew in his own juice.

From the above lines, we can say that To suffer the results of one's own actions is the correct meaning of the given phrase.

43(A). **Burning question:** an important question that requires an answer or a question whose answer is of great interest to everyone.

For example: Real estate taxes are always a burning question for the town leaders.

44(D). The meaning of the given idiom 'Let sleeping dogs lie' is 'to avoid restarting a conflict or ignore a problem because trying to deal with it could cause an even more difficult situation'.

Examples:

- I thought about bringing up my concerns but decided instead to let sleeping dogs lie.
- If he hasn't said anything about the incident, just let sleeping dogs lie.

45(C). The correct meaning is "to give enough space to move or work in".

'Elbow room' is a phrase coined by Shakespeare that refers in the physical sense to the literal space around a person, which enables them to move and function in some enterprise.

Example: With five people in my little car, there won't be enough elbow room.

46(C). "As unstable as mercury" is common metaphor in English, used to describe a character or situation that is unpredictable

47(B). The correct figure of speech in the sentence "Fair is foul and foul is fair" is Oxymoron. An oxymoron is a figure of speech in which two contradictory terms or ideas are combined to create a new meaning.

48(D). An open vowel is a vowel sound in which the tongue is positioned as far as possible from the roof of the mouth. Example: How, stout. The letter 'o' in these two words are pronounced like the open vowel sound 'a'.

49(D). IPA stands for the International Phonetic Association which was first published in 1888. Its objective is to define sounds of speech that apply to all languages. The phonetic symbol of the word 'water' is '/wɔːtə(r)/'.

50(B). Stressed syllable in tempestuous: tem- pes -tu-ous.

Ques (1-6): Direction : Read the passage given below and answer the questions that follow by choosing the correct/most appropriate options.

For the past two weeks, China has locked down Shanghai, its financial center. Many of its 26 million residents, confined to their apartments, have complained of acute food shortages. The government has struggled to supply every household with daily necessities, with the supply chain paralyzed by China's stringent measures under which every COVID-19 case, even if asymptomatic, is confined in government-run quarantine facilities. Food shortages are not the only problem. Many have said they are running out of medicines. Children who tested positive have been separated from their parents. The crisis has now ignited a debate on whether this strategy that enabled China to avoid a major second wave, still remains relevant when much of the rest of the world has returned to some form of normalcy thanks to vaccines. China is the only country still closed off from the rest of the world.

Signs are Beijing has no intention of changing course. The official Xinhua news agency on Sunday rebutted criticism over the policy saying "a dynamic zero-COVID approach remains crucial..." and "the repercussions of lowering the guard could be disastrous for... 1.4 billion people, including 267 million aged 60 or above". With those numbers, it argued, China's medical system "would risk a collapse". Chinese officials point to Hong Kong's experience. After two successful "zero COVID" years that allowed for normalcy, an Omicron outbreak this year led to 8,000 deaths there. Most were unvaccinated elderly residents. Beijing now finds itself in a bind. Opening up, it is feared, would mean many deaths among the elderly who have refused to get vaccinated. However, experts say one major reason for vaccine hesitancy is the "zero COVID" strategy, with the wide perception that risks from vaccines outweigh the risk of catching COVID. Zero COVID, in a sense, has become a victim of its own success. Politics is also as much a factor as public health. For two years, China's government has hailed its model as a contrast to the West which saw high deaths and continues to tell its population that COVID is a dangerous disease that requires everyone to be hospitalized. Changing course now would not suit that narrative, particularly with President Xi framing China's COVID response as one of his big legacies. Continuing on the current path, however, will bring rising economic and social costs. Rather than trumpet zero COVID and criticize living with the virus as irresponsible, China would be better served looking at the examples of countries that have successfully opened up and followed the science, as in Singapore, which aggressively vaccinated its population and incentivized it to do so by setting a timetable for opening. Otherwise, as the continued suffering in Shanghai has shown, the cure risks becoming worse than the disease.

1. **According to the passage, how China's "zero COVID" strategy could backfire?**
   (a) It will bring rising economic and social costs.
   (b) It will bring increase the use of the medicines and vaccines.
   (c) It will make every person in China opportunistic.
   (d) It will bring a huge increase in the price of vaccines.

2. **Read the sentence to find out whether there is any grammatical error in it.**
   Children who tested (A)/ positive have been (B)/ separated from (C)/ their parent. (D)
   (a) A
   (b) B
   (c) C
   (d) D

3. **What is the central theme of the passage?**

(a) China should continue its zero COVID strategy.
(b) India should learn the zero COVID strategy from China.
(c) The cure risks becoming worse than the disease in China.
(d) The zero COVID strategy has become a success throughout China.

4. **Choose the antonym of the word ' Stringent '.**
   (a) Draconian
   (b) Rigorous
   (c) Strict
   (d) Lenient

5. **Which of the following is/are incorrect according to the given passage?**
   A. Asymptomatic persons are also confined in China.
   B. People confined to their apartments in China have complained of the shortage of medicines.
   C. The Chinese government has taken care of every household with daily necessities.
   (a) Only A
   (b) Both A and B
   (c) Only B
   (d) Only C

6. **Choose the synonym of the word ' Hesitancy '.**
   (a) Reluctance
   (b) Resolution
   (c) Willingness
   (d) Certainty

Ques (7-13): Direction: Read the passage given below and answer the questions/complete the statements that follow with the help of given options.

1. The havoc the October super cyclone caused in Orissa could have been avoided had its mangrove forests not been destroyed to develop shrimp farms. New Scientist magazine, quoting coastal geographers from Cambridge University, recently said: "The (Orissa) coastline was once covered with mangrove forests and these would have dissipated the incoming wave energy."

2. Indeed, considering the unbridled human activity along the Indian coast, more Orissas can be expected at greater frequency. For, the delicate environment balance has been upset, compounding Nature's abnormalities.

3. India isn't alone in targeting its coastal areas for economic activates like ports, shrimp farms, oil refineries, luxury hotels and holiday resorts. In a few years, nearly 80 percent of the US population will be living within 50 miles of the coast. In India too, coastal populations are growing.

4. The emergence of megacities along the sea is seen as the single greatest threat to the world's coastal environment. Today, mangrove forests cover just 15.8 million hectares, and are declining at an assumed rate of 2 per cent every year. In the last few decades, feverish human activity has either destroyed or transformed nearly 50 per cent of the world's total mangrove forest area. Worse, only about one per cent of the global mangrove area is protected.

5. Mangroves are flowering plants, which grow on tidal coasts between the high and low water marks in clay and silt. They possess unusual "prop and knee" root system which enables them to trap sediments in their roots and provide the seabed a shallow slope. This helps it to absorb the energy of waves and tidal surges, and acts as a shield for the hinterland. The trees themselves form a barrier against wind.

6. Since mangrove areas are ideal for shrimp fams, they are being 'colonised' and mindlessly destroyed. India is among the top four shrimp exporters, with production growing at 15 per cent a year. But this has extracted its price- in the past 40 years, India is estimated to have lost half its mangrove forests, rendering states like Orissa and Andhra Pradesh vulnerable to the fury of cydones.

7. **Read the following statements.**

(A) The damage caused by the October cyclone could have been prevented by the mangrove forests.
(B) Shrimp farms are responsible for the October cyclone.
(C) The incoming waves could have arrested the October cyclone.
1. (A) is true and (B) and (C) are false.
2. (A) and (B) are true and (C) is false.
3. (A) and (C) are true and (B) is false.
4. (A) and (C) are false and (B) is true.
(a) 1   (b) 2
(c) 3   (d) 4

8. The destruction of the mangrove forests cannot be attributed only to:
1. Waves and tidal surges
2. Unbridled human activity
3. The development of shrimp farms
4. Economic activities
(a) 1   (b) 2
(c) 3   (d) 4

9. The single greatest threat to the world's coastal environment is:
1. The unbridled human activity along the coast.
2. The emergence of megacities along the sea.
3. The reduction of mangroves.
4. Teverish human activity.
(a) 1   (b) 2
(c) 3   (d) 4

10. 'Pop and knee' root system means that they-
(a) trap sediments in their roots.
(b) provide the sea bed with a shallow slope.
(c) act as a shield for the hinterland.
(d) allow wind to cross finally.
1. a, b, c are true.
2. b, c, d are true.
3. a, b, d are true.
4. a, c, d are true.
(a) 1   (b) 2
(c) 3   (d) 4

11. 'In coming' in para 1 is used as a/an-
1. noun
2. adverb
3. adjective
4. verb
(a) 1   (b) 2
(c) 3   (d) 4

12. 'Unbridled' in para 2 means the same as:
1. Uncontrolled
2. Undesired
3. Unexpected
4. Unforeseen
(a) 1   (b) 2
(c) 3   (d) 4

13. Mangroves are flowering plants\(A) which grow on tidal\(B) coasts among the high and low water\(C) marks in clay and silt.\(D)
The above sentence has an error in part:
1. A
2. B
3. C
4. D

(a) 1   (b) 2
(c) 3   (d) 4

Ques (14-20): Direction : Read the following passage carefully and answer the questions given below it.

Most people spend (on average) half of their day tapping away at their hand-held devices. Either, surfing the net or checking notifications. Facebook ranks the highest in all social networking platforms, followed by Twitter, Instagram and so forth.

Social media is addictive- which is why so many people are 'hooked'. Often referred to as Social networking addiction, this phrase is often used to describe someone who spends too much time on Facebook, Twitter, Instagram and other channels. A blog post, Instagram post, tweet, or youtube video can be produced easily by anyone and shared, which can then be viewed by millions for free. Psychologists and scientists have now taken the time to study social media in terms of why they believe it interferes with aspects of our daily life.There is no official medical term that identifies addiction and social networking. It cannot be deemed as a disease or disorder as the cases are not severe and the habit can easily be maintained or prevented. Furthermore, instead of spending long periods of time on social media, we dip into and out of these sites all day long. We check for updates from friends and family as well as news and information. However, the behavior associated with the excessive use of these channels has become the subject of much public and sociological debate.We actively post, like, comment and share personal posts. Not only that, we tend to share and reshare expressions (of either negative or positive) contagiously. But, why?

Scientists believed some years ago that, dopamine was simply a pleasure chemical in the brain. Recent studies have shown that; dopamine actually produces the desire in people to 'want' by drawing out the need for us to -seek and search. Creating the ultimate drive to find what is that what we want.

Dopamine is spontaneous. It's stimulated by unpredictability and small bits of information as well as reward cues which are the same conditions that social media presents to all users. In addition, the pull of dopamine is so strong that recent studies have shown that tweeting, for example, can be harder to resist than cigarettes and alcohol!

Researchers at Chicago University studied the effects of social media. They concluded quite quickly that people presented higher levels of addiction to social media than the need to smoke or drink. Media cravings ranked higher.

And, let's not forget oxytocin, many call it the cuddle chemical because the brain releases pleasure chemicals that transpire usually when you kiss and hug- or tweet. It is also known as the hormone that builds the strong yet unique bond between mothers and their babies. Oxytocin is now regarded as the human stimulant of empathy, generosity, trust, and more. These are factors which many advertisers and marketers play on when promoting a brand or business over social media.

Nevertheless, problems have arisen most commonly with school kids - whereby mobile phone devices have been confiscated because exam results have fallen severely due to lack of attention on homework or studies. Schools in many westernized countries have had to take drastic action - banning smartphones, iPad and most portable devices from school premises- as it is claimed to be a huge distraction. Whereas, other schools use it for educational purposes and as a rewards system for their pupils.

Research has also indicated unsurprisingly that Facebook is the most common activity that university students switch to, when studying. Worryingly, it has also found that those who most engage in this type of internet browsing tend to have lower levels of educational achievement.

Also, there have been many cases of students posting or sharing content that is unethical, which has caused parents and academic institutions to limit the use of these online networking channels.

14. **Which is the most common activity that university students switch to when studying?**
    - (a) Youtube
    - (b) Facebook
    - (c) Twitter
    - (d) Whatsapp

15. **Why is there no real medical term that identifies addiction and social networking?**
    - (a) Research is not yet done on the subject
    - (b) It cannot be deemed as a disease or disorder as cases are not severe.
    - (c) The habit can easily be maintained or prevented
    - (d) (B) and (C)

16. **Which of the following words is the most similar in meaning to the word 'contagiously' as given in the passage?**
    - (a) Assail
    - (b) Ambivalent
    - (c) Arboreal
    - (d) Malignant

17. **What actions are taken by schools for students regarding mobile phone devices as mentioned in the passage?**
    - (a) Punish students who bring mobile phones to schools.
    - (b) Use it for educational purposes and as a rewards system for their pupils.
    - (c) Banning smartphones, iPad and most portable devices from school premises.
    - (d) (B) and (C)

18. **What does the phrase 'Social Networking Addiction' mean?**
    - (a) Stalking People Socially
    - (b) Creating Fake profiles for fun
    - (c) Finding your Friend Circle Online
    - (d) Someone who spends too much time on social websites

19. **Which of the below sentences summarizes the key idea of the passage?**
    - (a) The Psychology of Social Addiction
    - (b) The Addiction in Students
    - (c) The Science behind Addiction
    - (d) Beliefs of Scientists for Social Life

20. **Why is Oxytocin regarded as the cuddle chemical?**
    - (a) The brain releases pleasure chemicals that transpire usually when you kiss and hug- or tweet.
    - (b) It builds the strong yet unique bond between mothers and their babies.
    - (c) It produces the desire in people to "want" by drawing out the need for us to -seek and search.
    - (d) None of these

21. **Direction: Out of the four alternatives, choose the one which express the right meaning of the word.**
    Consolation
    - (a) Comfort
    - (b) Problem
    - (c) Sadness
    - (d) Solution

22. **In the following question, four words are given out of which one word is incorrectly spelt. Find the incorrectly spelt word.**
    - (a) Macabre
    - (b) Anachronistic
    - (c) Coalscade
    - (d) Panoply

23. **Four words are given, out of which only one word is spelled correctly. Choose the correctly spelt word.**
    - (a) Guarantee
    - (b) Guarenty
    - (c) Gurantee
    - (d) Garantee

24. **Direction : In the following question, out of the four alternatives, choose the alternative which best expresses the meaning of the idiom/Phrase.**
    We must work with all our might and main , otherwise we cannot succeed.
    - (a) Full force
    - (b) Complete trust
    - (c) Exceptional skill
    - (d) Full unity

25. **Directions : In the following question, sentences are given with blanks to be filled in with an appropriate word(s).**
    My younger sister constantly misbehaves and is always causing _____.
    - (a) hostility
    - (b) violence
    - (c) mischief
    - (d) courtesy

Ques (26-28): Direction: The following sentence is divided in to four parts. Any of the parts may contain an error. Select the part that has an error.

26. **Looking back I find that (a)/ among the many renditions of the Indians (b)/ engrossed while I lived among them are (c)/ their respect for great men and women (d).**
    - (a) (a)
    - (b) (b)
    - (c) (c)
    - (d) (d)

27. **To expedite exports and enhance sales (a)/ in the indigenous market some (b)/ of the improvised fabrics and garments fabricated out from them (c)/ are displayed in the main dome (d).**
    - (a) (a)
    - (b) (b)
    - (c) (c)
    - (d) (d)

28. **He could not (a)/ convince them because (b)/ they persisted to suggest (c)/ that he was lying (d).**
    - (a) (a)
    - (b) (b)
    - (c) (c)
    - (d) (d)

Ques (29-31): Direction: Fill the blank given in the question with appropriate word.

29. **I_____ to go there when I was a student.**
    - (a) Liked
    - (b) Used
    - (c) Use
    - (d) Denied

30. **She was angry _____ me.**
    - (a) at
    - (b) about
    - (c) with
    - (d) in

31. **You should not laugh ____ the poor.**
    - (a) on
    - (b) at
    - (c) with
    - (d) over

Ques (32-33): Direction : In the following questions, a sentence is given with two blanks. You have to find the pair of words from the given options that fit both the blanks in the given order and make the sentence grammatically and contextually correct.

32. **It is now important for the central bank to _____ that the discipline in the system does not _____.**
    - (a) command, wrecked
    - (b) notice, week
    - (c) maintain, exist
    - (d) ensure, slacken

33. **It is possible that this piece of _____ is likely to be used against him by his electoral _____.**
    - (a) advice, clans
    - (b) information, rivals

(c) garbage, opponents   (d) paper, allies

34. **In the following question, any part of the sentence may have errors. Find out which part of the sentence has an error and select the appropriate option. If a sentence is free from error, select 'No Error'.**
I have watched many movies (1)/ of Rajnikanth's who is called the (2)/ Amitabh Bachchan of Tollywood. (3)/ No error
(a) 1   (b) 2
(c) 3   (d) No error

35. **In the following question, any part of the sentence may have errors. Find out which part of the sentence has an error and select the appropriate option. If a sentence is free from error, select 'No Error'.**
There are some people who believe (1)/ asking for government assistance is (2)/ akin with admitting one is a failure. (3)/ No error
(a) 1   (b) 2
(c) 3   (d) No error

Ques (36-40): Direction: In the following question two statements have been given with connectors given as options. You have to select that option which could connect both the sentences and make them grammatically and contextually correct.

36. **I. Higher interest rates make equity investments unattractive as it weighs on earnings growth.**
II. Higher interest rates lead to tightening of earnings yield spread over bond yields.
(a) Not only, besides   (b) Even though, for
(c) In addition, least   (d) Similarly, Otherwise

37. **I. Instead of confiscating all properties belonging to a fugitive economic offender, a prudent step would be to quantify the outstanding loan amount.**
II. Only those properties must be confiscated that have been acquired through proceeds of crime.
(a) Also, too   (b) Presently, finally
(c) Accordingly, hence   (d) Nearby, adjacent to

38. **I. GDP measures income but fails to measure poverty, income inequality, health and quality of life.**
II. GDP has become the single most important tool for Governments, financial institutions and policymakers since its inception in the 1930s.
(a) Nonetheless, Moreover
(b) Conversely, Thus
(c) In spite of this, for one thing
(d) Nevertheless, Although

39. **I. The GIFT City has already attracted close to $2 billion in real estate investment**
II. It is expected that this number could rise to nearly $11 billion.
(a) Afterwards, beforehand
(b) At some point, immediately
(c) Eventually, in time
(d) One day, even so

40. **I. Determining the sex of a fetus has been banned since 1994.**
II. Parents wanting sons have continued to find ways to abort girls.
a. Although
b. In spite of
c. Yet
d. Equally
(a) Only I   (b) Only I, III and IV
(c) Only I, II and IV   (d) Only I, II and III

41. **Direction: Choose the most appropriate meaning of the given idiom in bold.**
She's got the gift of gab , she should work in sales and marketing.
(a) Ability to work hard
(b) Ability to speak impressively
(c) In a good position
(d) At the top of

42. **Direction : Select the most appropriate meaning of the given idiom.**
Bad blood
(a) Ill feeling   (b) Poor quality
(c) Low status   (d) Hard luck

43. **Direction : Select the most appropriate meaning of the given idiom.**
Hold your horses
(a) Not get upset   (b) Aim high
(c) Fight trouble   (d) Slow down

44. **Direction: Select the most appropriate meaning of the given idiom.**
Over one's head
(a) something totally unexpected
(b) being at a disadvantage
(c) unable to function as before
(d) beyond one's capability to understand something

45. **Direction: Select the most appropriate meaning of the given idiom.**
Take exception
(a) appreciate   (b) object to
(c) care for   (d) deny

46. **Which of the following is an example of simile?**
(a) I wandered lonely as a cloud.
(b) Life is a dream.
(c) Anxiety is sitting on her face.
(d) A lie has no legs.

47. **Direction : Choose the most appropriate option that best explains the figure of speech in this line.**
In rivers the water that you touch is the last of what passed and the first of that which comes: so, with time present.
(a) Personification of the tangible and the intangible
(b) Simile that compares water and time
(c) Hyperbole that reveals elements of similarities
(d) Metaphysical analogy that divides time past from time future

48. **The number of pure vowels is:**
(a) 9   (b) 10
(c) 11   (d) 12

49. **The correct transcription of the word 'chain' is:**
(a) /cheɪn/   (b) /tʃeɪn/
(c) /tʃaːn/   (d) /chæn/

50. **The sounds of English have been divided into two parts:**
    (a) Vowel sounds and diphthongs.
    (b) Diphthongs and monophthongs.
    (c) Vowels and consonant sounds.
    (d) Short vowel and long vowels

// Smart Answer Sheet //

Correct Percentage of students who answered correctly.

Skipped Percentage of students who skipped.

Q.	Ans.	Correct / Skipped	Q.	Ans.	Correct / Skipped	Q.	Ans.	Correct / Skipped
1	A	84.53% / 0.0%	2	D	88.22% / 0.0%	3	C	46.24% / 1.27%
4	D	80.73% / 0.0%	5	D	47.32% / 1.17%	6	A	88.39% / 0.0%
7	B	85.97% / 0.0%	8	A	62.08% / 1.75%	9	D	77.73% / 0.0%
10	A	46.19% / 1.19%	11	C	83.97% / 0.0%	12	A	82.98% / 0.0%
13	C	53.45% / 1.08%	14	B	58.39% / 1.95%	15	D	80.52% / 0.0%
16	D	64.37% / 1.51%	17	D	68.18% / 1.84%	18	D	48.49% / 1.5%
19	A	86.17% / 0.0%	20	A	46.89% / 1.83%	21	A	63.45% / 1.98%
22	C	12.05% / 4.19%	23	A	76.01% / 0.0%	24	A	56.89% / 1.82%
25	C	78.86% / 0.0%	26	C	83.57% / 0.0%	27	C	59.17% / 1.91%
28	C	76.43% / 0.0%	29	B	89.65% / 0.0%	30	C	63.35% / 1.74%
31	B	56.93% / 2.0%	32	D	68.84% / 1.56%	33	B	65.95% / 1.2%
34	B	80.74% / 0.0%	35	C	50.24% / 1.86%	36	A	43.54% / 1.11%
37	C	56.15% / 1.58%	38	D	52.59% / 1.97%	39	C	66.39% / 1.55%
40	D	55.09% / 1.1%	41	B	59.36% / 1.86%	42	A	16.02% / 3.84%
43	D	61.48% / 1.13%	44	D	55.69% / 1.3%	45	B	63.95% / 1.64%
46	A	45.98% / 1.07%	47	D	51.4% / 1.61%	48	D	56.34% / 1.01%
49	B	66.54% / 1.9%	50	C	55.0% / 1.06%			

// Hints and Solutions //

1(A). According to the passage, "Continuing on the current path, will bring rising economic and social costs''.

From the above sentence, we can say that according to the passage , China's ''zero-covid'' will bring rising economic and social costs .

2(D). In the fourth part of the given sentence, the singular form of the noun 'parent' is incorrect.
- In the given sentence, the pronoun 'their' is a plural possessive pronoun.
- We know that a plural pronoun always takes a plural noun .
- The plural form of the noun ' parents ' should be used with the plural possessive pronoun 'their' .
- Therefore, the plural form of the noun ' parents ' should be used in place of the singular form of the noun 'parent' .

3(C). The second-last sentence of the first paragraph says '' The crisis has now ignited a debate on whether this strategy that enabled China to avoid a major second wave, still remains relevant when much of the rest of the world has returned to some form of normalcy thanks to vaccines '', the second-last sentence of the second paragraph says '' Rather than trumpet zero COVID and criticize living with the virus as irresponsible, China would be better served looking at the examples of countries that have successfully opened up and followed the science, as in Singapore, which aggressively vaccinated its population and incentivized it to do so by setting a timetable for opening '' and the last sentence of the passage concludes " Otherwise, as the continued suffering in Shanghai has shown, the cure risks becoming worse than the disease ".

From the above sentences, we can say that the central theme of the passage is '' The cure risks becoming worse than the disease in China ''.

4(D). The antonyms of the word ' Stringent ' is "Lenient".
Stringent: The word 'Stringent' means Not allowing for any exceptions or loosening of standards; very strict.
Example: Stringent safety regulations were introduced after the accident .
L enient - More merciful or tolerant than expected; not as strict as expected.
Example: The police are sometimes more lenient with female offenders .

5(D). The first paragraph says "The government has struggled to supply every household with daily necessities, with the supply chain paralyzed by China's stringent measures under which every COVID-19 case, even if asymptomatic, is confined in government-run quarantine facilities'' And first paragraph says "Many have said they are running out of medicines''.

From the above sentences, we can say that statements A and B are correct according to the given passage.

The first paragraph says "The government has struggled to supply every household with daily necessities, with the supply chain paralyzed by China's stringent measures under which every COVID-19 case, even if asymptomatic, is confined in government-run quarantine facilities''.

From the above sentence, we can say that statement C is incorrect according to the given passage.

6(A). The synonyms of the word ' Hesitancy ' is "Reluctance .
Hesitancy : The word 'Hesitancy' means A lack of willingness or desire to do or accept something.
Example: I noticed a certain hesitancy in his voice .
Reluctance : Unwillingness or disinclination to do something.
Example: He showed great reluctance to reveal his whereabouts .

7(B). According to the passage, statement (A) & (B) are true. "The havoc the october super cyclone caused in Orissa could have been avoided had its mangrove forests not been destroyed to develop shrimp forms." The given statement (C) is false.

8(A). As per the passage, the destruction of the mangrove forests cannot be attributed to below given activities.
(1) The development of shrimp forms.
(2) Unbridled human activity
(3) Economic activities
Waves and tidal surges can't be attributed to the destruction of the mangrove forests.

9(D). According to the passage, the emergence of megacities along the sea is seen as the single greatest threat to the world's coastal environment.

10(A). According to the para (5) management are flowering plants, which grow on tidal coasts between the high and low water marks in clay & silt. They possess unusual "Prop and knee" root system which enables them to trap sediments in their roots and provide the seabed a shallow slope. This helps it to absorb the energy of waves and tidal surges, and acts as a shield for hinterland. The trees themselves form a barrier against wind.

We can conclude that it supports statement (a), (b) & (c) and does not support statement (d).

11(C). The word 'Incoming' is an adjective. Britannica dictionary definition of incoming always used before a noun, Coming in Such as a arriving at as coming to a place.

Synonym of 'incoming' word-Arriving, entering, approaching, coming.

12(A). The similar meaning of the word 'unbridled' is uncontrolled.
Meaning of the given words:
- Unbridled - not controlled and therefore extreme
- Uncontrolled - not controlled
- Undesired - not wanted or desired
- Unexpected - not expected and therefore causing surprise
- Unforeseen - not expected

13(C). In the given sentence, part (C) has an error, as 'between' should be used in place of among because this sentence talks about only two thing-between the high & low water.
Among: Among is used for more than two things.

14(B). According to the passage, "Facebook is the most common activity that university students switch to when studying." Hence, the correct option is (B)

15(D). According to the passage, "There is no official medical term that identifies addiction and social networking because it cannot be deemed as a disease or disorder as cases are not severe and the habit can easily be maintained or prevented."

16(D). The meaning of the given words:
- Contagiously: (an emotion, feeling, or attitude) likely to spread to and affect others
- Malignant: very virulent or infectious
- Assail: to criticize strongly
- Ambivalent: having mixed feelings or contradictory ideas about something or someone
- Arboreal: related to trees
- Cogent: clear, logical, and convincing

From the meanings of the given words, we can conclude that Malignant is the most appropriate synonym of contagiously.

17(D). According to the passage, "Schools in many westernized countries have had to take drastic action- banning smartphones, iPad, and most portable devices from school premises- as it is claimed to be a huge distraction. Whereas, other schools use it for educational purposes and as a rewards system for their pupils."

18(D). 'Social Networking Addiction' mean someone who spends too much time on social websites.

19(A). The passage can be divided into four subheadings:
- It begins with the Science behind Social Addiction talking about how it interferes with the basic aspects of our life.
- It continues telling that there is no medical term that

identifies addiction and social networking.
- Furthermore, it talks about Dopamine and Oxytocin and how they contribute to social media addiction.
- The passage ends with a brief discussion of addiction in students nowadays.

Thus, all these subsections can be put together into one major heading which would be 'The Psychology of Social Addiction'.

20(A). According to the passage, "Many call it the cuddle chemical because the brain releases pleasure chemicals that transpire usually when you kiss and hug- or tweet."

So, it is concluded that oxytocin regarded as the cuddle chemical because the brain releases pleasure chemicals that transpire usually when you kiss and hug- or tweet.

21(A). Consolation means 'cthe comfort received by a person after a loss or disappointment,' so 'comfort' is the correct option.

For example, Here is a new philosophy of life, offering solid consolation amid the ruin of a world.

22(C). Here, option C is incorrectly spelt. Its correct spelling is coalesced.

Let's find out the meaning of the following words:-
Coalesced - come together to form one mass or whole; unite; join together.
Macabre - Being disturbed because concerned with or causing fear of death; horrific; horrible.
Anachronistic - belonging or appropriate to an earlier period.
Panoply - an extensive or impressive collection.

24(A). all our might and main means :With as much effort or strength as one can muster.

25(C). My younger sister constantly misbehaves and is always causing **mischief**.

26(C). The verb should be 'is' because it refers to one impression.

27(C). In the second part of the sentence replace "out from" by 'with'.
With is used in the company of somebody/something; in or to the same place as somebody/something.

28(C). Here in part (c) we replace persisted to suggest, it should be "persisted in suggesting".

29(B). 'Use to' is used when any habit is to be shown.
Here, in the sentence, the narrator had a daily habit to go somewhere he is referring to.
Complete sentence: I used to go there when I was a student.

30(C). 'Angry' agrees with the preposition 'with', because generally, we are angry with someone.
Complete sentence: She was angry with me.

31(B). Laugh agrees with the preposition 'at'.
Grammatically 'laugh at someone' is the correct phrasal verb, when we are referring to a person.
Complete sentence: You should not laugh at the poor.

32(D). It is now important for the central bank to **ensure** that the discipline in the system does not **slacken**.
In option A, "wrecked" is grammatically incorrect because it uses the past participle form of verb as well as does not fit the context.
In option B, week is contextually incorrect.
In option C, "exist" is exactly opposite to what is being required. RBI is a governing authority and it would try to maintain discipline rather than removing it.

Both the words of option D suit the context as well as fulfill the grammar rules.

33(B). It is possible that this piece of **information** is likely to be used against him by his electoral **rivals** .
Clans means group of kin, which is simply not related to the context. Thus option A is eliminated.
Any information can be misused by the opponents only, thus both the words of option B absolutely fit to the blanks.
In option C, garbage is completely wrong.
In option D, allies is just opposite to the context, allies means friends, which will not do anything against him.

34(B). "Rajnikanth" will come instead of "Rajnikanth's" because in the sentences which have the construction like "Many + Noun + of ", we don't use an apostrophe. So, the correct sentence is,
I have watched many movies of Rajinikanth who is called the Amitabh Bachchan of Tollywood.

35(C). 'Akin' is always used with the preposition 'to' instead of 'with'. So, the correct sentence is,
There are some people who believe asking for government assistance is akin to admitting one is a failure.

36(A). Both the statements talk about the effects of the same thing i.e., higher interest rates. We need connectors that can portray this relationship.
Only option (A) fits in well:
I. Not only do higher interest rates make equity investments unattractive as it weighs on earnings growth, they lead to tightening of earnings yield spread over bond yields.
II. Higher interest rates make equity investments unattractive as it weighs on earnings growth besides tightening of earnings yield spread over bond yields.

37(C). Statement I talks about a situation while statement B talks about dealing with it in an appropriate manner.
Only Option (C) fits in:
I. Instead of confiscating all properties belonging to a fugitive economic offender, a prudent step would be to quantify the outstanding loan amount and accordingly, only those properties must be confiscated that have been acquired through proceeds of crime.
II. Instead of confiscating all properties belonging to a fugitive economic offender, a prudent step would be to quantify the outstanding loan amount and hence, only those properties must be confiscated that have been acquired through proceeds of crime.

38(D). The two statements above are contradicting in nature and hence need the correct connectors to convey this relationshiop.
Only option (D) fits in:
I. GDP measures income but fails to measure poverty, income inequality, health and quality of life nevertheless, GDP has become the single most important tool for Governments, financial institutions and policymakers since its inception in the 1930s.
II. Although GDP has become the single most important tool for Governments, financial institutions and policymakers since its inception in the 1930s, it measures income but fails to measure poverty, income inequality, health and quality of life.

39(C). Both the statements talk about the same subject over a different time period- present and future. We need appropriate connectors to depict this.
Only option (C) fits in:

The GIFT City has already attracted close to $2 billion in real estate investment and eventually, it is expected that this number could rise to nearly $11 billion.

40(D). Both statements convey contradicting points.
Equally does not fit in here as it is used where the statements complement each othet.
The other connectors fit in well and are used to convey contradicting things.
I. Although determining the sex of a fetus has been banned since 1994, parents wanting sons have continued to find ways to abort girls.
II. In spite of determining the sex of a fetus being banned since 1994, parents wanting sons have continued to find ways to abort girls.
III. Determining the sex of a fetus has been banned since 1994 yet, parents wanting sons have continued to find ways to abort girls.

41(B). Gift of the gab means ability to speak impressively.
The ability to speak easily and confidently in a way that makes people want to listen to you and believe you.

42(A). The ill feeling is the most appropriate meaning of the given idiom.
Bad blood - Ill feeling (Bitterness)
• There's been a lot of bad blood between them since their quarrel.
• There's been bad blood between the two families for years.

43(D). Slow down the most appropriate meaning of the given idiom.
Don't get mad: Not get upset
Aim high: to be ambitious
Example: Just hold your horses, Bill! Let's think about this for a moment.

44(D). The most appropriate meaning of the given idiom is "beyond one's capability to understand something".
Over someone's head: without someone's knowledge or involvement, especially when they have a right to it.
Example: He went over his supervisor's head to complain to the company's president about the policy.

45(B). The most appropriate meaning of the given idiom is "object to".
Take exception: Disagree with, object to, or to be offended or made angry by something or someone.
Example: Why did you take exception to what he said? He was only joking.

46(A). The correct answer is "I wandered lonely as a cloud".
Simile means a figure of speech involving the comparison of one thing with another thing of a different kind, used to make a description more emphatic or vivid.
From the given options, only in the first option the comparison of "wandered lonely" has been done with "cloud".

47(D). In the given line, there exists an analogy between an idea or a thought and an object in the physical world. Such an analogy is called Metaphysical analogy. Here, a relationship exists between time and river. Thus, the metaphysical analogy that divides past time from future time.

48(D). Pure vowels are also called as monophthong. It's pronunciation is fixed from the beginning till the end and it do not glide to new position of articulation. The 12 pure vowels are /iː/, /ɪ/, /ʊ/, /uː/, /e/, /ə/, /ɜː/, /ɔː/, /æ/, /ʌ/, /ɑː/ and /ɒ/.

49(B). Transcription of the word 'chain' is /tʃeɪn/, here, it can be seen that 'ch' in the word 'chain' is represented as 'tʃ' and 'ai' is represented as 'eɪ' because the phonetic symbol 'eɪ' is a diphthong and used whenever there is a sound of 'ey', 'ay', or 'ai'. For. e.g. train, say, plane, etc.

50(C). The sounds of English have been divided into two parts: Vowels and consonant sounds.

Ques (1-7): Direction: Read the passage carefully and answer the questions given beside it.

India is blessed with an extraordinary richness of life. A myriad of unusual and exquisite species occur in the countless ecosystems spread across our vast lands, rivers, and oceans. Woven into this rich fabric of biodiversity is a stunningly vibrant and colorful tapestry of peoples, cultures, and traditions. This unique bio-cultural tapestry has been resilient to change for centuries, but with the unleashing of unprecedented economic and environmental forces, it is now subject to increasing wear and tear. Ultimately, these forces could even destroy our tapestry of life, cultures, and traditions — and in the process, ourselves.

Biologists all over the world have been documenting the ongoing loss of life forms. Modern extinction rates are more than a thousand times greater than the rates of the geological past. We have entered what scientists are calling the Anthropocene era — a new period in earth's history when humans have begun to impact our environment on a global scale. We have seen our forests degrade and diminish, our rivers vanish, and our air becomes unfit to breathe. We constantly talk about cleaning up the Ganga, as if it were the sole festering wound, but we overlook that the whole tapestry covering our body is slowly disintegrating. All life requires nurturing.

To protect life on earth, the famous American biologist E.O. Wilson has described an ambitious project he calls "Half-Earth". He calls for formally protecting 50% of the earth's land surface in order to conserve our rapidly disappearing natural heritage. Others have rightly argued that in the past conservation efforts have often disregarded issues of social justice and equity. Thus the goals of "Half-Earth" should not compromise the rights of indigenous people.

Clearly, we must do more to safeguard biodiversity and the ecosystem services that support all human endeavors. India's forest policy calls for forests to cover almost a third of the country, and if we include other natural systems such as grasslands and wetlands, the area to be protected could amount to almost 40%. In a populous country such as ours, that would be a huge achievement. Some areas could be fully protected while others might be managed by stakeholders for sustainable use and enrichment of biodiversity. We need a massive new effort to catalog, map, and monitor life, using fundamentally different approaches. Current efforts to map India's biodiversity are largely restricted to forestlands, while plans for species monitoring are even more inadequate. We have the digital tools and artificial intelligence today to efficiently catalog, map, and monitor life's fabric in a manner never before attempted — and with the potential engagement of millions of students and citizens. This mapping effort would include not only all life, including cultures, ethnicities, and dialects but also the use of biodiversity and its vulnerability to changes in land use and climate.

Cataloging, mapping, and monitoring life will give us a glimpse of what we have, and what is most vulnerable. But how do we reconcile the growing needs of society with the need to sustain our vanishing natural heritage? We still have only the most basic understanding of how society interacts with biodiversity, and how economic, social, and political forces can erode the biodiversity that ultimately sustains us. We are just beginning to learn how myriad species interact to drive our ecosystems, and how these systems in turn maintain our soils, water, and breathable air. Wild pollinators, the microbiota of soils, and the many enemies of agricultural pests — these and many other natural services underpin our agricultural productivity and mitigate climate change.

1. Which of the following is/are true with respect to the passage?

I. Nowhere on Earth is natural and human systems tied together more inextricably than on the Indian subcontinent.

II. Several non-government think tanks in the civil society sector have strong interdisciplinary programs in environmental sustainability in India.

III. It has been observed that conservation efforts have often focused on issues of social justice and equity.

(a) Only I
(b) Only III
(c) Only I and II
(d) None of the above

2. Which of the following is the main idea conveyed by paragraph 1?

(a) Life is a unique asset of our planet.
(b) India is the only nation to have a unique bio-cultural tapestry.
(c) The unique environmental and cultural mix in India has been static for centuries.
(d) Unparalleled economic forces are causing a lot of damage to India - a land of biocultural diversity.

3. Which of the following is/are example/s of the 'loss of life forms' mentioned in paragraph 2?

I. Population of 40% of large mammals has declined.

II. Huge number of whales dying due to ingesting plastic bags.

III. Natural habitats all over the world have shrunk.

(a) Only I
(b) Only II
(c) Only I and III
(d) All of the above

4. Which of the following is/are true with respect to the Anthropocene Era mentioned in the passage?

I. Both marine and continental faunas are essentially modern but with many more large land mammals such as Mammoths etc.

II. Human beings have started to have a huge impact on the Earth.

III. It covers most of the latest period of repeated glaciation, up to and including the Younger Dryas cold spell.

(a) Only II
(b) Only III
(c) Only I and II
(d) Only II and III

5. As per the passage, what is meant by 'Half-Earth'?

(a) It is when the capacity of Earth to sustain life would become half of what it was when it was formed.
(b) It is the time when half of Earth would become unsuitable for living and life would face mass extinction.
(c) It is a project which would involve protecting about half of Earth's land to conserve natural heritage.
(d) It is a project which would ensure the Oceans of the world are made habitable for humans in the foreseeable future.

6. As per the passage, what is/are some flaws in the current efforts to map India's biodiversity?

I. They are mainly restricted to forestlands and other natural systems that are not fully catered to.

II. The monitoring of species is insufficient.

III. There is a lack of digital tools and artificial intelligence.

(a) Only I
(b) Only I and II
(c) Only II and III
(d) Only III

7. Why is it difficult to reconcile the needs of society with

the need to sustain our natural heritage?

(a) We do not yet possess an understanding of the intricacies of how species, biodiversity, and society interact with each other.

(b) Our institutions need to place far more emphasis on the scientific study of life at higher levels.

(c) We lack a comprehensive inquiry into how our society is shaping as well as responding to changes in biodiversity.

(d) In many of our academic institutions, the 'Life Sciences' are still restricted largely to the study of cells and molecules — life at microscopic and submicroscopic levels.

Ques (8-13): Directions: Read the passage given below and answer the questions that follow by selecting the most appropriate options:

Your attitudes are the perspectives from which you view life. Some people seem to have a good attitude towards most things. Some people seem to have a bad attitude towards everything. But when you look closer, you will find that most of us have a combination of attitudes, some good, some not so good.

Whatever attitude we have towards anything will affect how we feel about it, which in turn determines whether or not we will do well. So our right attitudes play a very important part in helping us become successful.

In fact, as we can see, a good attitude is essential for achievement of any kind ! We so often hear of someone who is said to have a "bad attitude". The term is often applied to young people, especially to teenagers who frequently get into trouble, but we often hear it about adults, too. The implication is always that the individual in question is not going to make it if he doesn't change his attitude.

I would agree, without a good attitude it is not possible to see the opportunities ahead and set one's sights to reach them. But even more important is the fact that in order to possess the kind of feelings which work for us, we've got to have the right attitude to start with.

But where do we get our attitudes from? Are we born with them or do they just appear out of nowhere? Our attitudes are no accident. They don't just happen. Our attitudes are created and influenced entirely by our beliefs.

8. The term "bad attitude" is used for young people because they:

(a) defy all kinds of authority.

(b) behave irresponsibly.

(c) often get into difficulty.

(d) are unpredictable.

9. Right attitudes are absolutely essential to:

(a) succeed in life.

(b) win the goodwill of our peers and superiors.

(c) have harmonious relations with others.

(d) promote our mental well-being.

10. Which one of the following statements is correct?

(a) We are born with our attitudes.

(b) Our attitudes are influenced by our parents only.

(c) Our attitudes are created and controlled by our beliefs.

(d) Our attitudes are the results of our personal experience.

11. The word 'determine' most nearly means:

(a) govern   (b) influence

(c) overcome   (d) engage

12. Which part of speech is the underlined word in the sentence given below?

'Some people seem to have a good attitude <u>towards</u> most things.'

(a) Adverb   (b) Preposition

(c) Adjective   (d) Conjunction

13. A/An ______ attitude is absolutely necessary for attainment of any kind.

(a) virtuous   (b) cheerful

(c) optimistic   (d) good

Ques (14-20): Directions: Read the passage given below and answer the questions that follow by choosing the correct/most appropriate options:

Freedom is one of the most important factors in life. Man has fought politically for freedom all over the world. religions have promised freedom, not in this world but in another. In the capitalist countries, individual freedom exists to some degree, and in the communist world it has been denied. From ancient times freedom has meant a great deal to man, and there have been its opponents, not only political but religious- through the Inquisition, by excommunication, tortures and banishments, and the total denial of man's search for freedom. There have been wars and counter-wars fought for freedom. This has been the pattern of man's endeavours for freedom throughout history.

Freedom of self-expression and freedom of speech and thought exists in some parts of the world, but in others it does not. Those who have been conditioned revolt against their backgrounds, and react in immature ways. This reaction, which takes different forms, is called "freedom". The reaction to politics is often to shun the field of politics.

One economic reaction is to form small communities based on some ideology or under the leadership of some one person, in which authority is denied and an attempt is made to be self-supporting, but these generally disintegrate. The religious reaction against established organizations of belief is to revolt, either by joining other religious organizations or by following some guru or leader or by joining some cult or one denies the whole religious endeavour.

One thinks of freedom only as freedom of movement, either physical or movements of thought. It appears that one always seeks freedom on the surface. Surely, this is rather a limited freedom, involving a great deal of conflict, wars and violence. Inner freedom is something entirely different. It has its roots not in the idea of freedom but in the reality of freedom. It covers all the endeavours of man. Without inner freedom life will always be an activity within the limited circle of time and conflict.

14. Which methods do authorities not use to suppress people fighting for freedom?

(a) Inquisition   (b) Excommunication

(c) Persuasion   (d) Tortures

15. Real freedom, according to the author, is:

(a) economic freedom   (b) inner freedom

(c) political freedom   (d) religious freedom

16. Read the following sentences:

A. Individual freedom does not exist at all in capitalist countries.

B. People do not have individual freedom in communist countries.

(a) A is false, B is true   (b) A is true, B is false

(c) Both A and B are true   (d) Both A and B are false

17. Which word is most similar in meaning to the word 'endeavours' as used in the passage ? (Para 1)

(a) movements   (b) attempts

(c) actions   (d) challenges

18. Which word is the most opposite in meaning to the word, 'shun' as used in the passage ? (Para 2)
- (a) prefer
- (b) rehabilitate
- (c) welcome
- (d) rejoice

19. Which part of the following sentence contains an error? There is no doubt(a)/ that hard work (b)/ paves the way(c)/ to success(d)
- (a) (d)
- (b) (a)
- (c) (b)
- (d) (c)

20. Which of the following statements is not true?
- (a) Man can enjoy life only in an environment of freedom
- (b) Material progress cannot be achieved without freedom
- (c) Freedom is not one of the most important factors in life
- (d) Freedom helps man evolve morally and spiritually

21. Direction : In the following question, out of the four options, select the option which is the best substitute of the phrase given below-
Average in amount or quality.
- (a) Moderate
- (b) Supernatant
- (c) Hobble
- (d) Hum

22. Select the correctly spelt word.
- (a) Cleaver
- (b) Centiment
- (c) Taelant
- (d) Serenity

23. Select the incorrectly spelt word.
- (a) Inefficent
- (b) Independence
- (c) Influence
- (d) Inequality

24. Direction: Select the most appropriate word for the given group of words.
Persons working at the same place
- (a) Fellows
- (b) Colleagues
- (c) Contemporaries
- (d) Homogeneous

25. Direction: Select the most appropriate word for the given group of words.
A wooden drum in which beer or oil is stored
- (a) Cache
- (b) Gale
- (c) Bale
- (d) Barrel

26. Compounding is:
- (a) stringing together older words like the formation of earthquake from earth and quake.
- (b) removing seeming affixes from existing words, such as forming edit from editor.
- (c) joining parts of two or more older words, such as forming smog, which comes from smoke and fog.
- (d) forming new words from existing ones by adding affixes to them, like shame + less + ness →shamelessness

27. Examples of irregular verbs are:
- (a) break - broke
- (b) train - trainer
- (c) walk - walked
- (d) happy - happier

28. The following is a conditional sentence-
- (a) I have to go to work
- (b) If the sea is stormy, the waves are high
- (c) Shut, the door
- (d) It's a sunny day, isn't it?

Ques (29-30): Direction: In the following question, out of the four alternatives, select the alternative which is the best substitute for the phrase.

29. Put off for a future time
- (a) Codify
- (b) Reticent
- (c) Procrastinate
- (d) Retaliate

30. Greedy for money
- (a) Agnostic
- (b) Rapacious
- (c) Oblation
- (d) Celibacy

Ques (31-33): Directions: Identify the segment of the sentence given below that contains error(s). If no segment of the sentence has the error(s), please choose 'No improvement'

31. If he is not prepared, he will badly perform in the exam
- (a) If he is not prepared,
- (b) he will badly perform
- (c) in the exam
- (d) No improvement

32. If I was the Prime Minister, I would abolish red-tapism
- (a) If I was the Prime Minister,
- (b) I would abolish
- (c) red-tapism
- (d) No improvement

33. The employee as well as his colleagues were present
- (a) The employee as well as
- (b) his colleagues
- (c) were present
- (d) No improvement

Ques (34-37): Direction: The following sentence in this section has a blank space and four words or group of words are given after the sentence. Select the most appropriate word or group of words for the blank space. and indicate your response accordingly.

34. Abhishek's first _________ is to find a place to live.
- (a) Prior
- (b) Priority
- (c) Possess
- (d) Pause

35. Rahul will be given a reading test at the time of ______.
- (a) Sponsor
- (b) Engage
- (c) Enrollment
- (d) Encourage

36. Virat Kohli is a talented and _______ player.
- (a) Compound
- (b) Catchy
- (c) Conflict
- (d) Composed

37. S.C Bore was _________ as the president of the Congress Party in 1939.
- (a) Selected
- (b) Praised
- (c) Elected
- (d) Nominated

Ques (38-40): Direction: In the given question, a sentence has been broken into four parts and the parts are jumbled. Choose the option which provides the correct way to re-arrange the parts to form a grammatically and contextually meaningful sentence.

38. where the river meets the sea 1 / that are carried downstream 2 / by rivers and eventually deposited 3 / deltas are built from sediments 4.
- (a) 3421
- (b) 3214
- (c) 4231
- (d) 4132

39. An imbalanced consumerist culture spawned 1 / Buddha believed that self-sufficient local communities 2 / by those who believe that bigger is better. 3 / would serve the purpose much better than 4.
- (a) 2134
- (b) 2413

(c) 3142   (d) 4321

40. **She filled out a simple online form. 1 / until curiosity got the best of her and 2 / she would work online 3 / she never thought that 4.**
(a) 4321   (b) 4231
(c) 4132   (d) 4213

Ques (41-45): Direction : Below the idiom/phrase is followed by four alternative meanings. Choose the most appropriate meaning from these and mark your answer.

41. **Bolt from the blue**
(a) An event or piece of news which is unexpected
(b) Desirable event or news
(c) An event which takes place as planned
(d) News which has been long expected, but arrives late

42. **Run wild**
(a) To run like a wild animal
(b) To treat anyone like a wild creature
(c) To feel like a wild animal
(d) To behave without any control

43. **Take something with a "grain of salt"**
(a) Taking something under consideration
(b) Taking responsibility to maintain privacy
(c) Not taking something too seriously
(d) Not taking something easily

44. **Achilles heel**
(a) Runaway
(b) Soft feet
(c) A small problem or weakness in a person or system that can result in failure
(d) Walk slowly

45. **To have an axe to grind**
(a) A private end to serve   (b) To fail to arouse interest
(c) To have no result   (d) To work for both sides

Ques (46-47): Direction: Observe the following sentences where some changes are made in the sentence but keeping the sense of the sentence same. In the following questions, the sentences have some element of similarity.

46. **You have to find out the similarity and choose the option which is odd one out.**
(a) His behaviour displeased his officers. His officers were displeased at his behaviour.
(b) One must respect one's elders. One's elders must be respected.
(c) I said, "Do not speak of the past." I advised him not to speak of the past.
(d) A crash radio message was handed over to me. They handed over a crash radio message to me.

47. **You have to find out the similarity and choose the option which is odd one out.**
(a) I don't expect to see him back here. I don't expect that I will see him back here.
(b) In spite of his poverty, he is satisfied. He is poor but he is satisfied.
(c) He gave them not only food but some money also. Besides food, he gave him some money also.
(d) Escaping arrest, he ran away. He ran away in order to escape arrest.

48. **Which of the Following does not have O sound?**
(a) Put   (b) Wood
(c) Boot   (d) Could

49. **Which of the following does not have / ia / sound?**
(a) Near   (b) Deer
(c) Ear   (d) Pray

50. **Which of the following contains the words beginning with the same consonant sound?**
(a) charm-choice   (b) Church-chemistry
(c) Cheap - keep   (d) ship - chip

// Smart Answer Sheet //

Correct — Percentage of students who answered correctly.

Skipped — Percentage of students who skipped.

Q.	Ans.	Correct / Skipped	Q.	Ans.	Correct / Skipped	Q.	Ans.	Correct / Skipped
1	D	16.32% / 3.62%	2	D	25.54% / 3.59%	3	D	13.7% / 3.26%
4	A	19.89% / 4.62%	5	C	25.82% / 4.62%	6	B	18.88% / 3.18%
7	A	15.22% / 4.4%	8	C	50.85% / 1.67%	9	A	54.71% / 1.52%
10	C	63.75% / 1.52%	11	B	47.92% / 1.42%	12	B	12.78% / 3.82%
13	D	45.28% / 1.3%	14	C	50.84% / 1.41%	15	B	62.5% / 1.26%
16	A	67.11% / 1.92%	17	B	66.61% / 1.75%	18	C	53.32% / 1.13%
19	A	53.46% / 1.8%	20	C	77.96% / 0.0%	21	A	58.32% / 1.46%
22	D	45.44% / 1.43%	23	A	79.21% / 0.0%	24	B	69.27% / 1.89%
25	D	85.23% / 0.0%	26	C	48.86% / 1.86%	27	A	26.18% / 4.42%
28	B	46.36% / 1.12%	29	C	47.53% / 1.07%	30	B	49.28% / 1.78%
31	B	49.69% / 1.83%	32	A	43.23% / 1.13%	33	C	41.7% / 1.47%
34	B	56.01% / 1.51%	35	C	85.65% / 0.0%	36	D	59.08% / 1.27%
37	C	50.21% / 1.03%	38	C	47.94% / 1.52%	39	B	45.45% / 1.14%
40	A	50.31% / 1.54%	41	A	60.58% / 1.48%	42	D	42.5% / 1.99%
43	C	45.2% / 1.42%	44	C	55.66% / 1.82%	45	A	43.84% / 1.84%
46	C	66.76% / 1.24%	47	A	80.65% / 0.0%	48	C	57.21% / 1.26%
49	D	50.92% / 1.88%	50	A	58.96% / 1.35%			

// Hints and Solutions //

1(D). Refer to: ' In the past conservation efforts have often disregarded issues of social justice and equity . Thus the goals of "Half-Earth" should not compromise the rights of indigenous people.'
Statements I and II have not been mentioned in the passage anywhere while statement III is the opposite of what has been stated in the passage.
None of the statements are correct.

2(D). Option (D) is correct. Here, the paragraph has been neatly summarized by picking up the main points of India being a rich nation in terms of ecology and culture but the same being affected by relentless economic forces.
Option (A) cannot be the main idea as the paragraph does not talk about 'life' as such.
Option (B) is incorrect as although only India is being talked about, it is not enough to conclude that it is the only nation to have a 'unique bio-cultural tapestry.'
Option (C) is incorrect as the paragraph merely mentions that biocultural diversity has been resilient to changes. Also, it is not the main idea expressed.

3(D). All the statements convey the fact that 'life forms' are suffering and decreasing due to human activities.
III is correct as it directly causes the extinction of species.

4(A). Refer to: 'We have entered what scientists are calling the Anthropocene era — a new period in earth's history when humans have begun to impact our environment at the global scale.'
Only II is correct while I and III have not been mentioned in the passage.

5(C). Refer to: 'To protect life on earth, the famous American biologist E.O. Wilson has described an ambitious project he calls "Half-Earth". He calls for formally protecting 50% of the earth's land surface in order to conserve our rapidly disappearing natural heritage.'
Out of all the options, option (C) is the best fit. The rest are clearly incorrect.

6(B). Refer to: '.Current efforts to map India's biodiversity are largely restricted to forestlands, while plans for species monitoring are even more inadequate. We have the digital tools and artificial intelligence today to efficiently catalog, map, and monitor life's fabric in a manner never before attempted — and with the potential engagement of millions of students and citizens.'
As per the highlighted fragments, only I and II can be seen. III is the opposite of what the passage mentions and is incorrect.

7(A). Refer to: 'But how do we reconcile the growing needs of society with the need to sustain our vanishing natural heritage? We still have only the most basic understanding of how society interacts with biodiversity, and how economic, social, and political forces can erode the biodiversity that ultimately sustains us. We are just beginning to learn how myriad species interact to drive our ecosystems, and how these systems in turn maintain our soils, water, and breathable air. Wild pollinators, the microbiota of soils, and the many enemies of agricultural pests — these and many other natural services underpin our agricultural productivity and mitigate climate change.'
The entire highlighted fragment showcases that we do not have an adequate understanding of how everything is correlated. Option (A) is the best fit here.
Option (C) is close but incorrect as it focuses more on society and how it changes with respect to biodiversity but does not answer why it is difficult to reconcile the needs of society with the need to sustain our natural heritage.

8(C). From the passage, it can be inferred that t he term "bad attitude" is used for young people because they often get into difficulty.

9(A). From the passage, it can be inferred that r ight attitudes are absolutely essential to succeed in life.

10(C). From the passage, it can be inferred that "Our attitudes are created and controlled by our beliefs." is the correct statement.

11(B). The word 'determine' most nearly means 'influence'. 'Determine' means to control or influence something directly, or to decide what will happen.

12(B). 'Towards' is a preposition which means in the direction of, or closer to someone or something. In our sentence, 'towards' is used before the noun 'things' and connects 'things' (the noun) to the people with good attitude.

13(D). A good attitude is absolutely necessary for attainment of any kind.

14(C). Persuasion method is not used by authorities to suppress people fighting for freedom. It is mentioned that "From ancient times, freedom has meant a great deal to man, and there have been its opponents, not only political but religious through Inquisition, by excommunication, tortures and banishments, and the total denial of man's search for freedom."

15(B). Real freedom, according to the author, is inner freedom. It is mentioned that "Inner freedom is something entirely different. It has its roots not in the idea of freedom but in the reality of freedom. It covers all the endeavours of man."

16(A). It is mentioned that "In the capitalist countries, individual freedom exists to some degree, and in the communist world it has been denied." It can clearly be deduced that statement A is false and statement B is true.

17(B). Attempts is most similar in meaning to the word 'endeavours' as used in the passage.

18(C). Shun means persistently avoid, ignore, or reject (someone or something) through antipathy or caution whereas p refer means like (one thing or person) better than another or others. So prefer is the opposite in meaning to the word, 'shun.

19(A). Part (d) of the sentence, contains an error. The use of the preposition 'to' in part (d) is incorrect. It should be replaced by 'for' in order to indicate that for which thing hard work paves the way.

20(C). It is mentioned that "Freedom is one of the most important factors in life." All other options are given in the comprehension.

21(A). Moderate means average in amount, intensity, quality, or degree.
Average in amount or quality is Moderate.

22(D). Option (D) has the correctly spelt word. 'Serenity' meaning 'the state of being calm, peaceful, and untroubled'.
The correct spelling of other words along with their meanings:
Clever = mentally quick and resourceful
Sentiment = tender, romantic, or nostalgic feeling or emotion
Talent = a person who possesses unusual innate ability in some field or activity

23(A). The wrongly spelt word is given in option (A). The correct word is inefficient which means lacking skills.
Independence means freedom.
Influence means charm or tempt.
Inequality means lacking equality.

24(B). Fellows means associate or companion.

Colleague means an associate that one works with.
Contemporaries means people living at the same time or generation.
Homogeneous means same kind or consistent.

25(D). Cache is a secret store of valuables or money.
Gale means an outburst of laughter.
Bale means a large bundle bound for storage or transport.
Barrel is a cylindrical container that holds liquids.
Therefore, out of all the options, option (D) is the most appropriate word for the given group of words.

26(C). Compounding is joining parts of two or more older words, such as forming smog, which comes from smoke and fog.
Compounding: This process involves combining two or more existing words in order to form a new word. Compounds are made up of two or more parts which can also occur independently as words.

27(A). Examples of irregular verbs are break - broke.
Irregular verbs can be defined as a verb in which the past tense is not formed by adding the usual -ed ending.

28(B). The following is a conditional sentence- ' If the sea is stormy, the waves are high '.
There are always two parts to a conditional sentence – one part beginning with 'if' to describe a possible situation, and the second part which describes the consequence. For example: If it rains, we'll get wet.

29(C). Let' find out the meaning of given options:
Codify- arrange (laws or rules) into a systematic code.
Reticent- not revealing one's thoughts or feelings readily.
Procrastinate- delay or postpone action; put off doing something.
Retaliate- make an attack in return for a similar attack.
Clearly, postpone is done to do something in a future time.

30(B). Rapacious- aggressively greedy or grasping, especially for money.
Agnostic- a person who believes that nothing is known or can be known of the existence or nature of God.
Oblation- a thing presented or offered to God or a god.
Celibacy- the state of abstaining from marriage and sexual relations.

31(B). Let's look at each option:
If he is not prepared: This phrase introduces the Type 1 conditional nature of the sentence (A possible condition and its probable result) representing the subject and its adjective in a grammatically correct manner
he will badly perform:
- This phrase tries to convey the result of the condition presented in the preceding phrase
- Here, the verb is 'perform' and the adverb is 'badly', that is, the latter tells us the quality of the verb
- Conventionally, an adverb is placed after the verb
- However, sometimes, adverbs can be placed before the verb. In such a case, there is an emphasis on the adverb, e.g., She quickly finished her dinner.
- But some adverbs are always placed after the verb. These adverbs are: well, badly, hard, fast
in the exam: This phrase introduces the object ('exam'') of the verb and is grammatically correct
Thus the correct sentence is: If he is not prepared, he will perform badly in the exam.

32(A). Let's look at each option:
If I was the Prime Minister:
- This phrase introduces the sentence as an Unreal Conditional, that is, it expresses events that are hypothetical or improbable.
- Typically, an unreal conditional sentence begins with an if clause containing the past tense or past perfect tense of a verb followed by a conditional clause containing a modal verb such as "would.", e.g., If I had told you the answer, I would have been cheating.
- There is one exception to this rule, however. If the verb in the if-clause is "to be," use "were," even if the subject of the clause is a third-person singular subject (i.e., he, she, it), e.g., If I were a rich man, I would make more charitable donations.
- This exception applies only to unreal conditionals—that is, situations that do not reflect reality or possible reality.
I would abolish: This phrase represents the outcome part of the conditional with the modal verb ('would') - verb ('abolish') combination and is grammatically correct
red-tapism: This is the object of the verb 'abolish' and it means 'the practice of requiring excessive paperwork and tedious procedures before official action can be considered or completed'. This phrase is grammatically correct.
Thus the correct sentence is: If I were the Prime Minister, I would abolish red-tapism

33(C). Let's look at each option:
The employee as well as: This phrase introduces the first subject ('employee') followed by the adverbial phrase 'as well as' and is grammatically correct
his colleagues: This phrase introduces the second subject ('colleagues') preceded by a pronoun ('his') relating it to the first subject, and is grammatically correct
were present:
- This phrase uses the auxiliary verb 'were' and the adjective 'present' to convey that there was the presence of both the employee and his colleagues
- However, when the adverbial phrase 'as well as' connects two subjects, the rule of the English language says that the verb proceeding them should agree with the first subject (in this case, 'employee')
- So, the correct auxiliary verb to be used here should be the singular 'was'
Thus the correct sentence is: "The employee as well as his colleagues was present"

34(B). Priority is something that is regarded as more important than others. So, the correct answer is: Abhishek's first priority is to find a place to live.

35(C). Enrollment is the action of being register as a member of an institution. So, the correct answer is: Rahul will be given a reading test at the time of enrollment.

36(D). Composed is used for someone who has a control over his/her feelings or expressions. So, the correct answer is: Virat Kohli is a talented and composed player.

37(C). The correct sentence with the appropriate word from the given options is: S.C. Bore was elected as the president of the congress party in 1939.

38(C). The correct rearrangement is 4231.
The correct sentence: Deltas are built from sediments that are carried downstream by rivers and eventually deposited where the river meets the sea.

39(B). The correct rearrangement is 2413.
The correct sentence is: Buddha believed that self-sufficient local communities would serve the purpose much better than an imbalanced consumerist culture spawned by those who believe that bigger is better.

40(A). The correct rearrangement is 4321.
The correct sentence is: She never thought that she would work online, until curiosity got the best of her and she filled out a simple online form.

41(A). Bolt from the blue: A sudden, unexpected event
For example: The resignation of the chairman came like a bolt from the blue.

42(D). Run wild: to run, go, behave, etc., in a wild and uncontrolled way
For example: The mob was running wild in the streets.

43(C). The meaning of phrase "take something with a grain of salt" means not taking something too seriously.
Example: The Indian players took the issue of racism with a grain of salt.

44(C). Achilles heel means 'a small problem or weakness in a person or system that can result in failure'. Someone's Achilles heel is the weakest point in their character or nature, where it is easiest for other people to attack or criticize them.
Example- His Achilles heel is his quick temper.

45(A). To have an axe to grind: have a private reason for doing or being involved in something.
Example: He has no political axe to grind
Hence, the correct option is (C).

46(C). All three options (A), (B) and (D) are in passive voice, and option (C) is in reported speech.
Direct speech:
- I said, "Do not speak of the past. Is there not something in every life which it is happiness to forget? I have so much to remember in this world, so much to learn and so much to repay."

Indirect speech:
- I advised him not to speak of the past and asked whether there was not something in every life which it was happiness to forget, and added that I had so much to remember in this world, so much to learn and so much to repay.

47(A). In option (B), (C) and (D) using co-ordinating conjunction i.e., in option (B) but, in option (C) besides, and in option (D) in order to.
Only option (A) is the odd one because in the second line it has a relative clause (that).
So, option (A) is the odd one out.

48(C). Boot does not have O sound.

49(D). Pray does not have / ia / sound.

50(A). Charm-choice contains the words beginning with the same consonant sound.

Ques (1-7): Directions : Read the passage given below and answer the question.

Edison, the prince of inventors was born on 11 th February, 1847, in Milan, Ohio, USA. His father, Samuel Edison, was in the lumber and grain business. His mother Nancy was a former school teacher. Young Edison's eccentricities were evident quite early in life. Energetic, argumentative and hard to discipline, he was promptly labelled by his teachers as difficult. But his mother Nancy had the insight to realise that her child was special and required deft handling. She took him out of school, taught him herself at home and gave him a free hand to pursue his interests. It was a very wise decision. Formal education and rigid discipline might have extinguished the spark of creativity in this gifted child, and the loss would have been the world's.

Young Edison made full use of the freedom given by his mother. He eagerly devoured books on physics, chemistry, etc., but never accepted any statement without testing it out for himself. Designing and constructing gadgets by himself was an all-consuming passion with him.

At the age of twelve, Edison decided it was time to face the world on his own. He began earning by selling newspapers and food in trains. He then launched a small newspaper of his own, printing it in a railway carriage. He had to give it up when a reader incensed at his gossip column threw him fully clothed into a pool of water! He, however, continued to use his railway carriage as a mini physics-and-chemistry laboratory. But this too came to an end when there was an explosion in the carriage and the railway staff dumped him, along with his paraphernalia, at the nearest level crossing!

1. **Which of the following options is not correct ?**
   Edison's teachers labelled him as difficult because he was:
   (a) recalcitrant   (b) agrumentative
   (c) eccentric   (d) unmannerly

2. **Realising that her child was special, Edison's mother:**
   (a) encouraged him to visit science fairs and exhibitions.
   (b) gave him complete freedom to pursue his interests.
   (c) provided him with all the necessary gadgets.
   (d) engaged the best private tutors for him.

3. **Edison showed great interest in:**
   (a) setting up a printing press.
   (b) designing and building appliances.
   (c) all kinds of machines.
   (d) reading biographies of scientists.

4. **Read the following statements:**
   (A) The young Edison had great entrepreneurial skills.
   (B) Setbacks did not deter the young Edison from pursuing his interests.
   (a) (A) is true and (B) is false
   (b) (B) is true and (A) is false
   (c) Both (A) and (B) are false
   (d) Both (A) and (B) are true

5. **The word 'evident' in para 1 means the same as:**
   (a) provident   (b) diligent
   (c) obvious   (d) transparent

6. **The word opposite in meaning to the word 'incensed' in para 4 is:**
   (a) puzzled   (b) frustrated

(c) happy   (d) annoyed

7. **The word 'too' in "But this too came to an end" is a/an:**
   (a) Pronoun   (b) Adverb
   (c) Adjective   (d) Noun

Ques (8-14): Direction : Read the passage given below and answer the following question.

Peoples' faces light up when I say I taste chocolate for a living, but it is not always delicious. I also have to taste defective chocolate, which might have a bitter or burnt flavour. I'm usually in a small room, not allowed to talk, and parked in front of a computer to log information. Sometimes the room has red lighting to disguise the appearance of the chocolate, so I can evaluate it only by taste, not appearance. I can sample as man as 30 chocolates per day, so as to keep my palate active, I spit the sweets back out. That's another not-so-glamorous part of the job. Between samples, I wait 30 seconds to let my senses rest, and I chew half an unsalted cracker biscuit and drink plain warm water, as carbonated water and ice numb one's senses.

First I smell the chocolate and log its aroma. I also listen: if chocolate doesn't sound crisp when broken, it may be a sign it's old or was improperly stored. Then I place one inch bit in my mouth and leave it there for a few seconds, I press it against my palate and let it melt, recording the four basic tastes-sweet, sour, bitter and salty. Then I blow out short puffs of air through my nose. Certain sense receptors in the back of our head are stimulated by oxygen. They allow us to smell food when we chew. Exhaling sharply can bring out aromas like berry, mushroom, tea, citrus, beeswax, toast, cinnamon, and savoury spices that are sometimes too subtle for the nose to catch. I log these attributes, too, along with the texture.

8. **There is no glamour in his job as:**
   (a) he has to blow out short puffs
   (b) he keeps on spitting out chocolate
   (c) his place of work is narrow
   (d) he never ate burnt chocolate

9. **The narrator cannot eat and enjoy the chocolate:**
   (a) as it has not been stored properly
   (b) as it has not been stored properly
   (c) to keep his palate active
   (d) as it has a burnt flavour

10. **The process of chocolate tasting runs in the order of ____ and again smelling.**
    (a) breaking, smelling, listening, melting
    (b) breaking, listening, smelling, melting
    (c) smelling, breaking, listening, melting
    (d) melting, listening, breaking, smelling

11. **"Leave it there."**
    When the above sentence is changed into <u>passive voice</u>, it becomes:
    (a) Let it was left there.   (b) It is left there.
    (c) It was left there.   (d) Let it be left there.

12. **"Peoples' faces light up _____"**
    The word 'light' here is a/an
    (a) adverb   (b) noun
    (c) verb   (d) adjective

13. **The word 'parked' (Para 1) means:**

(a) ran   (b) managed
(c) operated   (d) seated

14. The word 'log' (Para 2) means:
(a) taste   (b) record
(c) cut   (d) enjoy

Ques (15-20): Direction : Read the following passage and answer the questions given after it.

The Celts who lived in Britain before the Roman invasion of 43 AD could be said to have created the first towns. Celts in southern England lived in hill forts, which were quite large settlements. (Some probably had thousands of inhabitants). They were places of trade, where people bought and sold goods and also places where craftsmen worked. The Romans called them oppida.

However, the Romans created the first settlements that were undoubtedly towns. Roman towns were usually laid out in a grid pattern. In the centre was the forum or market place. It was lined with public buildings. Life in Roman towns was highly civilized with public baths and temples.

From the 5th century Angles, Saxons and Jutes invaded England. At first, the invaders avoided living in towns. However, as trade grew some towns grew up. London revived by the 7th century (although the Saxon town was, at first, outside the walls of the old Roman town). Southampton was founded at the end of the 7th century. Hereford was founded in the 8th century. Furthermore, Ipswich grew up in the 8th century and York revived. However, towns were rare in Saxon England until the late 9th century. At that time, Alfred the Great created a network of fortified settlements across his kingdom called 'burhs'. In the event of a Danish attack, men could gather in the local burh. However, burhs were more than forts. They were also market towns. Some burhs were started from scratch but many were created out of the ruins of old Roman towns. Places like Winchester rose, phoenix-like, from the ashes of history.

The thing that would strike us most about medieval towns would be their small size. Winchester, the capital of England, probably had about 8,000 people. At that time a 'large' town, like Lincoln or Dublin had about 4,000 or 5,000 inhabitants and a 'medium sized' town, like Colchester had about 2,500 people. Many towns were much smaller.

However, during the 12th and 13th centuries most towns grew much larger. Furthermore, many new towns were created across Britain. Trade and commerce were increasing and there was a need for new towns. Some were created from existing villages but some were created from scratch. In those days you could create a town simply by starting a market. There were few shops so if you wished to buy or sell anything you had to go to a market. Once one was up and running, craftsmen and merchants would come to live in the area and a town would grow.

15. Match the words with their meaning.
   a. founded 1. protected
   b. declined 2. created
   c. fortified 3. dwindled
(a) a-1, b-3, c-2   (b) a-2, b-3, c-1
(c) a-3, b-2, c-1   (d) a-2, b-1, c-3

16. The hill forts of Celts were called:
(a) Oppida   (b) Burhs
(c) Centres   (d) Forums

17. Who were the first creators of towns in England?
(a) Celts   (b) Angles
(c) Saxons   (d) Romans

18. "Some were created from scratch." The towns which started from scratch were created by first:

(a) starting a market
(b) establishing a settlement
(c) building houses
(d) building a fort

19. Which of the following was the capital of England during medieval times?
(a) Dublin   (b) Winchester
(c) London   (d) Colchester

20. "At first, the invaders avoided living in towns." Who is/are being referred to here as 'invaders'?
(a) Saxons, Angles and Jutes (b) Alfred the Great
(c) Celts   (d) Romans

21. Direction: Choose the option that best expresses the meaning of the idiom which is underlined.
   Diana took to swimming like a duck to water even before she was 3 years old.
(a) Like an expert
(b) Having natural ability
(c) Swim the way a duck does
(d) Showing passion for

22. Direction: Choose the alternative that explains the given idiomatic expression.
   To shed crocodile tears
(a) To weep bitterly and long
(b) To pretend to feel sadness
(c) To behave like a clever person
(d) To deceive by telling tales of misfortune

23. Direction: Choose the alternative that explains the given idiomatic expression.
   To tempt providence
(a) To invite punishment   (b) To achieve a fortune
(c) To take reckless risks   (d) To have god's favour

24. In the following question, out of the four alternatives, select the alternative which best expresses the meaning of the Idiom/Phrase.
   In black and white
(a) Useless   (b) In writing
(c) In short   (d) In full swing

25. In the following question, out of the four alternatives, select the alternative which best expresses the meaning of the Idiom/Phrase.
   Stick one's neck out
(a) Interfere   (b) Look outside
(c) Move   (d) Invite trouble

Ques (26-27): Direction : A part of sentence is underline. Balance are given alternatives to the underlined part A, B, C and D which may improve the sentence. Choose the correct alternative.

26. It was not possible to drag any conclusion so he left the case.
(a) Fetch   (b) Find
(c) Draw   (d) No improvement

27. I am looking after my pen which is missing.
(a) Looking for   (b) Looking in
(c) Looking back   (d) No improvement

**28. Identify the segment in the sentence which contains the

grammatical error.
Neither Amit nor Raju are staying with his parents in Mumbai.
(a) are staying   (b) in Mumbai
(c) with his parents   (d) Neither Amit nor Raju

29. Identify the segment in the sentence, which contains the grammatical error.
Economics is one of the subject which I have found very difficult since school.
(a) Economics is
(b) which I have found
(c) very difficult since school
(d) one of the subject

30. Identify the segment in the sentence, which contains a grammatical error.
If I join a software company I am getting a good deal of experience.
(a) If I join
(b) a software company
(c) I am getting
(d) a good deal of experience

31. Direction : A sentence is given with a blank to be filled in with an appropriate and suitable word. Four alternatives are suggested for each question. Choose the correct alternative out of the four.
When Indians from the South move North, they find certain aspects of life quite .... from their own.
(a) strange   (b) separate
(c) different   (d) divergent

32. Direction: Choose the option that is the indirect form of the sentence.
She said to Mohit, "Rohit arrived on Sunday."
(a) She told Mohit that Rohit has arrived on Sunday.
(b) She told Mohit that Rohit arrived on Sunday.
(c) She told Mohit that Rohit had arrived on Sunday.
(d) She said to Mohit that Rohit had arrived on Sunday.

33. Direction: Select the correct form of the tense for the given sentence.
Does Rahul often go to the library?
(a) Simple Present   (b) Past simple
(c) Future continuous   (d) None of the above

Ques (34-36): Direction: In the following question, out of the four alternatives, select the alternative which will improve the underlined part of the sentence. In case no improvement is needed, select "No improvement".

34. **None of the employees of this organization <u>are serious about the</u> growth of the company.**
(a) have been serious for the
(b) is serious about the
(c) were serious about the
(d) No improvement

35. **Loneliness has become increasingly prevalent among adolescents, <u>who spent longer</u> and longer periods of time online.**
(a) who spend longer
(b) who spends longer
(c) who used to spend longer

(d) No improvement

36. **Gaurav Jain recovered from a mild Covid-19 attack around Diwali and <u>begins a normal life</u> after a short bout of weakness.**
(a) have begun a normal life   (b) began a normal life
(c) begin a normal life   (d) No improvement

Ques (37-39): Direction: Fill in the blank with the correct word.

37. **I like _____ this book again and again as it strengthens my mind in tough times.**
(a) To reading   (b) Reading
(c) Read   (d) Reads

38. **I _____ the essay by tomorrow afternoon by this time.**
(a) Finished   (b) Would finished
(c) Finishes   (d) Will have finished

39. **Her birthday is ____ the month of November so we have only two weeks in hand to prepare for the party.**
(a) In   (b) On
(c) For   (d) By

40. **Which of the following sentences is negative?**
(a) I come from a rich family
(b) You can do all this in no time
(c) He does not listen to me
(d) They are very gentle people

41. Direction: In the given sentence, one phrase has been printed in bold. Select the correct meaning of the phrase from the options given below.
The investors began to smell a rat when the company ceased paying dividends and delayed the mandatory audit.
(a) Suspicion   (b) Deceive
(c) Incorrect   (d) Wonder

42. Direction : In the given sentence, one phrase has been printed in bold. Select the correct meaning of the phrase from the options given below.
When he heard the bad news, he kept a stiff upper lip.
(a) Stoic demeanor   (b) Emotional outburst
(c) Physical injury   (d) Agitated state

43. Direction: Select the most appropriate idiom (in the context) to fill in the sentence.
In my parents' time, we mostly ate at home and family outings happened _____.
(a) in fine feather   (b) shoulder to shoulder
(c) behind the back   (d) once in a blue moon

44. Direction: In the following question, out of the four alternatives, select the alternative which is the best substitute for the phrase.
Something causing shock or dismay
(a) Mischievous   (b) Remarkable
(c) Frivolous   (d) Appalling

45. Direction: In the following question, out of the four alternatives, select the alternative which is the best substitute for the phrase.
Something happening by chance in a happy and beneficial way
(a) Fortitude   (b) Serenity

(c) Misadventure   (d) Serendipity

46. Which figure of speech is used in the following sentence?
All the world's a stage.

(a) Metaphor   (b) Euphenism

(c) Metonymy   (d) Metalepsis

47. Which figure of speech is used in the following sentence?
Swords clanged and guns boomed.

(a) Hyperbole   (b) Metaphor

(c) Oxymoron   (d) Onomatopoeia

48. Which of these terms refer to the study of speech process?

(a) Phonology   (b) Phonetic substances

(c) Phonetics   (d) Semantics

49. What is the full form of IPA?

(a) Indian Phonetic Alphabet

(b) International Phonetic Alphabet

(c) International Phonetic Agreement

(d) Indian Phonetic Agreement

50. Which of the following is voiced sound?

(a) /p/

(b) /t/

(c) /t/

(d) /tʃ/

// Smart Answer Sheet //

Correct	Percentage of students who answered correctly.	
Skipped	Percentage of students who skipped.	

Q.	Ans.	Correct / Skipped	Q.	Ans.	Correct / Skipped	Q.	Ans.	Correct / Skipped
1	D	44.46% / 1.98%	2	B	86.1% / 0.0%	3	B	41.41% / 1.76%
4	D	88.4% / 0.0%	5	C	43.9% / 1.81%	6	C	41.87% / 1.08%
7	B	40.11% / 1.28%	8	B	56.25% / 1.05%	9	C	55.37% / 1.39%
10	C	58.33% / 1.87%	11	D	66.85% / 1.06%	12	C	47.01% / 1.58%
13	D	84.92% / 0.0%	14	B	46.4% / 1.5%	15	B	56.12% / 1.81%
16	A	76.74% / 0.0%	17	A	77.98% / 0.0%	18	A	46.58% / 1.4%
19	B	86.94% / 0.0%	20	A	89.37% / 0.0%	21	B	60.86% / 1.43%
22	B	67.19% / 1.51%	23	C	12.0% / 3.21%	24	B	82.57% / 0.0%
25	D	66.68% / 1.56%	26	C	61.7% / 1.45%	27	A	44.04% / 1.27%
28	A	16.98% / 4.3%	29	D	88.23% / 0.0%	30	C	50.32% / 1.88%
31	C	48.99% / 1.84%	32	C	43.04% / 1.57%	33	A	48.88% / 1.27%
34	B	68.74% / 1.45%	35	A	50.1% / 1.62%	36	B	66.23% / 1.94%
37	B	78.42% / 0.0%	38	D	49.31% / 1.72%	39	A	81.24% / 0.0%
40	C	61.49% / 1.03%	41	A	42.64% / 1.22%	42	A	78.93% / 0.0%
43	D	52.26% / 1.28%	44	D	86.66% / 0.0%	45	D	40.22% / 1.55%
46	A	40.37% / 1.18%	47	D	68.75% / 1.58%	48	C	85.64% / 0.0%
49	C	51.97% / 1.96%	50	C	45.76% / 1.14%			

// Hints and Solutions //

1(D). Edison's teachers labelled him as difficult because he was unmannerly.

2(B). Realising that her child was special, Edison's mother gave him complete freedom to pursue his interests.

3(B). Edison showed great interest in designing and building appliances.

4(D). Both (A) and (B) are true.

5(C). The word 'evident' in para 1 means the same as obvious.

6(C). The word opposite in meaning to the word 'incensed' in para 4 is happy.

7(B). The word 'too' in "But this too came to an end" is a/an a dverb.

8(B). There is no glamour in his job as he keeps on spitting out chocolate.
- Refer to the line: 'I can sample as man as 30 chocolates per day, so as to keep my palate active, I spit the sweets back out. That's another not-so-glamorous part of the job.'
- Thus, we can conclude that the narrator has to keep spitting chocolates which is another not-so-glamorous part of his job.

9(C). The narrator cannot eat and enjoy the chocolate to keep his palate active.
- Refer to the lines: 'I can sample as man as 30 chocolates per day, so as to keep my palate active, I spit the sweets back out. That's another not-so-glamorous part of the job. Between samples, I wait 30 seconds to let my senses rest, and I chew half an unsalted cracker biscuit and drink plain warm water, as carbonated water and ice numb one's senses.'
- Thus, we can conclude that the narrator cannot enjoy eating chocolates as he has to sample around 30 chocolates per day and for that he keeps his palate active, chew unsalted cracker biscuit and drink plain warm water as well.

10(C). The process of chocolate tasting runs in the order of smelling, breaking, listening, melting and again smelling.
- Refer to the lines: ' First I smell the chocolate and log its aroma. I also listen : if chocolate doesn't sound crisp when broken , it may be a sign it's old or was improperly stored. Then I place one inch bit in my mouth and leave it there for a few seconds, I press it against my palate and let it melt, recording the four basic tastes-sweet, sour, bitter and salty. '
- It can be inferred from the above lines that the first step was smelling, second was breaking after which he listened the crisp sound of the chocolate and then he let the chocolate melt.
- Thus, the process is - smelling, breaking, listening, melting.

11(D). When the above sentence is changed into <u>passive voice</u>, it becomes Let it be left there.
- An imperative sentence does not normally have a subject. It is used to express a command or request.
- The instructions given below should be followed while

changing an imperative sentence to passive voice .
- It takes the following form:
  ◦ Let + Object + be + Past Participle.
- Example : Leave him. (Active Voice)
  Let him be left. (Passive Voice)
  So, the final sentence is - Let it be left there.

12(C). The word 'light' here is a verb.
- Light up is a phrasal verb. If someone's face or eyes light up, they express a strong emotion, usually happiness or excitement.
- Example: Antony's eyes lit up when Keiko walked into the room.
- Phrasal verbs are verb phrases that have idiomatic meanings—that is, the meaning is not obvious from the individual words that make up the phrase. Phrasal verbs are made up of a verb + a preposition , an adverbial particle, or both.
- According to the above explanation, light is a verb and up is a preposition.

13(D). The word 'parked' (Para 1) means seated.
- Refer to the line: 'I'm usually in a small room, not allowed to talk, and parked in front of a computer to log information.'
- Thus, we can infer that he was made to sit or had to sit in front of a computer to log information.
So, parked means seated according to the context.

14(B). The word 'log' (Para 2) means record.
Refer to the line: 'I log these attributes, too, along with the texture.'
Here, log refers to recording the attributes of the chocolate along with the texture.
Thus, log means record.

15(B). The correct answer is "a-2, b-3, c-1".
Founded means establish or originate (an institution or organization), especially by providing an endowment; created.
Declined means become smaller, fewer, or less; dwindled
Fortified means provide (a place) with defensive works as a protection against attack; protected
Therefore, from the given meanings, we find that the option with the correct match of the words with their meanings is the option (B).

16(A). According to the first paragraph, "Celts in southern England lived in hill forts, which were quite large settlements. (Some probably had thousands of inhabitants). They were places of trade, where people bought and sold goods and also places where craftsmen worked. The Romans called them oppida.".
Upon perusal of the above statement, it can be concluded that the hill forts of Celts were called oppida by the Romans.
Therefore, the correct answer is "Oppida".

17(A). According to the first paragraph, "The Celts who lived in Britain before the Roman invasion of 43 AD could be said to have created the first towns".
Upon perusal of the above statement, it can be concluded that Celts were the first creators of towns in England.
Therefore, the correct answer is "Celts".

18(A). According to the last paragraph, "In those days you could create a town simply by starting a market".
Upon perusal of the above statement, it can be concluded that the towns which started from scratch were created by first starting a market.
Therefore, the correct answer is "starting a market".

19(B). According to the fourth paragraph, "Winchester, the capital of England, probably had about 8,000 people".
Upon perusal of the above statement, it can be concluded that Winchester was the capital of England during medieval times.
Therefore, the correct answer is "Winchester".

20(A). According to the third paragraph, "From the 5th century Angles, Saxons and Jutes invaded England. At first, the invaders avoided living in towns".
Upon perusal of the above statement, it can be concluded that Saxons, Angles and Jutes are being referred to as invaders.
Therefore, the correct answer is "Saxons, Angles and Jutes ".

21(B). 'Take to something like a duck to water' means 'to adapt to or learn something very quickly and naturally, as if it were innate or one has a natural ability to do it'.

22(B). 'To shed crocodile tears' means 'to display false, insincere, or hypocritical sadness or remorse', to pretend to be sad or to sympathize with someone without really caring about them.
For Example: The sight of George shedding crocodile tears made me sick.

23(C). If you tempt fate or providence by doing something, you take a silly risk by doing it and depend too much on your good luck.
For example, You're tempting providence by riding your bike without wearing a helmet.

24(B). The idiom "in black and white" means in writing or in print.

25(D). The idiom "stick your neck out" means risk incurring criticism or anger by acting or speaking boldly, to take a risk or invite trouble by your actions.

26(C). Use of 'draw' is more suitable for using before word 'conclusion', because generally, we draw a conclusion, not drag it.
Correct sentence: It was not possible to draw any conclusion so he left the case.

27(A). Use of 'looking for' is proper because look for means to search for something which suits here, not 'looking after' which is used to take care of someone or something.
Correct sentence: I am looking for my pen which is missing.

28(A). The correct sentence is:
Neither Amit nor Raju is staying with his parents in Mumbai.
When there are 2 different subjects that are joined by either___or/ neither___nor / not only___but also/ _or_ ,and are different in numbers, the subject closer to the verb decides whether the verb will be singular or plural.
Examples:
- There is / are either some boys (subject closer to the verb) or a girl in the class.
- Neither the ministers nor the King (subject closer to the verb) have / has been arrested.
- Not only Sapna but also her friends (subject closer to the verb) has / have come.
Here, the subject closer to the verb is 'Raju' and thus the verb 'are' will be replaced by 'is' to agree with the singular subject.

29(D). When we refer to one among many items, we always use the plural of the noun in question.

This is because, out of the many subjects, there is only one subject that the speaker has found difficult.

So, the correct sentence will be:

"Economics is one of the subjects which I have found very difficult since school."

30(C). The correct sentence is:

"If I join a software company I will get a good deal of experience."

The sentence represents conditional sentences type 1.

Its structure is: if + Simple Present, will-Future.

From reading the sentence itself, it becomes clear that the person is going to get 'a good deal of experience' in the future.

Since the sentence contains the word 'if' (which signifies probability), we use the modal verb 'will'.

31(C). Let's have a look at the meanings of the given words:

different (Adj.): not the same as somebody

strange (Adj.): unusual

separate (Adj.): different; not connected (used before Nouns)

divergent (Adj.): different (of opinions, views, etc.)

Thus, the most suitable word here is 'different.'

Complete sentence: When Indians from the South move North, they find certain aspects of life quite different from their own.

32(C). The indirect speech of the given sentence is 'She told Mohit that Rohit had arrived on Sunday.'

When the reporting speech is in Simple Past Tense then all the speech Changes to Past Perfect tense.

- Arrived - Had arrived
- Said to of the reporting verb changed into told.
- Replace comma (,) and inverted commas (" ") with the conjunction 'that'.
- The third person(Rohit) of the reporting speech remains unchanged.

So, the final sentence is: 'She told Mohit that Rohit had arrived on Sunday.

33(A). The given sentence Does Rahul often go to the library? is in the Simple Present tense.

We know that the structure of the Simple Present tense for the interrogative sentence is

Structure: do/does + Sub + V1 + Obj?

Example: Do you sleep in the afternoon?

34(B). 'None of, one of, each of, etc.' is followed by a plural noun but the verb in the latter of the sentence should be singular.

Example,

One of the guests has come.

According to the rule and example that are given above, "is serious about the' will be used in the underlined part of the sentence.

35(A). The given sentence is in the present tense as is clear from the helping verb 'has'.

Therefore, we cannot use V2 i.e. spent.

If a subject and the verb are joined by a relative pronoun, the verb will agree with the antecedent to the relative pronoun.

E.g. He is one of the bravest soldiers that have ever lived on this earth.

According to the rule and example that are given above, 'who spend longer' will be used in the underlined part of the sentence.

36(B). The verb 'recovered' used in the first part of the sentence shows that the given sentence is in the past indefinite tense.

In the past indefinite tense V2 is used.

E.g. I saw you in the market yesterday.

According to the rule and example that are given above, 'began a normal life' will be used in the underlined part of the sentence.

37(B). The correct word here is the participle 'reading' as the sentence has been structured.

Correct sentence: I like reading this book again and again as it strengthens my mind in tough times.

38(D). The future perfect tense is used to express an action that, the speaker assumes, will have completed or occurred in the future. The other options are incorrect.

Correct sentence: I will have finished the essay by tomorrow afternoon by this time.

39(A). The correct preposition here is 'in' as 'in' is used for expressing a period of time during which an event happens or a situation remains the case.

Correct sentence: Her birthday is in the month of November so we have only two weeks in hand to prepare for the party.

40(C). A sentence is negative when it contains a negative word in it and expresses a negative idea. 'He does not listen to me' sentences is negative because it has a negative word 'not'.

41(A). Smell a rat: It means to suspect that something is not right. If you smell a rat, you begin to suspect or realize that something is wrong in a particular situation, for example, that someone is trying to deceive you or harm you.

Example: When he made that offer, I smelt a rat. It sounded too good to be true.

From the meaning above, options (B) and (C) are incorrect. Out of (A) and (D), (A) is a better choice as wonder means the desire to know something; feel curious.

42(A). To keep a stiff upper lip: It means to act as though you are not upset. Someone who has a stiff upper lip does not show their feelings when they are upset.

Example: Even though she was only two years old, Jill kept a stiff upper lip the whole time she was in the hospital recovering from the surgery.

From the meaning given above, option (A) is the best fit here.

43(D). In my parents' time, we mostly ate at home and family outings happened once in a blue moon.

The speaker wants to convey that family outings occurred rarely . So, once in a blue moon is correct.

Once in a blue moon means to do very rarely.

44(D). Appalling means something causing shock or dismay.

Example: She suffered appalling injuries in the accident.

45(D). Serendipity is the best substitute for the phrase " Something happening by chance in a happy and beneficial way".

Serendipity: Serendipity means the occurrence and development of events by chance in a happy or beneficial way.

Example: It was a fortunate incident of serendipity.

46(A). The figure of speech in "All the world's a stage" is "Metaphor".

In the lines, All the world's a stage- All men and women are merely players there is an implied comparison between two different things. In this poem, Shakespeare compares life to a stage.

A metaphor is a figure of speech that, for rhetorical effect, directly refers to one thing by mentioning another. It may provide clarity or identify hidden similarities between two different ideas.

47(D). The figure of speech in "Swords clanged and guns boomed." is "Onomatopoeia".

Onomatopoeia is the use or creation of a word that phonetically imitates, resembles, or suggests the sound that it describes. Such a word itself is also called an onomatopoeia. Common onomatopoeias include animal noises such as oink, meow, roar, and chirp.

48(C). Phonetics refer to the study of speech process.

49(C). International Phonetic Agreement is the full form of IPA.

50(C). /t/ is voiced sound.

Ques (1-7): Direction: Read the following passage and answer the questions given after it.

Mrs. Baroda was a little provoked to learn that her husband expected his friend, Gouvernail, up to spend a week or two on the plantation.

They had entertained a good deal during the winter; much of the time had also been passed in New Orleans in various forms of mild pursuits of pleasure. She was looking forward to a period of unbroken rest, now, and undisturbed company with her husband, when he informed her that Gouvernail was coming up to stay a week or two.

This was a man she had heard much of but never seen. He had been her husband's college friend; was now a journalist, and in no sense a society man or "a man about town," which were, perhaps, some of the reasons she had never met him. But she had unconsciously formed an image of him in her mind. She pictured him tall, slim, cynical; with eye-glasses, and his hands in his pockets; and she did not like him. Gouvernail was slim enough, but he wasn't very tall nor very cynical; neither did he wear eyeglasses nor carry his hands in his pockets. And she rather liked him when he first presented himself.

But why she liked him she could not explain satisfactorily to herself when she partly attempted to do so. She could discover in him none of those brilliant and promising traits which Gaston, her husband, had often assured her that he possessed. On the contrary, he sat rather mute and receptive before her chatty eagerness to make him feel at home and in face of Gaston's frank and wordy hospitality. His manner was as courteous toward her as the most exacting woman could require; but he made no direct appeal to her approval.

Once settled at the plantation he seemed to like to sit upon the wide portico in the shade of one of the big Corinthian pillars, smoking his cigar lazily and listening attentively to Gaston's experience as a sugar planter.

"This is what I call living," he would utter with deep satisfaction, as the air that swept across the sugar field caressed him with its warm and scented velvety touch. It pleased him also to get on familiar terms with the big dogs that came about him, rubbing themselves sociably against his legs. He did not care to fish, and displayed no eagerness to go out and kill sparrows when Gaston proposed doing so.

1. **Which of the following Gouvernail didn't like much?**
   - (a) sitting upon the wide portico in the shade of one of the big Corinthian pillars
   - (b) big dogs rubbing themselves sociably against his legs
   - (c) fishing and hunting birds
   - (d) smoking his cigar lazily and listening attentively to Gaston's experience

2. **The word 'provoked' in the passage means:**
   - (a) Pursuit
   - (b) Irritated
   - (c) Encouraged
   - (d) Pleased

3. **Identify the part of speech of the underlined word:**
   He sat rather mute and receptive before her <u>chatty</u> eagerness to make him feel at home.
   - (a) Adverb
   - (b) Adjective
   - (c) Verb
   - (d) Noun

4. **When Mrs. Baroda met him she liked him. Why?**
   - (a) Her husband liked him.
   - (b) He had all the qualities that her husband had told her about.
   - (c) She herself didn't know why she liked him.

   - (d) He was frank and courteous to her.

5. **Find the error in a part of the sentence:**
   He did not care to fish, (a)/ and has no eagerness to go out (b)/and kill sparrows (c)/ when Gaston proposed doing so.(d)/
   - (a) a
   - (b) b
   - (c) c
   - (d) d

6. **Which of the following characteristics of Gouvernail matched with the image that Mrs. Baroda had formed of him in her mind?**
   - (a) he was tall
   - (b) he wore eyeglasses
   - (c) he was slim
   - (d) he was cynical

7. **What were Mrs. Baroda's plans while on the plantation?**
   - (a) to look after the plantation along with her husband
   - (b) to rest and have undisturbed company of her husband
   - (c) to spend the time with her husband and his friend
   - (d) to entertain people on the plantation

Ques (8-13): Direction: Read the passage and answer the question that follow.

The word 'depressed' in common usage means sad, frustrated, fed up, bored up, and pessimistic. The mood of a depressed person is much lower at his or her best moments than the mood of a normal person at his or her worst. Depression is a state of mind. It is specifically a mental disorder characterized by a lowering of the individual's vitality, his mood, desires, hopes, aspirations and of his self-esteem.

Depression arising out of environmental factors is called reactive depression whereas depression arising out of some biochemical changes in the brain is called endogenous depression. If depression is mild or moderate and if the individual is in touch with his surroundings, it is known as neurotic depression. If the individual is severely disturbed and is not able to comprehend what is happening around, such a state is called psychotic depression.

Old age is one of the stages of human development, where a person attains wisdom, maturity, social and economic stability with social recognition and emotional fulfillment. Generally, societies show great respect and consideration for the aged. In ancient times old people were considered as the guiding stars in Indian families since they were symbols of tradition, respect, wisdom, and experience. In primitive, ancient, and medieval cultures, old persons had a recognized social role. They were of great value because they could impart knowledge and skill to youngsters. The old people were considered as repositories of wisdom and traditions and were not perceived as problems.

At present, social structures and values are undergoing a transformation from traditional to modern. There is a rapid stride in urbanization and industrialization leading to the breaking up of joint families and property. This has ultimately weakened the traditional families, social position, and status of the aged in the family. From time to time changes in the institutions of marriage and family have diminished the control of parents over their children.

It has increased the freedom of children and they view the aged as a useless and non-productive entity. Modernization has eventually led to the degradation of their status and authority. Consequently, the integrity of the family and the existence of the elderly as an integral part of the family are being uprooted. The importance of their functional positions thus declines and consequently their authority and much of the respect and prestige that they enjoyed earlier get faded. These changes generally bring about depression in older people.

As old age advances, events at home may also contribute more to their problems. The 'empty nest' feeling arising as a result of the grown-up children leaving the home, daughters departing as a result of wedlock and sons leaving the station in pursuit of higher education or jobs may make the aged more lonely. The loneliness also arises because of the premature loss of a spouse. This would deprive the person of a long-standing emotional bond that had provided plenty of emotional succour and security. The loss wherever it might occur in the later years leaves the individual terribly lonely and at the mercy of the sons and daughters-in-law.

Added to these the increasing gap and interactional stress and strain in the family may leave the elderly without peace of mind. The elderly as a result of these developments feel marginalized, alienated, and left out of the mainstream. The foregoing are the common problems faced by most of the elderly. These either directly or indirectly lead to a state of depression and make aging for many an unwanted and unpleasant event to be abhorred.

Usually, mild depression which is caused due to environmental factors is temporary. The person reconciles within a short time and tries to forget the loss. Kind words and timely support of friends, relatives, and family members help one recover from depression.

8. The author has focussed mostly on-
   (a) Disrespect of old people
   (b) Depression in old age
   (c) Old age
   (d) Depression as a major problem

9. Why were old people greatly valued?
   (a) They were respectable in the society
   (b) Children were forced to listen to thim
   (c) There was no urbanization at that time
   (d) They could pass on knowledge and skill

10. What does the author mean by "Usually, the mild depression which is caused due to environmental factors is temporary"?
   (a) Mild depression has an ever-lasting effect
   (b) Mild depression does has a short-term effect
   (c) One can control mild depression
   (d) Environmental factors can be the cause of temporary depression

11. Which word in the passage means the same as 'support'?
   (a) Mercy   (b) Abhorred
   (c) Reconcile   (d) Succour

12. Which problems are highlighted in the given sentence? "The foregoing are the common problems faced by most of the elderly".
   (a) Disrespect   (b) Loneliness
   (c) Health problems   (d) Depression

13. What is depression called when the patient does not understand what is going on around him?
   (a) Psychotic depression   (b) Reactive depression
   (c) Endogenous depression (d) Neurotic depression

Ques (14-20): Direction : Read the passage given below and answer the questions that follow by selecting the correct/most appropriate options.

Buddha's method was one of psychological analysis and, again, it is surprising to find how deep was his insight into this latest of modern sciences. Man's life was considered and examined without any reference to a permanent self, for even if such a self exists, it is beyond our comprehension. The mind was looked upon as part of the body, a composite of mental forces. The individual thus becomes a bundle of mental states, the self is just a stream of ideas. 'All that we are is the result of what we have thought'. There is an emphasis on the pain and suffering of life, and the 'Four Noble Truths' which Buddha enunciated deal with this suffering, its cause, the possibility of ending it, and the way to do it. Speaking to his disciples, he is reported to have said: 'and while ye experienced this (sorrow) through long ages, more tears have flowed from you and have been shed by you, while ye strayed and wandered on this pilgrimage (of life), and sorrowed and wept, because that was your portion which ye abhorred, and that which ye loved was not your portion, than all the water which is in the four great oceans' Buddha told his disciples what he thought they could understand and live up to. His teaching was not meant to be a full explanation of everything, a complete revelation of all that is. Once it is said, he look some dry leaves in his hand and asked his favourite disciple, Ananda, to tell him whether there were any other leaves besides those in his hand. Ananda replied: The leaves of autumn are falling on all sides, and there are more of them than can be numbered, Then said the Buddha: 'In like manner I have given you a handful of truths, but besides these are many thousand of other truths, more than can be numbered.'

14. After the emergence of new scientific approaches the self', came to be considered as:
   1. a permanent entity in physical body
   2. beyond comprehension
   3. a composite of conflicting mental forces
   4. a stream of ideas
   (a) 1   (b) 2
   (c) 3   (d) 4

15. The most important characteristics of the Buddha's teaching is:
   1. complete explanation of the fact
   2. emphasis on cleansing oneself of what is base
   3. realization with the help of an illustration
   4. involving people in discussion
   (a) 1   (b) 2
   (c) 3   (d) 4

16. Choose the nearest antonym of the word - 'abhorred'.
   1. flattered
   2. entertained
   3. loved
   4. admonished
   (a) 1   (b) 2
   (c) 3   (d) 4

17. Identify the clause used in the underlined part of the sentence "Buddha told his disciples <u>what he taught they could understand and live up to</u> ".
   1. Noun clause
   2. Adjective clause
   3. Adverb clause
   4. Principal clause
   (a) 1   (b) 2
   (c) 3   (d) 4

18. Which of the following words has the same meanings as the word, 'permanent' used in the passage?
   1. unending
   2. lasting
   3. remaining
   4. sustaining
   (a) 1   (b) 2

(c) 3   (d) 4

19. Buddha's method of understanding 'the self' can be described as:
1. metaphysical
2. philosophical
3. moralistic
4. scientific
(a) 1   (b) 2
(c) 3   (d) 4

20. Which of the following is not one of the 'Four Noble Truths' as enunciated by the Buddha?
1. There is suffering in the world
2. There is a cause of this suffering
3. The suffering has a demoralising effect on us
4. There is possibility of ending the suffering
(a) 1   (b) 2
(c) 3   (d) 4

21. **Direction: Select the most appropriate word to fill in the blank.**
Unlike most ruler in the _____ age, Akbar believed in religious tolerance.
(a) historical   (b) ancient
(c) feudal   (d) aristocratic

22. **Direction: Select the most appropriate word to fill in the blank.**
The census gives _____ of the size, distribution and socio-economic, demographic and other characteristics of the country's population.
(a) information   (b) news
(c) facts   (d) acknowledgement

23. **Direction : Select the most appropriate word for the given group of words.**
Full of cheerful excitement or enthusiasm.
(a) Ebullient   (b) Eccentric
(c) Egoist   (d) Elegiac

24. **Select the correctly spelt word.**
(a) Riteous   (b) Righteous
(c) Rightious   (d) Richeous

25. **Direction : Select the word which means the same as the group of words given.**
A solution or remedy for all difficulties or diseases.
(a) Riddle   (b) Panacea
(c) Ailment   (d) Dilemma

Ques (26-27): Direction: Sentence Completion.

26. They were afraid _____ the lion, so they dropped the idea of hunting in the jungle.
(a) in   (b) for
(c) from   (d) of

27. Our company signed a profitable ____ last month.
(a) issue   (b) agenda
(c) deal   (d) paper

Ques (28-30): Direction: Read the following sentence to find out the error in it. The error will be in one part of the sentence. The number corresponding to that part will be your answer.

28. Psychologists has done a (A)/ considerable amount of research (B)/ to assess the effectiveness of various strategies (C)/ for behaviour modification. No Error(D)/
(a) (A)   (b) (B)
(c) (C)   (d) (D)

29. A great part of the information (1)/ I have, am acquired by (2)/ looking up something and (3)/ finding something else on the way. (4)
(a) 1   (b) 2
(c) 3   (d) 4

30. Yesterday, the three tax inspectors of the local government (1)/ is accused of (2)/ aiding and abetting the (3)/ men charged with fraud. (4)
(a) 1   (b) 2
(c) 3   (d) 4

Ques (31-32): Direction: Select the most appropriate indirect form of the given sentence.

31. **Mary says, "My younger brother wants to be a radio jockey."**
(a) Mary says that her younger brother wants to be a radio jockey.
(b) Mary says that my younger brother wanted to be a radio jockey.
(c) Mary said that her younger brother wanted to be a radio jockey.
(d) Mary says that my younger brother wants to be a radio jockey.

32. **"We will wait for you if you are late," they said to me on the telephone.**
(a) They told me on the telephone that they would wait for me if I am late.
(b) They told me on the telephone that they would wait for me if I was late.
(c) They said to me on the telephone that we will wait for you if you are late.
(d) They said to me on the telephone that they will wait for me if you were late.

33. **Direction:** In the following question, some parts of the sentence may have errors. Find out which part of the sentence has an error and select the appropriate option. If a sentence is free from error, select 'No Error'.
Unless you don't obey (A)/ your elders you (B)/ will not succeed in your life. (C)/ No Error (D)
(a) (A)   (b) (B)
(c) (C)   (d) (D)

Ques (34-36): Direction: In the following question, out of the four alternatives, select the alternative which will improve the underlined part of the sentence. In case no improvement is needed, select "No improvement".

34. **If you had intimated us about the arrival of guests, we <u>would had made</u> arrangements.**
(a) would have made   (b) will have made
(c) would have been made   (d) No improvement

35. **They barely knew each other, <u>do they</u>?**
(a) did they   (b) does they
(c) didn't they   (d) No improvement

36. **Shivam is <u>going to meeting</u> some of his friends, from his hometown, after work.**
(a) going meeting   (b) going to meet

   (c) go to meet   (d) No improvement

Ques (37-40): Direction: In the question given below, rearrange the parts of the sentence in the correct order, and choose the correct option.

37. Since the first eggs laid on land (A)/ thicker, harder shells that prevented moisture loss (B)/ of birds and reptiles started laying eggs with (C)/ were vulnerable to drying out, the ancestors (D).
    (a) ACDB
    (b) ADCB
    (c) BADC
    (d) BCAD

38. With jungle zip-lining, white-water rafting (A)/ and fire spewing from the (B)/ Arenal volcano, Costa Rica offers plenty (C)/ of thrilling adventures and sights (D).
    (a) ADBC
    (b) ABDC
    (c) CDBA
    (d) No rearrangement required

39. Which of the following is/are synonyms of farcical?
    I. Skeptical
    II. Preposterous
    III. Ludicrous
    IV. Perplexed
    (a) Only I
    (b) Only II and III
    (c) Only I, III and IV
    (d) Only II, III and IV

40. Which of the following is/are antonyms of complacent?
    I. Vitriolic
    II. Slack
    III. Humble
    IV. Gloat
    (a) Only IV
    (b) Only III
    (c) Only I, III and IV
    (d) Only II and IV

41. Which among the following phrase describes someone who comes up with a counter argument contrary to what other people have been saying?
    (a) Midnight's Children
    (b) Dark Sheep
    (c) Devil's Advocate
    (d) Satan's Sword

42. Choose the correct meaning of the given idiom: "To tie the knot"
    (a) Get married
    (b) Playing with a coir rope
    (c) Give a death penalty
    (d) Commit suicide

43. Which of the given words describe Yashpal's state most appropriately?
    "I am feeling under the weather, today", said Yashpal.
    (a) Brightness
    (b) Hardness
    (c) Wellness
    (d) Illness

44. Complete the sentence with appropriate phrase. To help you, the meaning of the phrase is given in the bracket: Sharmila has a _______ approach to management. She gets things done very efficiently, rather than following theory (practical).
    (a) baneful
    (b) rabid
    (c) speculative
    (d) pragmatic

45. Choose the correct option to complete the idiom which means to overcome a barrier:
    "To ______ through the glass ceiling".
    (a) crack
    (b) break

   (c) beat   (d) melt

Ques (46-47): Direction: Point out the figure of speech used in the sentence given below.

46. 'She let such beautiful pearls of wisdom slip from her mouth without even knowing.' What figure of speech is "pearls of wisdom"?
    (a) Metaphor
    (b) Simile
    (c) Personification
    (d) None of the above

47. I was so hungry that I could eat a cat.
    (a) Personification
    (b) Metaphor
    (c) Hyperbole
    (d) Alliteration

48. Monophthong _______
    (a) is called as a pure vowel
    (b) is marked by its steady quality
    (c) is a single vowel sound
    (d) All of above

49. In the production of vowel sounds, there is _______
    (a) complete closure of the air passage between speech organs.
    (b) no closure of the air passage between any speech organs.
    (c) partially closure of the air passage between speech organs.
    (d) All of above

50. Diphthong falls under the category of _______ sounds.
    (a) Consonant
    (b) vowel
    (c) Both
    (d) None

// Smart Answer Sheet //

Correct — Percentage of students who answered correctly.

Skipped — Percentage of students who skipped.

Q.	Ans.	Correct / Skipped	Q.	Ans.	Correct / Skipped	Q.	Ans.	Correct / Skipped
1	C	83.56% / 0.0%	2	B	89.94% / 0.0%	3	B	87.64% / 0.0%
4	C	80.19% / 0.0%	5	B	68.09% / 1.33%	6	C	82.56% / 0.0%
7	B	89.45% / 0.0%	8	B	22.04% / 3.33%	9	D	25.93% / 3.72%
10	B	50.31% / 1.13%	11	D	19.5% / 3.73%	12	B	24.38% / 4.29%
13	A	29.7% / 4.06%	14	D	42.15% / 1.11%	15	C	45.36% / 1.25%
16	C	58.46% / 1.03%	17	A	48.06% / 1.37%	18	B	87.75% / 0.0%
19	D	82.23% / 0.0%	20	C	78.93% / 0.0%	21	A	84.14% / 0.0%
22	A	44.47% / 1.2%	23	A	53.06% / 1.46%	24	B	81.08% / 0.0%
25	B	46.71% / 1.24%	26	D	81.13% / 0.0%	27	C	84.6% / 0.0%
28	A	81.92% / 0.0%	29	B	76.54% / 0.0%	30	B	85.3% / 0.0%
31	A	43.18% / 1.39%	32	B	43.18% / 1.39%	33	A	80.14% / 0.0%
34	A	66.1% / 1.12%	35	A	52.78% / 1.88%	36	B	56.49% / 1.71%
37	B	49.26%	38	D	40.01%	39	B	27.96%

		1.93%				1.77%			3.47%
40	B	40.11%	41	C		24.16%	42	A	58.03%
		1.91%				4.16%			1.14%
43	D	61.37%	44	D		48.09%	45	B	47.41%
		1.99%				1.33%			1.59%
46	A	52.67%	47	C		59.02%	48	D	87.16%
		1.61%				1.38%			0.0%
49	B	56.17%	50	B		60.48%			
		1.25%				1.39%			

// Hints and Solutions //

1(C). Gouvernail didn't like fishing and hunting birds much. According to the last paragraph (last line), He did not care to fish, and displayed no eagerness to go out and kill sparrows when Gaston proposed doing so.

2(B). The word 'provoked' in the passage means Irritated.
Provoked: To try to make a person or an animal angry or annoyed, to irritate
Example: He was trying to provoke me into a fight.
Irritated: Annoyed
Example: I began to get increasingly irritated by her questions.

3(B). The underlined word is an Adjective.
Eagerness is a noun meaning enthusiasm to do or to have something; keenness.
An adjective refers to a word which qualifies i.e., gives us more information about the noun.
Chatty is a word that is modifying the noun eagerness.

4(C). Mrs. Baroda liked Gouvernail but she didn't know why. She partly knew why. It is not stated clearly why she liked him. She thinks him to possess some traits her husband didn't was one of the reasons but not the entire reason.
According to the lines, Gouvernail was slim enough, but he wasn't very tall nor very cynical; neither did he wear eyeglasses nor carry his hands in his pockets. And she rather liked him when he first presented himself.
But why she liked him she could not explain satisfactorily to herself when she partly attempted to do so. She could discover in him none of those brilliant and promising traits which Gaston, her husband, had often assured her that he possessed.

5(B). In part b, has needs to be replaced by had.
Seeing the part a of the sentence, we can get an idea that the given sentence is in past tense. Has is in present tense and to change it into past tense, we need to make it had.
Correct sentence: He did not care to fish, (a)/ and had no eagerness to go out (b)/and kill sparrows (c)/ when Gaston proposed doing so.(d)/

6(C). The only characteristic of Gouvernail that matched with the image that Mrs. Baroda had formed of him in her mind was that he was slim. But, he wasn't very tall nor very cynical; neither did he wear eyeglasses nor carry his hands in his pockets.
According to these lines:
- But she had unconsciously formed an image of him in her mind. She pictured him tall, slim, cynical; with eyeglasses, and his hands in his pockets; and she did not like him.
- Gouvernail was slim enough, but he wasn't very tall nor very cynical; neither did he wear eyeglasses nor carry his hands in his pockets.

7(B). Mrs. Baroda wanted to rest and have undisturbed company of her husband while on the plantation.

According to the lines:
Once settled at the plantation he seemed to like to sit upon the wide portico in the shade of one of the big Corinthian pillars, smoking his cigar lazily and listening attentively to Gaston's experience as a sugar planter.
It can be deduced that Mrs. Baroda wanted to smoke cigar lazily. The words 'lazily' show that she was in a mood to rest. And, she wanted to listen attentively to her husband i.e., wanted to have his company solely.(Solely means only and not involving anyone or anything else).

8(B). The author has first described depression in the passage. Then, he has described old age and given details of the reasons that are responsible for depression in old age.
So, the focus is mostly on 'depression in old age'.

9(D). The following is given in the passage: "In primitive, ancient, and medieval cultures, old persons had a recognized social role. They were of great value because they could impart knowledge and skill to youngsters. The old people were considered as repositories of wisdom and traditions and were not perceived as problems".

10(B). The given statement clearly means that mild depression is caused by environmental factors and does not have a deep or ever-lasting effect on a person. It only lasts for a brief period of time.

11(D). Meanings of the given words are-
Mercy means 'compassion or forgiveness shown towards someone whom it is within one's power to punish or harm'.
Abhorred means 'regarded with disgust and hatred'.
Reconcile means 'restore friendly relations between'.
Succour means 'assistance and support in times of hardship and distress'.

12(B). The following is given in the passage : "The elderly as a result of these developments feel marginalized, alienated, and left out of the mainstream. The foregoing are the common problems faced by most of the elderly".
'Alienated' means 'left alone; experiencing or inducing feelings of isolation'.
As the only problem mentioned in the options is 'loneliness'.

13(A). The following is given in the passage: "If the individual is severely disturbed and is not able to comprehend what is happening around, such a state is called psychotic depression".
This clearly means that in psychotic depression the individual fails to understand what is going on around him.

14(D). According to the passage, " The individual thus becomes a bundle of mental states, the self is just a stream of ideas. 'All that we are is the result of what we have thought'."
So, it can be concluded that after the emergence of new scientific approaches the self', came to be considered as a stream of ideas.

15(C). According to the passage, "Once it is said, he look some dry leaves in his hand and asked his favourite disciple, Ananda, to tell him whether there were any other leaves besides those in his hand. Ananda replied: The leaves of autumn are falling on all sides, and there are more of them than can be numbered, Then said the Buddha: 'In like manner I have given you a handful of truths, but besides these are many thousand of other truths, more than can be numbered.'"
So, it can be concluded that the most important characteristics of the Buddha's teaching is realization with

the help of an illustration.

16(C). The meaning of the given words:
- Abhorred: to hate something very much
- Loved: to like somebody/something in the strongest possible way
- Flattered: to say nice things to somebody, often in a way that is not sincere, because you want to please him/her or because you want to get an advantage for yourself
- Entertained: to interest and amuse somebody in order to please him/her
- Admonished: to tell somebody firmly that you do not approve of something that he/she has done

From the meanings of the given words, we can conclude that loved is the most appropriate antonym of abhorred.

17(A). Noun clause used in the underlined part of the sentence "Buddha told his disciples <u>what he taught they could understand and live up to</u> ".
A noun clause is a clause (a group of words with a subject and a verb) that serves as a noun in a sentence.
Example: <u>That she has won the prize</u> surprised me.

18(B). The meaning of the given words:
- Permanent: lasting for a long time or forever; that will not change
- Lasting: continuing for a long time
- Unending: having or seeming to have no end
- Remaining: to stay or continue in the same place or condition
- Sustaining: to keep somebody/something alive or healthy

From the meanings of the given words, we can conclude that lasting has the same meanings as the word, 'permanent'.

19(D). According to the passage, " Buddha's method was one of psychological analysis and, again, it is surprising to find how deep was his insight into this latest of modern sciences. Man's life was considered and examined without any reference to a permanent self, for even if such a self exists, it is beyond our comprehension."
So, it can be concluded that Buddha's method of understanding 'the self' can be described as scientific.

20(C). According to the passage, "There is an emphasis on the pain and suffering of life, and the 'Four Noble Truths' which Buddha enunciated deal with this suffering, its cause, the possibility of ending it, and the way to do it."
So, it can be concluded that the suffering has a demoralising effect on us is not one of the 'Four Noble Truths' as enunciated by the Buddha.

21(A). Unlike most ruler in the historical age, Akbar believed in religious tolerance.
'Historical' means pertaining to past events.
It forms a meaningful sentence: Akbar was one of the rulers belonging to a past age.

22(A). Information is the most appropriate word to fill the blanks.
Information means knowledge or facts.
News means information, headlines.
Facts mean details, factual data.

23(A). • 'Ebullient' is an 'adjective' which means 'cheerful and full of energy.'
  ○ Example: She sounded ebullient and happy.'
  Thus, the first option is the most appropriate choice.

WORDS	MEANING

Eccentric (noun)	A person of unconventional and slightly strange views or behavior.
Egoist (noun)	A self-centered or selfish person (opposed to altruist). an arrogantly conceited person.
Elegiac (adjective)	Relating to or characteristic of an elegy.

24(B). Let's look at the correct spelling and meaning of the marked option:
- **Righteous** - (of a person or conduct) morally right or justifiable; virtuous.

Example :
He was regarded as a righteous and holy man.

25(B). • The most appropriate one-word for the given group of words is 'Panacea'.
- Let's look at the meaning and examples of the given words:

Riddle	something that is confusing, or a problem that is difficult to solve	*Scientists may have solved the riddle of Saturn's rings.*
Panacea	something that will solve all problems	*Technology is not a panacea for all our problems.*
Ailment	an illness	*Treat minor ailments yourself.*
Dilemma	a situation in which a difficult choice has to be made between two different things you could do	*The president is clearly in a dilemma over how to tackle the crisis.*

- Therefore, by reading the above explanation we find that the correct answer is panacea.

26(D). Afraid agrees with the preposition 'of', so option (D) is correct.
Complete sentence: They were afraid of the lion, so they dropped the idea of hunting in the jungle.

27(C). Normally, a company signs a contract or deal, so the use of 'deal' is proper here.
Deal means an agreement entered into by two or more parties for their mutual benefit, especially in a business.
Complete sentence: Our company signed a profitable deal last month.

28(A). The error is in the first part of the sentence.
We need to replace 'has' with 'have'. The plural subject 'psychologists' should be accompanied by the plural auxiliary verb 'have' in accordance with the rule of subject-verb agreement.
Correct sentence: Psychologists have done a considerable amount of research to assess the effectiveness of various strategies for behaviour modification.

29(B). The auxiliary verb "am" is for the noun "part" which is a part of third person singular subject (a great part of the information). So, the corresponding verb should follow suit. It should be "is" instead of "am" in part (2).

30(B). "Inspectors" is a plural noun so the respective verb should be plural too. But in the given case, the verb "is" is singular. It should be "were" in part (2).

31(A). It is clear that the given sentence is in the present tense so the changes will be limited.

To convert from direct to indirect speech, there are some basic rules that we need to follow:
- Inverted commas (,") needs to be removed and use 'that' in the same place.

The subject of the Reported speech (My younger brother) has to be changed according to the Subject of Reporting speech (Mary says).
- The subject 'My younger brother' into 'her younger brother'.

If we follow the above changes, the indirect speech would be:
- Mary says that her younger brother wants to be a radio jockey.

32(B). To convert from direct to indirect speech, there are some basic rules that we need to follow:
- 'Said to' will be converted into 'told'.
- Inverted commas (,") needs to be removed and use 'that' in the same place.

The subject and verb of the Reported speech (We will wait for you if you are late) have to be changed according to the given Reporting speech (they said to me on the telephone). There are two underlined subjects in the reporting speech here - We will wait for you if you are late.
- The subject 'We' into 'They' and the next subject 'you' into 'I'.

There are two underlined verbs in the reporting speech here - We will wait for you if you are late
- The verb 'will wait' into 'would wait' and the verb 'are' into 'was'.
- The object 'you' into 'me'.

If we follow the above changes, the indirect speech would be:
- They told me on the telephone that they would wait for me if I was late.

33(A). The correct sentence should be unless you obey in part (A).

Unless means if this condition is not met. Don't use other negative words in the clause starting with conjunctions until and unless.

Correct sentence: Unless you obey your elders you will not succeed in your life.

34(A).
- Conditional sentences are statements discussing known factors or hypothetical situations and their consequences.
- One of the structures is mentioned below:
- This particular type is followed when something didn't happen as a certain condition wasn't fulfilled.

Correct Sentence: If you had intimated us about the arrival of guests, we **would have made** arrangements.

35(A).
- If the statement is negative , the question tag must be positive and vice versa.
- But if any of these words are used, the question tag will be positive :
- Hardly, Scarcely, seldom, rarely, barely.

Correct Sentence: They barely knew each other, **did they** ?

36(B). For events that will take place in the near future, Present Continuous Tense is used.

Correct Sentence: Shivam is **going to meet** some of his friends, from his hometown, after work.

37(B). The correct rearrangement is ADCB.

A begins the sentence by introducing the surrounding context and telling us about the first eggs laid by animals on land. D continues by telling us how these eggs were vulnerable to drying out. D also establishes the subject - the ancestors. C follows with the verb stem and tells us what the ancestors of birds and reptiles began to do - laying eggs with thick and hard shells (continued by B).

ADCB is the final order.

38(D). AB begins the sentence as a pair, by telling us the activities that Costa Rica offers - jungle zip-lining, rafting, and volcanic sights. C follows by establishing the subject - Costa Rica. D concludes with the verb stem by telling us how this nation offers adventures and sights.

Thus, ABCD is the final order.

39(B). Farcical: relating to or resembling farce, especially because of absurd or ridiculous aspects.

Eg: He considered the whole idea farcical.

Synonyms: Preposterous and Ludicrous.

Skeptical and perplexed both mean puzzled.

40(B). Complacent: showing smug or uncritical satisfaction with oneself or one's achievements.

Eg: We can't afford to be complacent about security.

Synonyms: Slack, gloat.

Thus, II and IV are incorrect.

Vitriolic means hurtful/spiteful.

Only humble is correct as the antonym of complacent.

Hence, the correct option is ().

41(C). Devil's advocate describes the given phrase, Devil's advocate is one who expresses a contentious opinion in order to provoke debate or test the strength of the opposing arguments.

42(A). "To tie the knot" is an idiom that means to get married. The expression is often used to describe the act of getting married and is a reference to the tying of a knot, which symbolizes the binding of two people together in marriage.

43(D). The idiom "feeling under the weather" is a common way of saying that someone is feeling ill or not feeling well. This phrase is often used to describe minor illnesses, such as colds or flu-like symptoms, rather than serious illnesses.

44(D). As practical is to be used in the given sentence, the word practical means something that is feasible and concerned with real circumstances. Thus, from the given options, option (D) i.e. pragmatic which means sensible and realistic approach, will be correct alternative to fill the blank.

45(B). 'To break through the glass ceiling' means to overcome a barrier.

46(A). In the given sentence "pearls of wisdom" is a metaphor. Metaphor: It is a figure of speech that describes an object or an action in a way that isn't literally true. It helps explain an idea or make a comparison.

In the given sentence "pearls of wisdom" means something that sounds very wise and useful. It doesn't literally mean pearls that are made of wisdom. Therefore, the figure of speech here is a metaphor.

47(C). Hyperbole is a figure of speech in which an author or speaker purposely and obviously exaggerates to an extreme.

In the given sentence, the speaker was extremely hungry and so the hunger is exaggerated in a way that he could eat a cat. So, hyperbole is the correct answer.

48(D). Monophthong: is called as a pure vowel; is marked by its steady quality; is a single vowel sound.

49(B). In the production of vowel sounds, there is no closure of the air passage between any speech organs.

50(B). Diphthong falls under the category of vowel sounds.

Ques (1-6): Direction: Read the passage given below and answer the following question.

The Kittur Fort

One can see today only the dilapidated walls and ruins of the great fort which was once known for its strength. The most important landmark as one goes towards the fort is the 'Bahadurgad'. Situated to the southwest of the fort and outside of it, on a natural hillock, the highest in the plain, the 'Bahadurgad', which was the watchtower, provides a most panoramic and commanding view of the sparsely wooded surrounding region of green grassland, fading, as if gradually, into soft contoured hills in the west and the horizons on the other sides. To the north of the tower is 'Ranagattikere' where Rani Chennamma fought her last stubborn fight against the British, with almost savage determination.

The actual fort, circular in plan, consisted of double walls, separated by moats on the outer sides, with semi-circular bastions on the exterior of the outer wall. It had originally the main gateway on the east, approached by the causeway across the outer moat known as ane honda which was used for bathing the elephants.

The entrances through the walls are deliberately not aligned, evidently in the interests of security. After passing by the winding path through the walls, one is led to the front side of the imposing main entrance of the palace located near the northern arc of the inner fort wall.

To the south of the palace, inside the fort, are the ruins of horse-stables and foundations of residential buildings, probably meant for the important officials of the palace. To the southwest is the heavily built watchtower relieved by a series of parallel buttresses at regular intervals.

1. **Which one of the following statements is true?**
   (a) Rani Chennamma ruled Kittur from here.
   (b) Bahadurgad is situated inside the Kittur Fort.
   (c) From it, one can enjoy a view of the hills in the east.
   (d) It was used as a watchtower.

2. **Rani Chennamma fought against the British:**
   (a) in Bahadurgad Fort
   (b) in the wooded grasslands
   (c) in the contoured hills
   (d) at Ranangattikere

3. **From Bahadurgad, one could easily get:**
   (a) to see a natural hillock
   (b) a commanding view of a dense forest
   (c) to see tall rugged hills in the west
   (d) a look at green grasslands

4. **Unaligned gates in the walls:**
   (a) make the walls look imposing
   (b) make the entry easy
   (c) make the fort secure
   (d) make the fort insecure

5. **"___ as one goes towards ____"**
   'one' in the above clause is a/an:
   (a) adjective
   (b) noun
   (c) verb
   (d) pronoun

6. **"___ and commanding view of ___."**
   'commanding' in the above phrase is a/an:
   (a) adverb
   (b) noun
   (c) verb
   (d) adjective

Ques (7-13): Direction : Read the passage carefully and answer the questions that follow by selecting the correct/most appropriate options.

Born out of the forces of globalization, India's IT sector is undertaking some globalization of its own. In search of new sources of rapid growth, the country's outsourcing giants are aggressively expanding beyond their usual stomping grounds into the developing world; setting up programming centres, chasing new clients and hiring local talent. Through geographic diversification, Indian companies hope to regain some momentum after the recession. This shift is being driven by a global economy in which the US is no longer the undisputed engine of growth. India's IT powers rose to prominence largely on the decisions made by American executives, who were quick to capitalize on the cost savings to be gained by outsourcing non-core operations, such as systems programming and call centres, to specialists overseas.

Revenues in India's IT sector surged from \$4 billion in 1998 to \$59 billion last fiscal, but with the recession, NASSCOM forecasts that the growth rate of India's exports of IT and other business services to the US and Europe will drop to at most 7% in the current fiscal year, down from 16% last year and 29% in 2007–08.

Factors other than the crisis are driving India's IT firms into the emerging world. Although the US still accounts for 60% of the export revenue of India's IT sector, emerging markets are growing faster. Tapping these more dynamic economies won't be easy, however. The goal of Indian IT firms for the past 30 years has been to woo clients outside India and transfer as much of the actual work as possible back home, where lower wages for highly skilled programmers allowed them to offer significant cost savings. With costs in other emerging economies equally low, Indian firms can't compete on price alone.

To adapt, Indian companies which are relatively unknown in these emerging nations are establishing major local operations around the world, in the process of hiring thousands of locals. Cultural conflicts arise at times while training new recruits. In addition, IT firms also have to work extra hard to woo business from emerging-market companies still unaccustomed to the concept of outsourcing. If successful, the future of India's outsourcing sector could prove as bright as its past.

7. **Which of the following factors made the services offered by the Indian IT attractive to the US?**
   A. Indian IT companies had expertise in rare core operations
   B. The US lacked the necessary infrastructure and personnel to handle mass call centre operations
   C. Inability of other equally cost-efficient developing countries to comply with their strict policies
   (a) None
   (b) Only A
   (c) Only A and B
   (d) Only C

8. **What has caused Indian IT firms to change the way they conduct business in developing countries?**
   (a) The volume of work being awarded cannot be handled by Indian firms
   (b) The demands of these markets are different from those of India's traditional customers
   (c) Wages demanded by local workers are far higher than what they pay their Indian employees
   (d) Stringent laws which are not conducive to outsourcing

9. **According to the passage, which one of the following is not a difficulty that Indian IT firms will face in emerging markets?**

(a) Mindset resistant to outsourcing
(b) Local IT services are equally cost-effective
(c) The US is their preferred outsourcing destination
(d) Conflicts arising during the training of local talent

10. **Which of the following is/are not true in the context of the passage?**
A. The recession severely impacted the US but not India.
B. India is trying to depend less on the US as a source of growth.
C. The future success of Indian IT firms depends on emerging markets.
(a) Only B and C
(b) Only A
(c) Only B
(d) All A, B and C

11. **Which one of the following words is most similar in meaning to the word 'chasing' as used in the passage?**
(a) Running
(b) Harassing
(c) Pestering
(d) Pursuing

12. **Which one of the following words is most opposite to the meaning of the word 'undisputed' as used in the passage?**
(a) Challenging
(b) Doubtful
(c) Deprived
(d) Emphasized

13. **Other than crisis, what is driving IT companies to seek other options?**
(a) The US makes more than 60% of India's export revenue
(b) Emerging markets
(c) None of the above
(d) Both (A) and (B)

Ques (14-20): Direction : Read the passage given below and answer the questions/ complete the statements that follow with the help of given options.

Our giant water tower was home to some big and menacing honey free colonies. We made all efforts to get rid of them for the safety of the human residents of the colony. Honey collectors were invited but were only able to destroy a few hives.

Actually they never wished to get rid of all the honey trees honey was their livelihood. Whenever we saw the honey collectors in their loin- dhoti, jute ropes, leaf baskets and flaming torches, the children would run home for fear of the bees and hail the honey collectors for their bravery from our balconies. For me as a kid bees did not belong to the urban environment.

Decades later, a thousand kilometres from the water tank, I accompanied honey collectors deep into the forest to study their harvesting technique. They carnied battery lights, ropes and bee suits. Climbing up the trees, protected by the bee suit, the collectors set to the task - they extracted the honey chamber leaving the hive intact. A few days before the extraction, they had inspected the hives to select those that looked full or healthy - ensuring that honey extraction does not damage the hives. This sustainable harvest ensured that the bees were not destroyed and the collectors retained their livelihood. For the biologist the bees belonged to the wilderness.

In between the water tower and the forest lie our gardens and fruit orchards. Here both humans and bees meet more intimately. Here our relationship with bees is give and take. They pollinate our flowers and help our fruit trees to get laden with fruit.

14. **'Only able to destroy a few hives' the word opposite in meaning to 'destroy' is:**
1. Enjoy
2. Enlarge
3. Build
4. Occupy

(a) 1
(b) 2
(c) 3
(d) 4

15. **The writer of this article is a:**
1. Biologist
2. Photographer
3. Honey collector
4. Bee keeper
(a) 1
(b) 2
(c) 3
(d) 4

16. **In the forest, the honey collectors-**
1. help pollinate the flowers.
2. carry flaming torches to distract the bees.
3. don't have to climb the trees.
4. collect more honey.
(a) 1
(b) 2
(c) 3
(d) 4

17. **Study the following statements:**
a. Honey collectors cheated the residents of the colony.
b. Safety of the colony residents was completely ensured.
c. Hailing the honey collectors by the residents was misplaced.
1. (a) is right and (b) is wrong.
2. (b) is right and (a) is wrong.
3. (b) is right and (c) is wrong.
4. (c) is right and (a) is wrong.
(a) 1
(b) 2
(c) 3
(d) 4

18. **And 'smouldering torches' the word 'smouldering' here means:**
1. Glowing
2. Burning
3. Bright
4. Shining
(a) 1
(b) 2
(c) 3
(d) 4

19. **'those that looked full' the underlined word is a/an:**
1. Adjective
2. Adverb
3. Pronoun
4. Preposition
(a) 1
(b) 2
(c) 3
(d) 4

20. **Study the following statements:**
(a) The trees are treated as a menace in the cities.
(b) Man derives a double benefit from the bees.
1. (a) is right and (b) is wrong.
2. (b) is right and (a) is wrong.
3. Both (a) and (b) are right.
4. Both (a) and (b) are wrong.
(a) 1
(b) 2
(c) 3
(d) 4

21. **From the given words in option, choose the word wrongly spelt:**
(a) Imperative
(b) Ilicit
(c) Imminent
(d) Immature

22. **Choose the word wrongly spelt:**
(a) Semester
(b) Senesent
(c) Sensory
(d) Salacious

23. Choose the word wrongly spelt:

(a) Teaser   (b) Teething

(c) Tedious   (d) Teatotaller

Ques (24-25): Direction: In the following question, out of the four alternatives, select the alternative which is the best substitute of the phrase/sentence.

24. Writing or drawings scribbled, scratched, or sprayed illicitly on a wall or other surface in a public place.

(a) Splotch   (b) Smudge

(c) Graffiti   (d) Streak

25. A person or thing that brings bad luck.

(a) Felicitous   (b) Adventitious

(c) Jinx   (d) Providential

26. Direction : In the given question, a sentence or a part of the sentence is emboldened. Below are given alternatives to that part that may improve the sentence. Choose the correct alternative. In case no improvement is required, choose the No improvement option.
He has composed a beautiful song.

(a) jotted down   (b) No improvement

(c) written   (d) penned

27. Direction: Choose the correct suffix to get meaningful word.
Coloni__.

(a) -y   (b) -al

(c) -less   (d) -ive

28. Direction: Select the correct form of the tense for the given sentence.
Had it been raining all night?

(a) Present perfect continuous

(b) Past perfect continuous

(c) Future perfect continuous

(d) Past perfect

29. Direction: Choose the correct meaning of the idiom and mark the answer.
By leaps and bounds

(a) very fast   (b) very slow

(c) in details   (d) aimlessly

30. Direction: Identify the underlined part of speech in the given sentence:
Isn't that a <u>new</u> jacket you're wearing?

(a) Adjective   (b) Noun

(c) Preposition   (d) Adverb

31. Direction: In the following question out of the four alternatives, choose the alternative which best expresses the meaning of the Idiom/Phrase.
Know the ropes

(a) Knowledge of braiding

(b) Death by hanging

(c) A long winding road

(d) Experience of procedures

Ques (32-33): Direction: Select the option that expresses the given sentence in the reported speech.

32. Harry said to me, "Don't wear this expensive watch to school".

(a) Harry told me that not to wear that expensive watch to school.

(b) Harry told me not to wear that expensive watch to school.

(c) Harry told me that don't wear that expensive watch to school.

(d) Harry told me to not wear this expensive watch to school.

33. She said, "It is my birthday next week".

(a) She said that my birthday was next week.

(b) She said that it is my birthday the following week.

(c) She said that it was her birthday the following week.

(d) She said that next week was her birthday.

Ques (34-36): Direction: Fill in the blank with the correct word.

34. Do not push her ____ the problem as she is too young to deal with all this.

(a) In   (b) Into

(c) Up   (d) At

35. Small kids carry heavy sacks which ____ their physical development.

(a) Is stunting   (b) Stunt

(c) Was stunt   (d) Stunts

36. Advertisements and promotional campaigns are being ____ by the company.

(a) Ran   (b) Run

(c) Running   (d) Runs

Ques (37-39): Direction: In question, a part of the sentence is made bold. Below are given alternatives to the bold part at (A), (B), (C) and (D) which may improve the sentence. Choose the correct alternative. In case no replacement is needed, mark (E) as your answer.

37. Though every boy and girl were present , the Principal did not turn down .

(a) Was present, turn up

(b) Was present, turned off

(c) Was present, turned about

(d) Were present, turned on

38. I am really sorry that he is latest ; you must are waiting for a long time.

(a) He is latest, had been waiting

(b) He is late, has been waiting

(c) He is late, have been waiting

(d) He is late, is waiting

39. I shall wait for you here till you will finish with your class in the college.

(a) Shall wait, shall finish   (b) Will wait, shall finish

(c) Wait, finish   (d) Shall wait, finish

40. Direction: Identify the best way to improve the underlined part of the given sentence. If there is no improvement required, select 'no Improvement'.
All the faces <u>bore same expression for</u> excitement and enthusiasm.

(a) bore the same expressive of

(b) bore same expression as

(c) bore the same expression of

(d) No Improvement

Ques (41-45): Direction: Given below are some idioms/phrases followed by four alternative meanings for each. Choose the most appropriate answer from among the options (A), (B), (C) and (D).

41. A queer fish:
(a) A strange person
(b) A good person
(c) An unlucky person
(d) A lucky person

42. Be in the pink:
(a) To be very healthy
(b) To be very colourful
(c) To be very sad
(d) To be very rich

43. Be in the running:
(a) In a very bad state to speak
(b) In a powerful position
(c) In a good position to win
(d) In a losing position

44. A sea change:
(a) Change in the sea tides
(b) A complete change
(c) Change like sea
(d) Changed sea with pollution

45. Be in seventh heaven:
(a) To be extremely sorry
(b) To be extremely wise
(c) To be extremely sad
(d) To be extremely happy

46. Direction : Choose the correct Figure of Speech in the following sentence:
'The wind lies asleep in the arms of dawn.'
(a) Metaphor
(b) Hyperbole
(c) Personification
(d) Oxymoron

47. Direction : Point out 'Figure of Speech' in the following sentence:
"And having nothing, he hath all."
(a) Onomatopoeia
(b) Oxymoron
(c) Simile
(d) Apostrophe

48. In BrE /ɔ/ in words such as Not, block, cross, stop, college is pronounced _____ in AmE.
(a) /ɑː/
(b) /o/
(c) /oɔ/
(d) None

49. The word 'Asia' is pronounced as /'eɪʒə/ in British English, whereas it is pronounced _______ in American English.
(a) /'eɪʃiːa/
(b) /'eɪʃə/
(c) /'eɪʃə/
(d) /'eɪʃːya/

50. RP is the abbreviation of the word _________.
(a) right pronunciation
(b) received pronunciation
(c) right practice
(d) received practice

// Smart Answer Sheet //

	Correct	Percentage of students who answered correctly.
	Skipped	Percentage of students who skipped.

Q.	Ans.	Correct / Skipped	Q.	Ans.	Correct / Skipped	Q.	Ans.	Correct / Skipped
1	D	60.06% / 1.33%	2	D	59.81% / 1.61%	3	D	87.73% / 0.0%
4	C	60.33% / 1.88%	5	D	56.95% / 1.37%	6	D	27.93% / 4.17%
7	D	65.05% / 1.48%	8	C	62.52% / 1.97%	9	D	85.78% / 0.0%
10	B	56.04% / 1.89%	11	D	58.34% / 1.97%	12	B	64.59% / 1.29%
13	D	88.12% / 0.0%	14	C	48.45% / 1.8%	15	A	83.25% / 0.0%
16	D	84.83% / 0.0%	17	A	89.23% / 0.0%	18	B	52.6% / 1.56%
19	C	50.55% / 1.96%	20	C	76.97% / 0.0%	21	B	53.53% / 1.24%
22	B	57.73% / 1.51%	23	D	43.31% / 1.1%	24	C	19.62% / 3.1%
25	C	64.61% / 1.19%	26	B	89.99% / 0.0%	27	B	60.08% / 1.8%
28	B	53.74% / 1.74%	29	A	40.35% / 1.34%	30	A	48.35% / 1.24%
31	D	58.22% / 1.59%	32	B	42.13% / 1.03%	33	C	63.28% / 1.63%
34	B	67.27% / 1.92%	35	D	46.28% / 1.52%	36	B	65.85% / 1.17%
37	A	48.25% / 1.0%	38	C	54.57% / 1.14%	39	D	42.85% / 1.6%
40	C	80.69% / 0.0%	41	A	55.33% / 1.52%	42	A	63.71% / 1.65%
43	C	50.22% / 1.52%	44	B	45.36% / 1.39%	45	D	83.17% / 0.0%
46	C	61.13% / 1.77%	47	B	44.02% / 1.26%	48	A	89.45% / 0.0%
49	B	81.54% / 0.0%	50	D	89.38% / 0.0%			

// Hints and Solutions //

1(D). A true statements is , It was used as a watchtower.
Look at the line: 'Situated to the southwest of the fort and outside of it, on a natural hillock, the highest in the plain, the 'Bahadurgad', which was the watchtower'
Thus, we can conclude that it was used as a watchover.

2(D). Rani Chennamma fought against the British at Ranangattikere.
- Refer to the line: 'To the north of the tower is ' Ranagattikere' where Rani Chennamma fought her last stubborn fight against the British, with almost savage determination.'
- Thus, we can conclude that Rani Chennamma fought against the British at Ranangattikere.

3(D). From Bahadurgad, one could easily get a look at green grasslands.
- Refer to the line: 'Situated to the southwest of the fort and outside of it, on a natural hillock, the highest in the plain, the 'Bahadurgad', which was the watchtower, provides a most panoramic and commanding view of the sparsely wooded surrounding region of green grassland '.
- Thus, we can conclude that one could look at the green grasslands from Bahadurgad.

4(C). Unaligned gates in the walls make the fort secure.
- Refer to the line: 'The entrances through the walls are deliberately not aligned, evidently in the interests of security'.
- Thus, we can conclude that unaligned gates acted as security for the fort i.e. made the fort secure.

5(D). 'one' in the above clause is a pronoun.
- Pronoun is a word that is used instead of a noun or a noun phrase. These are often used to refer to a noun that has already been mentioned. Eg: He, she, it etc.

- One may act as an indefinite pronoun in the English language.
- It is a gender-neutral, third-person singular pronoun. It mostly acts as as a subject (nominative case) like the case here.
- In the sentence, "_ _ _ as one goes towards _ _ _", one is a pronoun.

6(D). 'Commanding' in the above phrase is an adjective.
Adjectives are words that are used to describe or modify nouns or pronouns.
For example,
a red hat, the quick rabbit, a happy duck, an obnoxious person. Here, all the bold words are adjectives.
View is a noun which refers to a sight or prospect, typically of attractive natural scenery, that can be taken in by the eye from a particular place.
Commanding is an adjective which refers to (of a place or position) dominating from above; giving a wide view of an area.
Similarly, in the above sentence, 'commanding' is an adjective which describes the noun 'view'.

7(D). According to passage: "India's IT powers rose to prominence largely on the decisions made by American executives, who were quick to capitalize on the cost savings to be gained by outsourcing noncore operations, such as systems programming and call centres, to specialists overseas . "
Clearly, the inability of other equally cost-efficient developing countries to comply with the US's strict policies made the services offered by the Indian IT attractive to the US.

8(C). According to passage: "The goal of Indian IT firms for the past 30 years has been to woo clients outside India and transfer as much of the actual work as possible back home, where lower wages for highly skilled programmers allowed them to offer significant cost savings."
Wages demanded by local workers are far higher than what they pay their Indian employees has caused Indian IT firms to change the way they conduct business in developing countries.

9(D). According to passage: "Cultural conflicts arise at times while training new recruits."
So, according to the passage conflicts arising during the training of local talent is not a difficulty that Indian IT firms will face in emerging markets.

10(B). According to passage: "Through geographic diversification, Indian companies hope to regain some momentum after the recession."
Therefore, the recession also impacted India.

11(D). The meaning of the word 'chasing' is 'to run after or follow someone'.
The meaning of the other given words:
Running: racing
Harassing: to annoy someone continuously
Pestering: to trouble or annoy someone
Pursuing: to follow or run after someone or something
Clearly, option (D) is the word which is most similar in meaning to the word 'chasing' as used in the passage.

12(B). The meaning of the word 'undisputed' is 'not in doubt'.
The meaning of the given words:
Challenging: testing one's capacity
Doubtful: in question or in doubt
Deprived: poverty-stricken
Emphasized: give prominence to

Clearly, option (B) is the word which is most opposite in meaning of the word 'undisputed'.

13(D). According to passage: "Factors other than the crisis are driving India's IT firms into the emerging world. Although the US still accounts for 60% of the export revenue of India's IT sector, emerging markets are growing faster. "
Clearly, the IT companies are seeking other options because the US makes more than 60% of India's export revenue and emerging markets are growing faster.

14(C). The opposite meaning to 'destroy' is 'build'.
Meaning of the given words:
- Destroy - to damage something so badly that it cannot be used
- Build - to develop according to a systematic plan, by a definite process, or on a particular base
- Enjoy - to get pleasure from the situation
- Enlarge - to become bigger or to make something bigger
- Occupy - to fill, exist in, or use a place or period of time

15(A). The writer of this article is a biologist because he says that for biologist the bees belonged to the wilderness. And for him bees did not belong to the urban environment.

16(D). According to the passage, in the forest, the honey collectors collect more honey.

17(A). According to the passage, statement (a) is right and (b) is wrong.
Honey collectors cheated the residents of the colony as honey was their livelihood but statement (b) and (c) is incorrect.

18(B). In the phrase "Smouldering torches", the word "Smouldering" means burning.
Meaning of the given words:
- Burning - affecting with or as if with heat
- Glowing - shining with or as if with warmth or heat
- Bright - of high saturation or lightness
- Shining - to be eminent, conspicuous, or distinguished

19(C). In the given sentence, "Those that looked full", 'that' is a pronoun.
A relative pronoun is a pronoun that marks a relative clause. It serves the purpose of conjoining modifying information about an antecedent referent.
In the above sentence 'that' is used to conjoin those with 'full'.

20(C). According to the passage,
- Trees are treated as a menace in the cities as bees belong to trees.
- Man derives a double benefit from the bees they pollinate our flowers and help our fruit trees to get laden with fruit.

Therefore, both (a) and (b) are right.

21(B). Word ' Ilicit' is wrongly spelt. The correct word is Illicit.
Illicit - To manage to get information, facts, a reaction, etc. from somebody.

22(B). Word ' Senesent' is wrongly spelt. The correct word is Senescent.
Senescent - This means that the three main phases of life are there in every species-r-development.

23(D). Word 'Teatotaller' is wrongly spelt. The correct word is Teetotaller.
Teetotaller - A person who does not drink alcohol

24(C). Graffiti means words or drawings (especially humorous/

funny/rude in nature) made on walls or doors.
Splotch means a large uneven mark or stain.
Smudge means a mark with no particular shape.
Streak means a long thin line or mark which is usually different in color from its surroundings.

25(C). Jinx means someone or something that brings bad luck.
Other words:
Felicitous means used to describe something as suitable / right because it expresses the desired thought.
Adventitious means happening by chance or by accident.
Providential means happening exactly when needed.

26(B). The sentence is grammatically correct and needs no improvement.

27(B). A suffix is a letter or a group of letters that is usually attached to the end of a word to form a new word, as well as alter the way it functions grammatically.
The word Colonial consists of the root word 'Coloni' combined with the suffix '-al' which means 'relating to'.
There are some words related to the Suffix '-al' are - Fiscal, Thermal.

28(B). The given sentence 'Had it been raining all night?' is in the Past perfect continuous tense.
We know that the structure of the Past perfect continuous tense for the interrogative sentence is
Structure: had + Sub + been + V + ing + Obj + since/for + time
Example: Had he been finishing his homework since morning?

29(A). The most appropriate meaning of the given idiom 'By leaps and bounds' is 'very fast'.
By leaps and bounds: very quickly
Example: Her health is improving by leaps and bounds.

30(A). From the above definitions of different parts of speech, it is clear that 'new' is defining the quality of 'jacket' in the sentence which makes it an adjective.
Adjective - A word naming an attribute (quality, characteristic) of a noun, such as sweet, red, or technical.

31(D). To have experience of the appropriate procedures.
Example: Don't worry about Sara's taking over the reporter's job, she already knows the ropes.
Which means she is already experienced and knows the details of the situation or task.

32(B). The given sentence is in Direct Speech. As per the question we have to change it into Indirect Speech.
The process of transformation is as follows:
- The given sentence is an example of an imperative sentence.
- Let's look at the rules of transformation:
- While changing the narration of an imperative sentence, we need to follow the given steps:
- The conjunction 'to' should be used in place of a comma (,) and inverted commas (" ").
- Here, 'don't' will be changed into 'not to'.
- 'said to' will be changed into 'told'.
- 'to' is followed by 'V1 (wear)'.
- Lastly, the adverb 'this' will be changed into 'that'.
Example:
The queen said to his servant, "Cook me some delicious food today." (Direct Speech)
The queen ordered his servant to cook her some delicious food that day. (Indirect Speech)
Correct Sentence: Harry told me not to wear that expensive watch to school.

33(C). The given sentence is in Direct Speech. As per the given question, we have to change it into Indirect Speech.
The process of transformation is as follows:
- The conjunction 'that' will be added and comma and inverted commas will be removed.
- 'is' changes into 'was'.
- 'my' changes into 'her'.
- 'next week' will be changed into 'the following week'.
Correct Sentence: She said that it was her birthday the following week.

34(B). The correct preposition here is 'into' as someone pushes a person 'into' a problem. 'Push someone into a problem' means 'get someone involved in a problem.'

35(D). The correct form of the verb is simple present tense and it must be singular as the subject is small kids carrying heavy sacks, which is singular.

36(B). The verb 'run' is correct here as the tense is present progressive thus the other options cannot be placed here.

37(A). The given statement wants to imply that all the students were present but the Principal did not come and the given parts in bold have errors since turn down refers to rejecting something especially a proposal by somebody and also, if the subjects are preceded by every, the verb used with such subjects should be singular. Here were has been used with every boy and girl, this is not correct usage.
Hence, the correct sentence would be: <u>Though every boy and girl **was present**, the Principal did not **turn up**</u>.
Turned off refers to left one road to join another whereas turned on refers to attacked suddenly with full power.

38(C). The given sentence implies that he is late and somebody else has been waiting for a long time for me. It an action is still going on at the present time starting from some point of time in the past, the present perfect continuous tense is used for that action. Here, the person has been waiting for a long time but he is yet to come. That means the action is still in progress.
Now, he is latest is completely wrong since this does not imply anything meaningful. He is late makes senses in this context whereas are waiting is in present continuous tense and therefore, is not correct in the present context of the sentence, present perfect continuous tense should be used in this sentence i.e. have been waiting.
The correct sentence would be: <u>I am really sorry that **he is late**; you must **have been waiting** for a long time.</u>

39(D). According to the given sentence, it means that one will be waiting for another till the time the other is done with his class in the college.
In such sentence where there are two actions denoting two different points of time, we use the future indefinite tense for the action that will finish later whereas for the other action, the simple present tense is used in the sentence. Here, in the first part of the sentence, shall wait is correct but in the second part of the sentence will finish is not correct since here the simple present tense should have been used. The correct usage would have been finish with your class.
The correct sentence would be: <u>I shall wait for you till you finish with your class in the college.</u>

40(C). The underlined part is grammatically incorrect. Thus, the best suited is "bore the same expression of".

41(A). "A queer fish" is an idiom that means an odd or strange person, usually in a negative sense.

42(A). The phrase "be in the pink" is often used to describe someone who is in good health or good physical condition.

43(C). The phrase "be in the running" typically refers to being a strong contender or having a good chance of winning or achieving something.

44(B). A sea change means a complete change. The phrase comes from Shakespeare's play "The Tempest".

45(D). "Be in seventh heaven" is an idiomatic expression used to describe a feeling of extreme happiness or bliss.

46(C). The personification gives human-like qualities to non-human objects. The sentence does not contain oxymoron or hyperbole as they involve contradictory terms or exaggerated language.

47(B). The figure of speech in the given sentence is oxymoron because it contains contradictory terms appearing together, such as "having nothing" and "he hath all."

48(A). In BrE /ɔ/ in words such as Not, block, cross, stop, college is pronounced /ɑː/ in AmE.

49(B). The word 'Asia' is pronounced as /'eɪʒə/ in British English, whereas it is pronounced /'eɪʃːya/ in American English.

50(D). RP is the abbreviation of the word received practice.